MW00830297

PRA
AMERICA'S FINAL WAR

"Andrei Martyanov's latest work reinforces his status as one of the most important analysts of the rot that pervades the U.S. military and its failure to craft a workable national security strategy. He effectively uses the war in Ukraine to illustrate the arguments he presented in his first book, *Losing Mililtary Supremacy.* Any political or military leader keen on making America's military great again should read this."

—LARRY JOHNSON
Former CIA analyst and State Department counter-terrorism advisor

"This is the epic culmination of Martyanov's previous three books —taking his carefully calibrated analysis of Russia's real revolution in military affairs to a whole new level. From the—botched—possibility of a mutual security negotiation that would have prevented the Special Military Operation (SMO) in Ukraine to Russia's ISR and hypersonic capabilities, Martyanov expands into the finer details of the 'U.S. at war' enigma. We learn, concisely, why there can be no frontal U.S. v. Russia war; why the West is fundamentally incapable of war; and how inescapable facts and figures are formatting NATO's impending geopolitical humiliation. This is a Khinzal narrative that instantly blows up a painstakingly built, Western-controlled edifice of power, corruption and lies. Of course, a must read."

—PEPE ESCOBAR
Journalist, *AsiaTimes*

"Andrei Martyanov's book is a wake-up call. Set against the backdrop of the Ukraine, he provides an uncompromising and masterful analysis of the Western way of understanding war. With a simultaneously introspective and constructive eye, he highlights the fundamental weaknesses of the United States and its allies in their strategic and operational approach to warfare against Russia. He reminds us that victory depends on knowing one's opponent as well as oneself. The problem is that we tend to know neither."

—COL. JACQUES F. BAUD (Rtd.),
Former Swiss Strategic Intelligence Officer

AMERICA'S FINAL WAR

———///———

Andrei Martyanov

Clarity Press, Inc.

© 2024 Andrei Martyanov
ISBN: 978-1-963892-04-8
EBOOK ISBN: 978-1-963892-05-5

In-house editor: Diana G. Collier
Book design: Becky Luening

Library of Congress Control Number: 2024939496

Clarity Press, Inc.
2625 Piedmont Rd. NE, Suite 56
Atlanta, GA. 30324
http://www.claritypress.com

CONTENTS

PREFACE

ON MARCH 25, 2024, the Lebanese news site *Al Mayadeen* summarized the meaning of what has become known as Russia's Special Military Operation (SMO) for the peoples who today are now known as the Global South:

> All in all, Putin has done a remarkable job at defending his country's interests and national security. Not only have his contributions solidified his leadership within Russia, but they have also inspired the Global South towards new horizons. With that in mind, history has begun to shift in the right direction.[1]

It is this shift "in the right direction"—a euphemism for the end of Western liberalism—which now is leaving behind it a trail of destruction and bloodshed. This shift is why an overwhelming majority of ignorant Western elites and a substantial part of the West's populace, which has been completely insulated from the realities of the outside world, hate Russia and Russians. This is the hatred of a much larger scale than mere geopolitical contradictions between nations and states; this hatred is taking on a metaphysical dimension, rising from its racial, religious, and cultural components. It is also extremely intense.

A huge part of this hatred is based on the recognition of Russia as the power, as it has been throughout the history, which is not afraid of the West and which has not only resisted the West's latest assault on the Russian people but also has exposed the combined West to be a military paper tiger. By effectively annihilating several iterations of the Armed Forces of Ukraine (AFU), including the bulk of NATO's "volunteers" and Western military hardware, which for the first time faced an opponent with extremely advanced armed forces, a massive industrial economy, and a strategy which was birthed by arguably the greatest military school and thought in history, Russia's Real Revolution in Military Affairs drove a paradigm shift in warfare.

This proverbial 800-pound gorilla in the room which can no longer be ignored—the West's miscalculation of Russia is of epic proportions—is driven by utterly incompetent elites, most of whom have no background in warfare, diplomacy or economics. They built the empire of lies and now they cannot do anything to stop the West's degeneration into a dystopia of whatever passes for suicidal policies. I warned of this crisis in my previous three books and now it is upon us and not going to end well for the combined West.

At this stage, however, the main task which Russia's leadership faces is how to prevent the West and its crazed leadership in the United States from unleashing a global conflict, not least through sacrificing Europe, whose population will inevitably be brainwashed into a desire to fight Russia, once again. This plan by the globalist cabal is based around primitive, ignorant views of the modern economy, resources management and warfare. It is not surprising once one begins to look at the backgrounds of those people who are either the globalist elite or are its servants. None have the educational, professional and life experience backgrounds which are imperative for achieving tangible successes in economy, in science or on the battlefield. Hence their inability to achieve or generate anything but white board ideologies which breed destruction, including of the realm wherein they reside, which is geographically anchored in Western Europe and the United States.

These plans and ideologies represent a death knell for Western societies, some of which are likely, as the plan goes, to be sacrificed on the battlefields of Russia. They know they cannot defeat Russia on the battlefield, nobody can, but they still dream about making Russia spend its resources so that in the end, their dream of regime change in Russia might be realized, whatever the cost.

As insane as this plan is, it is also very instructive. It demonstrates that Russia cannot talk to anyone in the West, which has become a euphemism for the United States, which has already turned European states into its lapdogs and, possibly, into cannon fodder. This plan is also militarily impossible because, as the SMO has demonstrated, the U.S. military is simply not in the same league in terms of operational and strategic planning as the Russian General Staff and Russia's military-political leadership. The U.S. Armed Forces TOE (Table of Organization and Equipment) is that of the legacy force stuck in the 1990s. The realization of this fact by some in the United States has delivered a profound shock to the system which has been heretofore incapable of learning and adapting due to its falsified military history and the increasingly low standards of the American top brass.

Their record speaks for itself—it is one of numerous lost wars. The current U.S. economy and military will not be able to fight Russia conventionally; it would face defeat if it tried. So, the United States and combined West have resorted to terrorism—the weapon of the weak. Everything which is being done in the Western media and the sphere of public policy is being done with a view to obfuscate, to hide the fact of the West's weakness. As driven home by the dismal "performance" of NATO's equipment—from the U.S. made Patriot PAC3 air defense complexes and Abrams tanks to British Challenger and German Leopard 2 tanks among many other weapon systems—NATO is incapable of fighting a real war of the 21st century. Even America's shortly to be overcome superiority in satellite constellations and NATO's ability to fly with impunity in the international air space over Black Sea counts for little in real war, in which NATO would be made blind and its Command and Control disrupted.

And then there are losses which might be expected in any such future war. As determined by the U.S. Army itself, the projected losses of the U.S. Armed Forces in a real conventional war with Russia are of a scale which is beyond the comprehension of any Western political leader and most military professionals. Projected at 3,600 casualties daily, the U.S. Army will surpass the number of casualties it suffered in Iraq and Afghanistan in two decades in about two weeks.[2] In terms of Killed In Action in the Vietnam War, in 10 years the U.S. Army can reach this grim score within a month, give or take. Nobody in Russia takes the small and backward Bundeswehr, French, let alone British, armies, seriously.

There is another reason that the West cannot fight such wars. It's not just due to their military-industrial and technological deficiencies but for moral and psychological ones as well. Societies in the West, and especially in the U.S., will simply collapse, unless a totalitarian state is established to enforce order. The United States and Europe are well on the way to this terrifying dystopia.

This is the reality facing the West and its leader, the United States, which has been demonstrated to the rest of the world. The West doesn't know how to cope with this new reality—its lies have been exposed; its myths have been dispelled. The rest of the world, however, foresees a more stable and prosperous future in the event of the demolition of the West's real and perceived hegemony.

If the United States avoids a civil war and doesn't split into several political entities, there are some chances of survival of the West in some form. If not, Europe is doomed due to lack of affordable energy, deindustrialization and the loss of social cohesion. Europeans, with the exception of Hungary, consistently voted for the globalists and will continue to do so.

The United States 2024 elections, if they are held at all, may mark the start of the physical disintegration of the country. The question remains—can the United States, unlike Europe, survive its hubristic pursuit of globalism and the subjugation of its political institutions to Zionism? There is no clear answer to that. What is clear, however, is that the demolition of the best proxy the United States ever had on the battlefields of Ukraine has given birth to the new world.

This book addresses the core structural factors underpinning Russia's defeat of the combined West militarily—bringing about not just its immediate defeat, but forestalling its ability to launch major wars for decades to come, if not indefinitely—and what this means for the rest of the world. It reflects on the empirical evidence from the SMO battlefields of the West's humiliating military and political defeat and the demolition of its military mythology—the main pillar on which U.S. and the West's hegemony relied—just a few decades after the collapse of the Soviet Union.

The collapse of American hegemony and the end of Western global domination promise to eclipse the consequences of that Soviet collapse. We can only await in awe the reconstruction of the world disorder into something which promises to be more just, stable and diverse.

CHAPTER 1.

AN INTRODUCTION TO THE ECHO CHAMBER

THE DEFINITION OF AN ECHO CHAMBER is as simple as it is profound. An on-line dictionary provides the following definition pertinent to the subject of this book: *an environment in which the same opinions are repeatedly voiced and promoted, so that people are not exposed to opposing views.*[3] The current era is not the first time that the Western elites and mass media willingly insulate themselves from reality inside an echo chamber. The historic record of their similar insulation and lack of any desire to listen to opposing views since the end of World War Two is voluminous and is documented extremely well by historians and eyewitnesses of high caliber. Describing British 19th century blindness, precipitated by the utopian liberal confabulation and a sense of imperial greatness, to the reality of the world at large, the late Corelli Barnett noted:

> For other great powers did not see the world as one great human society, but—just as the British had done up to the nineteenth century—as an arena where, subject to mutual convenience of diplomatic custom, nation-states—the highest effective form of human society—competed for advantage. They did not believe in a natural harmony among mankind, but in national interests that might sometimes coincide with the interests of others, sometimes conflict.[4]

While British liberalism of the nineteenth century could have been viewed, by those insulated from the brutal realities of Empire's legal and military exploits, as relatively benign in its

1

aspirations, its 21st century version—or better yet, mutation—as is practiced by the United States and its coterie of clients, often labeled inter alia as the Davos Culture, G-7, World Economic Forum, represents nothing more than a post-modernist neoliberal cult in which nation-state is viewed as an obsolete construct which needs to be abolished. In the end, the guiding ideology of this culture, which is comprised primarily of the Western nations, is called globalism for a reason: it is built around the ideas of free trade, free flow of capital, and the eventual reduction of humanity to a gray mass of consumers with largely uniform tastes, aspirations, and an ersatz morality, subservient to the guidelines issued by the masters of discourse, sitting at the very top of the financial and political pyramid.

A lot has been written about this mutation and the emergence of such a set of views, later translated into the economic, military and cultural policies of neoliberalism, but one dominating feature of the algorithm of the Western political and media classes remains this very proclivity to insulate themselves inside an echo chamber of dubious ideas about themselves and the world outside. Assessing America's founding, Michael Brenner digs into the metaphysics of this echo chamber:

> Americanism provides a Unified Field Theory of self-identity, collective enterprise, and the Republic's enduring meaning. When one element is felt to be in jeopardy, the integrity of the whole edifice becomes vulnerable. In the past, American mythology energized the country in ways that helped it to thrive. Today, it is a dangerous hallucinogen that traps Americans in a time warp more and more distant from reality. There is a muted reflection of this strained condition in the evident truth that Americans have become an insecure people. They grow increasingly anxious about who they are, what they are worth and what life will be like down the road.[5]

Insecurity breeds the need for echo chambers as means of avoidance or insulation from "bad" news and provides an escape from the human compulsion for self-reflection—particularly if self-reflection could produce some very bitter pills for any individual to swallow. On the national level, moreover, the pain of facing reality could be excruciating, and sometimes even deadly. America was always insecure as a nation. This is not to say that other nations always feel secure, but America's insecurity is a special case. As Brenner posits:

> This is an individual and collective phenomenon. They are related insofar as self-identity and self-esteem are bound up with the civic religion of Americanism. To a considerable degree, it's been like this since the very beginning. A country that was "born against history" had no past to define and shape the present. A country that was born against tradition had no rooted and common sense of meaning and value that cut deeply into the national psyche. A country that was born against inherited place and position left each individual at once free to acquire status and obliged to do so for insignia of rank were few.[6]

This insecurity is America's birthmark and is in the foundation of a proverbial garrulous patriotism noted by Alexis De Tocqueville during his tour of 1830s United States.[7] This insecurity began to manifest itself across the board of what are a traditional nation's activities ranging from the economy, to the military, to foreign affairs, and to culture, of which I warned in all of my previous books, and today it has reached a grotesque form and scale, demolishing not only the ideas floating inside this echo chamber, but the chamber itself.

Two seemingly innocuous events may underscore this point. These are not the events directly associated with Russia's Special Military Operation in Ukraine, but they are very important because in some sense they serve as a Russian variation on a saying by the legendary H.R. Mencken: "It is the classic fallacy of our time that a moron run through a university and decorated with a Ph.D. will thereby cease to be a moron."[8] Speaking to students of Kostroma State University on March 13, 2020, Russia's Prime Minister Mikhail Mishustin, while by no means disparaging humanities education, noted nevertheless: "I know a large number of absolutely wonderful financiers, economists who used to be not very good engineers, but I don't know a single, even not a very good one, engineer who used to be good financier or economist."[9] The point Mishustin was getting across was very simple—Russia, which at that time was already living under the severe West's sanctions, didn't need more economists, financiers and sociologists; she needed engineers and STEM scientists, and she needed them badly.

Then, right after Russia launched her Special Military Operation (SMO), as if the political weight of its Prime Minister hadn't been enough, no less than President Putin himself made a statement which infuriated both Russia's and the Western "analytical" Parnassus. Vladimir Putin decided to jokingly challenge the status of what is called political science. As reported by TASS on July 7, 2022,

> Russian President Vladimir Putin doubted that political science can be classified as a science, because it is difficult to find a research method that is unique to this field of knowledge. He shared this assessment on Thursday at a meeting with the winners of the fourth season of the Leaders of Russia contest. Hearing that one of the contestants was going to defend her Ph.D. thesis in the field of political science, the head of state was surprised: "In the field of political science? Is there such a science—political science?" Hearing an affirmative answer, he added with a laugh: "A moot point....As I understand it, it has always been believed that for a certain field of knowledge to claim to be called a science, it must have its own subject of study and its own research method. In political science, it is

somehow difficult to find a research method inherent only to it," Putin shared his vision of the situation.[10]

It is worth noting that I personally had to bring up these points in 2018 while writing *The (Real) Revolution In Military Affairs,* a substantial part of which was based on the critique of noted American political scientist John Mearsheimer's work *The Great Delusion: Liberal Dreams and International Realities* in particular, and of the Western field of the political science in general. It would be a good idea to remind readers what I wrote back then in the Preface to that book:

> Just recently a respectable, conservative, and to their greatest credit, anti-war publication *The American Conservative* unleashed a scathing, well-justified, criticism on warmongers and Iran hawks such as David Brooks and Bret Stephens, who write primarily for the *New York Times.* Both Brooks and Stephens, among very many similar others, fancy themselves pundits, analysts, columnists and commentators with a focus on geopolitics and international relations. No doubt, they analyze and comment on those issues and, as is the case with any humanities-educated pundits among leading American mainstream media personalities, they boast an impressive (for media figures) set of credentials in all kinds of disciplines related to media—from history to political philosophy to journalism. What neither Brooks nor Stephens, as well as the vast majority of American political class, have as credentials is even an infinitesimally small background in the subjects on which all of them are trying to comment, analyze and (for those in position of political power) even make decisions—warfare.[11]

At that time such a description might have seemed a bit harsh or even farfetched, but the times did change dramatically in the last four years and today this critique seems almost subdued, because when speaking about the American echo chamber one fact cannot be ignored: the majority of people who are responsible in the United States for developing America's strategies, or what passes for strategies in the U.S. establishment, be they economic or military ones, are political scientists and economists. Lawyers and mainstream journalists—here, a euphemism for propagandists—follow. In all, in the United States the decisions which are vital for the existence of not only the United States, but the world, are made by people who by and large have zero serious academic and life experiences related to issues of war and peace, geopolitics, the real economy and statesmanship. These are precisely the types of people who in the combined West are in charge of narratives and, in the end, of erecting this very echo chamber whose existence threatens all life on Earth. So here, we must take a closer look at the *American Intellectual Class.*

Let us quote a definition of the intellectual class, which also is known as the intelligentsia: *the intelligentsia is a status class composed of the university-educated people of a society who engage in the complex mental labors by which they critique, shape, and lead in the politics, policies, and culture of their society; as such, the intelligentsia consists of scholars, academics, teachers, journalists, and literary writers.*[12] It warrants noting that the Western intelligentsia in general, and the American one in particular, in the last 30 years has become the embodiment of an echo chamber. It has exposed its rather very limited intellectual tool kit, which was not that impressive to start with, and as noted by Mencken, long ago has become a degree mill for people who were supposed to become part of the intellectual class but failed *en masse*, bar a few exceptions here and there.

While Western mainstream media have become the butt of jokes around the world, not to mention the fact that they are viewed primarily as propaganda outlets for Western governments, it is also worth pointing out that the large strata of Western journalists, especially at the start of Russia's SMO, demonstrated themselves to be utterly incompetent people in matters of warfare, strategy, the real economy, and geopolitics. This is not a new phenomenon. But the current time and circumstances have made it possible to finally arrive at a precise diagnosis of the West's intellectual class, and it is not an optimistic one. I have warned for years of the West's impending intellectual collapse and the fact that its "elite manufacturing machine" is utterly broken.

It took the SMO to remove a longstanding myth of American exceptionalists, which posits the existence of secret rooms where the "true" intellectual and government elites adeptly toil to develop serious long-term strategies. Thus, however crude, boorish, if not outright embarrassing and stupid the public behavior of American officials and intellectuals is, one can always surmise that some real masters of discourse are developing real, albeit invisible to the eyes of mere mortals, policies. The often outright idiotic public behavior of American officials exposed for all world to see might and likely have been countered with supposition that, in the end, they do not really represent *those who make decisions* and are but a disposable cadre of caretakers and fronts. Obviously, this argument suffers from a fundamental flaw; even the simple act of comparing the universally admired, even by enemies, highly educated and cultured spokesperson for Russian Foreign Ministry Maria Zakharova to spokespersons for the State Department or White House, ranging from the notorious Jan Psaki to Karine Jean-Pierre (embodying three facets of the woke agenda in one person), among many others, whose incompetence became legendary, reveals a profound professional abyss between them. Moreover, as is the case with American diplomats in general, they simply pale in professional competence compared to Russian or Chinese ones, a fact admitted by American diplomats themselves.[13]

This is not to say that those secret hidden rooms do not exist, both figuratively and physically, they surely do. They do exist in the White House complex, they do exist in CIA headquarters at Langley, they surely exist in the Pentagon, and they do exist in different iterations at upscale resorts and golf clubs where America's elites congregate. And surely, discussions are held there on matters of utter importance for the major stakeholders in modern globalism—but the reality of those stakeholders being as unqualified and as ignorant, if not worse, as those who allegedly serve as their avatars for public appearances, cannot be denied any longer. The rumbling of the imminent crisis of American competence has been heard long before the start of Russia's SMO and was registered, on one of many similar occasions, in the main publication of American foreign policy establishment, *Foreign Affairs,* in 2017, in the wake of Donald Trump's unlikely—as most pundits suggested—victory, which took him into the Oval Office. Tom Nichols, then a professor of National Security Affairs at the U.S. Naval War College. lamented America's loss of faith in expertise:

> It's not just that people don't know a lot about science or politics or geography. They don't, but that's an old problem. The bigger concern today is that Americans have reached a point where ignorance—at least regarding what is generally considered established knowledge in public policy—is seen as an actual virtue. To reject the advice of experts is to assert autonomy, a way for Americans to demonstrate their independence from nefarious elites—and insulate their increasingly fragile egos from ever being told they're wrong. This isn't the same thing as the traditional American distaste for intellectuals and know-it-alls. I'm a professor, and I get it: most people don't like professors. And I'm used to people disagreeing with me on lots of things. Principled, informed arguments are a sign of intellectual health and vitality in a democracy. I'm worried because we no longer have those kinds of arguments, just angry shouting matches.[14]

Nichols, who in the same year published a book with the title of *The Death of Expertise: The Campaign against Established Knowledge and Why it Matters,* in which he expounded on the mechanisms behind this death, quoted Richard Hofstadter who had already predicted in 1963 in his seminal *Anti-intellectualism in American Life:*

. . . the complexity of modern life has steadily whittled away the functions the ordinary citizen can intelligently and comprehendingly perform for himself. In the original American populistic dream, the omnicompetence of the common man was fundamental and indispensable. It was believed that he could, without much special preparation, pursue the professions and run the government. Today he knows that he cannot even make his breakfast without using devices, more or less mysterious to him, which expertise has put at his disposal; and when he sits down to breakfast and looks at his morning newspaper, he reads about a whole range of vital and intricate issues and acknowledges, if he is candid with himself, that he has not acquired competence to judge most of them.[15]

Hofstadter also pointed to the immense importance of trained intelligence in the modern world as it existed in 1963.[16] This was almost sixty years before the start of SMO and the world of internet, satellite constellations, smart phones, hypersonic weapons, and supercomputers. The irony of a political scientist and Ph.D in history from Columbia University warning about the complexities of the emerging world and the necessity for trained intellect was evidently completely lost on the Western intellectual establishment, which loves to associate itself with expertise, faced with the earthshaking exposure of this establishment's ignorance, intellectual impotence and lack of any expertise on any issue concerning modern humanity's activities ranging from the real economy, to science and technology, to warfare.

The American political "science" establishment and its associated pseudo-academe structures, such as Western journalism, or rather punditry, has served as a driving force, the engine, behind the crash-test car which is accelerated to a very high speed only to be smashed against the concrete wall with an enormous force, so that industrial scientists might sift through the mangled wreckage and crash-test dummies in order to understand the impact and to apply learned lessons to a design of a new vehicle. And indeed, the crashing of this Western intellectual class's test car of ideas, knowledge, or rather lack thereof, of the outside world, of its delusions of just about anything not related to the white board abstracts, against the immovable concrete wall of reality was devastating. This crash revealed the remnants of its already shaky reputation and of the pretense to relevance and integrity of the American intellectual class, those proverbial Mencken's Ph.D morons. The test car was completely wrecked with very little left for salvaging.

Anyone with more or less serious professional military and intelligence background who was reading the first edition of Zbigniew Brzezinsky's celebrated 1997 book, *The Grand Chessboard: American Primacy and Its Geostrategic Imperatives,* primarily within this very distinct American geopolitical echo chamber, ranging from credentialed "thinkers" to establishment publications, likely could not shake off a feeling of being in the presence of a geopolitical legerdemain. Brzezinski's opus came out in the wake of the two other celebrated works by American "experts"—Fukuyama's almost immediately discredited 1992 promise of *The End of History,* and Huntington's 1993 seminal *The Clash of Civilizations,* with much that is inaccurate despite some lucid thoughts. As with most of the previous writing of many celebrated American intellectuals, Fukuyama and Huntington demonstrated a complete ignorance of real war and the way it shapes societies. This was only natural for American political scientists struggling to grasp the nature and complexities of a real war, especially the way it serves as a primary tool of geopolitics as well as its increasing tactical, operational, and strategic complexity due to a scientific and technological revolution.

Degrees in political science, economics (a euphemism for finance), law or communications—dominant degrees among America's intellectual and power elite—do not provide the crucial knowledge and a tool kit required for a competent description of the balance of global power. In the world of people with serious professional skill sets, ranging from medicine, to STEM, to modern military, those degrees are known as "soft degrees" which do not require intellectual and physical effort to also be tested against practical outcomes. Rephrasing Mikhail Mishustin's dictum, one could easily find a good political scientist among former engineers or motor rifle battalion or air defense regiment commanders, but one would have been hard pressed to find even a mediocre heart surgeon, aerospace engineer or frigate commanding officer among former political scientists, albeit U.S. military is known to run its officers through such degree programs with less than stellar results.

Brzezinski stands here as a special figure not just because of his fanatical Russophobia, but because of his very prominent position as a foreign policy adviser to the Obama Administration and later, before his death, to Joe Biden and, in general, to the Democratic Party establishment going back to the times of Lyndon Johnson. In this respect this professional political scientist, who distinguished himself as a National Security Adviser in the Carter Administration, was a classic product of America's humanities academe in a sense that most of its "products" never had any serious understanding of either real scientific-technological developments or, as is the case even today, had any clear idea of the tsarist/Soviet or contemporary Russian history, economy, cultural idiosyncrasies and, especially, its military history. Remarkably, these very same people have very little understanding of their own country, the United States, precisely because modern American higher education does not provide a required tool kit for proper connection to that reality. The only tool this education provides is the ability to juxtapose accurately selected facts which serve politically expedient narratives, but not to engage with an objective picture.

In layman's terms, Brzezinski would have been described as a military amateur, as would be the majority of America's geopolitical thinkers, who have never had a systemic military and technological education and never served a day in military officer uniform. In other words, most American geopolitical thinkers who emerged in 1970s through the 1990s elucidated their views on geopolitics founded on an anecdotal image of military power—a defining tool of geopolitics. But the fountain of works on geopolitics in the United States in the 1990s had three fundamental features:

1. It was spurred to a large degree by the collapse of the Soviet Union and demonstrated a lack of understanding of the main causes of said collapse, due to a complete corruption of what became to be known as the American Russia Studies field.
2. It exhibited an irrational euphoria over and gross misrepresentation of both the operational-strategic and the technological aspects of the victory over the grossly incompetent and underequipped Iraqi army in the First Gulf War.
3. It maintained a profound conviction of its own ability to expound on matters of military doctrine and strategy despite lacking any serious military academic background and any tactical and operational experience.

Brzezinski offered the most extreme exhibit of all three causes wrapped into one. His inability to understand modern war for what it is—bar some popular general cliches about nuclear weapons—brilliantly exposed his lack of depth in this matter in his magnum opus. Writing in 1997 about American global preponderance, Brzezinski misidentified some of the factors:

America's economic dynamism provides the necessary precondition for the exercise of global primacy.... America's share of global GNP, and more specifically its share of the world's manufacturing output, had stabilized at about 30 percent, a level that had been the norm for most of this century, apart from those exceptional years immediately after World War II. More important, America has maintained and has even widened its lead in exploiting the latest scientific breakthroughs for military purposes, thereby creating a technologically peerless military establishment, the only one with effective global reach. All the while, it has maintained its strong competitive advantage in the economically decisive information technologies. American mastery in the cutting-edge sectors of tomorrow's economy suggests that American technological domination is not likely to be undone soon, especially given that in the economically decisive fields, Americans are maintaining or even widening their advantage in productivity over their Western European and Japanese rivals.[17]

This was a military delusion on a grand scale, one which would have a terminal effect on America's foreign policy and ensured a dramatic departure of the United States from the world arena as a self-proclaimed hegemon, having bought into own military supremacy mythology and rejecting all indications to the contrary. Brzezinski, who never served a day in uniform and had zero STEM background, which otherwise could allow him to weigh the veracity of his own statements on "the latest scientific breakthroughs for military purposes," was so busy with the fate of Central Europe and Poland that he simply overlooked the Soviet military-technological developments of the 1980s and lost his orientation on the scale of things. In other words, he exhibited a defining trait of the American intellectual elites who tend to learn about military affairs from the entertainment industry.[18]

Even against the raging economic crisis in the 1990s Russia and the chaos which ensued in the wake of the barbaric U.S.-directed economic reforms and the essential demolition of the Soviet Armed Forces, the military-technological heritage of the Soviet Union was preserved to a very substantial degree. This is precisely the point which the overwhelming majority of American geopolitical thinkers, even those who pass for the so-called realists with whom Brzezinski was mistakenly identified, cannot grasp because they do not have a proper background, reliable information, or both. Already in 1996–97 it had become clear that the truncated Russian military-industrial complex was still engaged with a backlog of highly advanced Soviet military R&D which was much more impressive than America's "technologically peerless military establishment" as proclaimed by Brzezinski, in the wake of euphoria from beating a backward third world military. Russia in 1994–95 was already offering on the international market systems such as:

- 3M54 Kalibr anti-shipping cruise missile (NATO reporting SS-N-27 Sizzler).
- S-300 PMU 1 and 2 Air Defense Complexes (NATO reporting SA-20 Gargoyle).
- P-800 Oniks supersonic cruise missiles (NATO reporting SS-N-26 Strobile).
- A variety of deeply modified combat aircraft such as international arms market-oriented SU-30MK, and Russian Air Force variant of SU-30, later SU-30SM.
- In 1997, demonstrating the SU-34 (as SU-32FN) prototype in Le Bourget, including first versions of R-73 long range AAM.
- Advanced radar and signal processing systems.
- Combat ships and diesel submarines.
- Since 1982, the GLONASS satellite constellation, while maintaining the use of *Parus* system.
- T-90 tanks.

This is just a short list of what Russia was offering on the international market, despite a marked decline in her arms sales due to the loss of the arms markets of the former Warsaw Pact countries. Even a brief look at the glossy Russian publication *Military Parade,* which saw its first issue published in 1994, in the 1990s could have given pause to real military professionals when reviewing what was being revealed by the Russian military-industrial complex. While Russia was lagging at that time in some fields related to the computers and communications behind the United States, in the field of air defense, cruise missiles and combat aviation Russia was already then leading the United States technologically, while in terms of submarine technologies she was either on par or beginning to lead in the most crucial aspects of submarine operations.

One of the best and most respectable American military observers with strong emphasis on naval issues, Norman Polmar, together with cadre officer of the Royal Dutch Navy Jurrien Noot, provided in 1991 an astonishing estimation of the growth of Soviet underwater capabilities compared to the American ones. In it, they assessed that by 1990 the U.S. Navy submarine force had only four advantages, out of a list of fourteen crucial submarine characteristics, over Soviet submarines. As Polmar and Noot concluded, Russian submarine development by 2000 would leave the U.S. with only two advantages, which have been identified as *manning quality,* a highly debatable estimate for this specific factor, and *passive sonar,* with the rest being equal or with the advantage, eight out of twelve, going to Russia.[19]

While the collapse of the Soviet Union arrested the overall shipbuilding program in 1990s Russia, Russian R&D for advanced submarine technologies never ceased. Russia continued to build advanced submarines of both types, diesel-electric and nuclear ones, even through the calamitous 1990s. This fact, among many other similar ones, went unnoticed by Brzezinski and his colleagues working on creating white-board geopolitical theories and waxing strategic without understanding the operational and technological implications. Yet, the strategic and geopolitical meaning of those developments which didn't fit the overall narrative of American military omnipotence, was immense.

In 1997, the precise year Brzezinski concluded that America "has maintained and has even widened its lead in exploiting the latest scientific breakthroughs for military purposes," U.S. Naval Institute Proceedings published an alarmist article about Russian submarine development in which it stressed: "The Russian submarine Navy's emphasis, much like our own, is now on quality not quantity. The Office of Naval Intelligence's estimate of the current Russian submarine order of battle reveals a formidable force of new or significantly overhauled (submarines)."[20] America's intellectual class was manifestly oblivious to all those complex details which are not taught in political science or international relations programs—precisely the body of knowledge which should have been seriously considered when preoccupied with

American intellectuals' favorite pastime—doctrine and strategy mongering. Here, the American intellectual class revealed fully its militant arrogance enabled solely by its ignorance.

Nor was the U.S. military, bathed in the glory of the Gulf War, willing to take a serious measure of its actual—as opposed to grossly exaggerated by media and "scholars"—military accomplishment, thus amplifying the echo-chamber effect. A sobering account, such as the 1994 (revised in 2013) work by Anthony Cordesman of the Center for Strategic and International Studies titled *Lessons of the Gulf War: 1990–1991,* was revealing and not in favor of the United States and its military. It concluded:

> The UN Coalition had five and one-half months to deploy, adapt, and train its forces. This was critical to integrating tactics, technology, training, and sustainability necessary to build up heavy armored and mechanized formations, and to giving the Coalition the ability to control and sustain intense air operations. In contrast, Iraq showed little ability to take the initiative, and could not obtain reinforcement or resupply. Iraq did nothing militarily to try to limit the Coalition build-up. It took no action against Saudi ports, and military facilities during the time that the Coalition had only token forces. More importantly, it seemed to have discounted the risk of actual large scale conflict, and to [have] assumed that a political solution would be found that would allow it to keep Kuwait. It failed to seriously study and assess the capabilities of Coalition forces, particularly in regard to advanced tactics and technology.[21]

Generally speaking, all 973 pages of this publication went on to describe, both explicitly and implicitly, including through a vast number of tables with available tactical and operational data, the utter military incompetence and backwardness of the Iraqi Army, despite the author's efforts to convince otherwise. Much noise at the time was made in the media all over the world about the Revolution in Military Affairs with constant references to the Gulf War as some kind of unheard-of military achievement. Any attempts at that time, in the 1990s, to point out the obvious—a historic strategic anomaly in circumstances surrounding the Gulf War, from Soviet cooperation to the sheer weakness of the enemy—had been ignored. Even thirteen years after the conclusion of the Gulf War, and with the United States starting its disastrous adventures both in Afghanistan and Iraq, the mythology and all the wrong lessons of the Gulf War had not been disposed of. As Stephen Biddle noted:

> The startingly low loss rate has had important policy consequences. In fact, it made the Gulf War a shaping event for defense planning today in much the way the painful defeat in Vietnam came to shape U.S. planning in 1980s. U.S. forces are now sized and structured against a Gulf War yardstick.[22]

There it was—a concise and terminal diagnosis and death sentence to America's self-proclaimed hegemony since this yardstick was to exercise a baneful influence on America's military and foreign policies and would serve as a pivot around which a host of utterly false narratives would be created and spun by people from America's media and academe, those proverbial "Ph.D. morons," who never knew what real war is and how it is fought.

Russians have not been keen on buying media hype. Already in 1992, the then Chief of the Strategy Department of Russia's Academy of General Staff, Lieutenant-General Klokotov, stated in his presentation:

> I would like to emphasize here that the Persian Gulf war was taken as the standard in studying the strategic nature of possible war. It would appear that this position, adopted in the draft "Fundamentals of Russian Military Doctrine," is dangerous. The fact

is that this war [was] "strange" in all respects [and] cannot serve as a standard.[23]

It could not and in the end, it did not—even though military reforms initiated by Anatoly Serdyukov seemed to be "inspired" by the U.S. performance in the Gulf. At least that is how many Western observers saw it. As Roger McDermott concluded, it was the attempt at Netcentric Warfare structure based on the brigade configuration and derived from the five-days war in August 2008 in which the Russian Army demolished NATO-trained and partially equipped Georgian one.[24] Needless to say, most Western observers have been wrong, because Russia learned proper lessons from her campaigns and from the performance of the U.S. Army, whose justified criticism was viewed by many in Western military academe and media as merely a result of professional jealousy and was followed by delusional statements of the Gulf War being a "game changer."[25]

The real game changer, however, was the fact that, initially cautiously and then increasingly assertively, many Russian military thinkers and serious analysts working in the defense field began to accept the fact of the West not just being generally badly informed about Russia in general, and its Armed Forces in particular, but to their surprise, discovered the growing incompetence of America's decision-making circles and the U.S. military in questions related to modern warfare. Not only geopolitical American thinking turned out to be a collection of hollow white-board doctrine mongering theories, but U.S. military performance even against subpar opponents elsewhere, as well as disastrous procurement policies, revealed a deep systemic crisis within America itself. Increasingly, Russians started to perceive what the late Angelo Codevilla pointed out when describing a catastrophe that the American foreign policy has become in the 21st century:

> Foreign nations are no longer impressed by our establishment's degrees and pedigrees. They now look to themselves. Our foreign policy establishment

gurus haven't noticed their own lack of international standing.[26]

Codevilla's diagnosis is precise, and it applies equally to all facets of American activity in the 21st century, be that in the economy, culture, foreign policy and especially so, in military affairs, which saw the United States producing a 70 years long record of lost wars marked by an inability to adapt to the everchanging realities of modern warfare. This rigidity is a result of an echo chamber whose only purpose is to serve the self-aggrandization of the increasingly incompetent American civilian and military elites who have learned absolutely nothing from Russia, whose military history and record dwarfs that of the United States. The result of the insularity of this echo chamber is America's strategic and historic in its scale miscalculation, which is now on full display in the process of Russia's Special Military Operation in Ukraine and elsewhere.

This book is written to demonstrate not only the realities of the modern warfare Russia conducts in Ukraine against the combined forces of NATO, but to validate, rephrasing Codevilla, why American establishment degrees and pedigrees are entirely incompatible and useless in the new emerging multi-polar world.

And why they have brought Western Civilization to its knees.

CHAPTER 2.

SVECHIN AND AMERICAN STRATEGY

STRATEGY IS A VERY POPULAR TERM; it is also one of the most abused and misapplied or misappropriated. Generally, the definition of strategy is as simple as it gets; per Cambridge Dictionary: "it is a detailed plan for achieving success in situations such as war, politics, business, industry, or sport, or the skill of planning for such situations."[27] Russian Academic Dictionary gives a more focused definition, concentrating on military strategy. Per this dictionary, strategy "is from Greek *strategos*—military art. In game theory, strategy is a plan of the game per any move by the other player."[28] One can actually play a good family game—similar to the popular game of finding alternative proofs of the Pythagorean Theorem in many schools around the world—which entails competing in providing the most comprehensive definition of strategy. But for the sake of the flow of our argument here, let's agree that in our particular case we are going to use the definition of strategy as:

1. In the military sense—a plan for achieving political objectives of a war.
2. In geopolitical sense—a plan for achieving national goals on the global arena.

These two parts are intertwined, because in the end the war is often the only tool for achieving national goals on the global arena and that requires exceptional planning in both the military and the broader geopolitical senses. No doubt, a lot has been written about strategy throughout history. Some writings on strategy aged extremely well and provided some of the greatest one-liners known to humanity. Kernels of strategic wisdom by Sun Tzu or Clausewitz are often quoted, even by people addressing subjects not related to war at all. Be that Sun Tzu's "If you know the enemy and know yourself" or Clausewitz's "war is a continuation of politics by other means," these one-liners give a layman some insight into the mind of a strategist, and many of them are applied even without reference to war as such. But of course, as is the case with any intellectual endeavor, some strategy theories didn't age well at all, especially when one considers the definition given to strategy by one of the most consequential Soviet/Russian strategists, Alexander Svechin, who in his most important work *Strategy* provided in 1927 a comprehensive *initial* definition and tied strategic and operational levels of war:

> Strategy is the art of military leaders, primarily the art of those persons called on to resolve the basic problems set forth by a wartime situation and to transmit their strategic decisions for execution by operational artists. Strategy is the art of the entire high command of an army, because not only front commanders and army commanders, but also corp commanders, would be incapable of accomplishing their operational missions if they are incapable of clear strategic thinking. Any time an operational artist must make a choice between two alternatives he will be unable to justify a particular operational method if he stays solely within the realm of operational art, and he will have to rise to a strategic level of thinking.[29]

One may ask, why the definition is "initial"? The answer lies in the exponentially increasing number of factors which any person who writes on strategy or does strategic planning must consider in order to avoid descending into tactical minutiae or coming across as trite. Examples from history abound.

In 1921 Italian general and military theorist Giulio Douhet wrote his magnum opus on aerial strategy, being, not without justification, fascinated with the potential of emerging and fast evolving combat aviation, as were many of his contemporaries. The problem with Douhet's writing, however, was his lack of technological foresight which led to him advocating for total war and envisioning fleets of bombers capable of bombing the enemy into utter submission—a theory taken to the heart by the United States Air Force, which even today cannot accept the realities of either modern air combat or modern air defenses due to having not encountered a capable enemy, either in the skies or on the ground. Douhet's writings didn't age well precisely for his failure to take account of the factor of technological development. He wrote:

> In discussing the unit of combat, let us first look into the possibility of aerial opposition, because it is the combat unit which will overcome the opposition. As for any opposition from ground forces, there can be none except antiaircraft guns; and I shall try to show how combat planes can counteract even the action of antiaircraft guns. But quite apart from this point, in actual fact the efficacy of antiaircraft guns can never be anything but very limited, both because of their inaccurate fire and because of the dispersion of means inherent in that kind of defense. Antiaircraft fire can certainly put out of action some planes in a bombing unit—a limited loss; but no one can hope to fight a war without taking some risks, especially when those risks can be reduced to a minimum. And that loss can easily be compensated for by simply keeping up the strength of the bombing units by a constant flow of replacement planes.[30]

That was the case in 1921 and it was true even in 1931. But that began to change with WW II when not only did air defense forces become a serious factor in mitigating the effects of strategic bombing, but anti-aircraft artillery became considerably more accurate in terms of targeting by means of improved sights and ballistics. With the development of the electro-mechanical computers and eventually radar directors, such as the M9 gun director with SCR-584 radar, the profile of air combat as conceived by Douhet started to change dramatically, not in favor of his vision. These improvements to AAA (anti-aircraft artillery) saw a noticeable increase in the kill ratio by British Air Defense forces during operation *Diver*—the battle against German V-1 flying bombs by both Royal Air Force and British AAA in 1944. The dramatic statistics of British AAA success was immediately noticed:

> Rapid progress was also made with the replacement of mobile guns by static guns of which 288 were in position by the end of July and a fortnight later that figure had reached 379. This redeployment of guns and aircraft solved the problem, and to the guns must go the lion's share of the credit. The improvement in the results they achieved leapt in the first week from sixteen per cent. to twenty-four per cent., and in the week of the 7th to 14th August they destroyed 120 out of 305 flying bombs, thus for the first time exceeding the claims of the fighters. ... The results grew steadily more and more noteworthy. Of the 1,124 bombs launched between 16th August and 5th September, only seventeen per cent. fell in the target area, and in the last four days of the attack only 28 bombs out of 192 fell in London. The climax was reached on the night of 27th/28th August when out of 97 bombs reported approaching the United Kingdom 87 were destroyed; 62 by the guns, 19 by the fighters, two by balloons and four by a combination of balloons and guns.[31]

Douhet, who died in 1930 and didn't see World War Two, would have been appalled by the rate of failure of his vision and his strategy of air warfare. His example inevitably leads to the conclusion that strategies are viable only when they account for a wide spectrum of economic, historical, cultural, technological, political, and very many other factors, which must be taken into account thus allowing the analyst to make the proper generalizations required for developing strategies which work in attaining political objectives, whether of the war or of national goals in a larger geopolitical context. When speaking about the world's major powers these two facets of strategy, as was pointed out above, are intertwined and the victory in war most of the time leads to achievement of the national goals globally.

Douhet's strategic vision, however, is far from the only instance of a fast (in historical terms) expiration of strategic ideas. Examples are very numerous, and military history buffs are well aware of some such military strategies which expired rather fast or never matured in their time period when faced with the developing economic and technological realities of their age. I emphasized the example of the *Jeune Ecole* (Young School) in one of my books, where I noted:

> The reasons for the Jeune Ecole springing to life were ideological, financial, and technological. The new technology of naval cannon shells and torpedoes, as opposed to cannonballs, seemed to be a good means for an anti-British, anti-commerce strategy in which, so Aube's thinking went, a coordinated attack of swarms of small torpedo and cannon boats, aided by commercial raiders, would be able to disrupt British shipping lanes. Young French naval officers, hence the Young School, were enthusiastic about those ideas, which were opening chances for their faster career advancement during the transformation of all navies from sailing ships to smaller steam and screw-driven naval forces. Some even called torpedo boats "democratic," increasing their acceptability along the lines of French press democratic rhetoric of the time.[32]

These ideas exercised a baneful effect on the development of the French Navy well into the 20th century.[33] *Jeune Ecole* strategy was driven by a misunderstanding of the complexities of the command and control of forces it envisioned and was a failure both operationally and tactically, which brought down the strategy of conducting *course de guerre* against British shipping. The technological capability to do what Aube and his journalist friend, Gabriel Chramez, envisioned wouldn't come around until WW II and especially after it, when communications and detection means had developed and improved sufficiently to the extent of allowing the remote control of groups of ships—and what was at the core of *Jeune Ecole,* groups of small ships whose striking power migrated from guns to anti-shipping cruise missiles. The arrival of the Network-Centric Warfare (NCW) made that possible through having a combination of a useful modern battlefield picture allowing for improved tactical and situational awareness, and effective command and control data links to fight, as Norman Friedman defined it, "in a new way."[34]

But it was the development of the weapons, namely the long-range supersonic and hypersonic anti-shipping missiles, that made possible what Aube dreamed about, and even more, allowing what is known as a mosquito fleet, a fleet of relatively small ships (boats), not only to disrupt shipping lanes but to attack and defeat what in the 21st century would have been termed as a modern equivalent of the Royal *Grand Fleet.*

In an ironic historic twist, *Jeune Ecole,* conceived as a romantic, if not fantastical vision by French naval and ideological thinkers as means to retain some French maritime influence in the wake of France's humiliating defeat in the Franco-Prussian War of 1870–71, came of age almost a century later with the sinking in October 1967 of the Israeli naval ship *Eilat* by two Egyptian Soviet-made *Komar-class* missile boats using Soviet anti-shipping missiles *P-15 Termit* (NATO *SS-N-2 Styx*). The idea of a 61-ton displacement boat sinking a combatant almost 30 times heavier (*Eilat's* displacement was 1,700 tons) seemed almost scandalous to the U.S. Navy, which rested on its massive experience of naval warfare in the Pacific in WW II and a strategic vision which profoundly shaped naval thinking in the world throughout most of the 20th century. The work which impacted every military thinker and even the lay public around the world was American

Admiral Alfred Thayer Mahan's magnum opus, *The Influence of
Sea Power upon History: 1660–1783.*

It is not only normal but highly desirable for any strategist
to refer to history. Looking for historical symmetries is natural for
any thinking person. This may, however, represent a problem for
a military strategist. As Alexander Svechin noted:

> A particular strategic policy must be devised for every
> war; each war is a special case, which requires its own
> particular logic, rather than any kind of stereotype or
> pattern, no matter how splendid it may be. The more
> our theory encompasses the entire content of modern
> war, the quicker it will assist us in analyzing a given
> situation. A narrow doctrine would probably confuse
> us more than guide us.[35]

Mahan's strategy was built on historic lessons he derived
from the wars in the time period embedded in the title of his
work, the 17th and 18th centuries, the times of sail and naval
cannons shooting cannonballs. But herein lay a problem: while
definitely influential, Mahan's work was published (1890) at the
time of revolutionary changes in naval ships' propulsion and
weapons, including modern optical rangefinders, the appearance
of the first submarines, and eventually, early 20th century radio
communications. Surely, the evolution and the influence of naval
power on the rise of Great Britain was interesting from the purely
historical point of view, and as the foundation for a discussion of
the merits of new naval technologies as applied to what Mahan
professed to be some of the keys to strategy—geography and
concentration of naval forces:

> Gibraltar was indeed a heavy weight upon the English
> operations, but the national instinct which clung to it
> was correct. The fault of the English policy was in
> attempting to hold so many other points of land, while
> neglecting, by rapidity of concentration, to fall upon
> any of the detachments of the allied fleets. The key of

the situation was upon the ocean; a great victory there would have solved all the other points in dispute. But it was not possible to win a great victory while trying to maintain a show of force everywhere.[36]

Mahan's work was not just that of a first-rate strategist but of an imperialist looking for proper tools to control the sea or the oceans—the sea lanes of trade, that is. Mahan's contention was that:

> Especially is it misleading when the nation against whom it is to be directed possesses, as Great Britain did and does, the two requisites of a strong sea power, —a wide-spread healthy commerce and a powerful navy. Where the revenues and industries of a country can be concentrated into a few treasureships, like the flota of Spanish galleons, the sinew of war may perhaps be cut by a stroke; but when its wealth is scattered in thousands of going and coming ships, when the roots of the system spread wide and far, and strike deep, it can stand many a cruel shock and lose many a goodly bough without the life being touched. Only by military command of the sea by prolonged control of the strategic centres of commerce, can such an attack be fatal; and such control can be wrung from a powerful navy only by fighting and overcoming it.[37]

Mahan's ideas buttressed the ideas of what is known today as *navalism*—a policy asserting the dominance of naval interests and naval class in the geopolitical affairs of a nation. Naturally, those policies were born on an island, Great Britain. In the 1880s Great Britain faced a new reality on the high seas, with French and Russian navies emerging as major forces, and with unjustified alarmism over ideas of *Jeune Ecole,* which sought to disrupt Britain's Sea Lanes of Communications (SLOC). As a result, British agitation over this grossly overstated threat led to

parliamentary investigation and ultimately resulted in the Naval
Defense Act of 1889. As is noted by Andrew K. Blackley:

> This groundbreaking legislation for the first time
> dictated the size of the Royal Navy, requiring that it be
> larger than the combined fleets of the two next-largest
> foreign navies, a standard that remained in effect until
> 1921. The act called for the construction of 10 new
> battleships and 38 cruisers within a five-year period.[38]

It was also through navalism and Mahan's ideas of
correlating naval supremacy with a global one that the United
States arrived on the international stage as a global player.[39]
Theodore Roosevelt's Great White Fleet's cruise around the world
in 1907–1909 was the embodiment of Mahan and Roosevelt's
own navalism, which sought through massive naval expansion to
validate Mahan's key point:

> . . . there is but one comment that need be made
> upon these arrangements. In any coming war their
> permanency would depend wholly upon the balance
> of sea power, upon that empire of the seas concerning
> which nothing conclusive had been established by the
> war.[40]

Navalism and its general ideas endured well into the 20th
century, until they were modified after World War Two. The
modification came from the Soviet Union and its Navy, built and
commanded by Admiral of the Soviet Union Sergey Gorshkov.
In his important work on naval strategy *The Sea Power of the
State*, Gorshkov described the naval requirements of a genuinely
continental power with immensely powerful ground armies which
neither Great Britain nor the United States could field in the 20th
century. While not denying the importance of naval power as
such, Gorshkov rebuked "island" navalists as follows:

Western strategists often give to sea power an unjustifiably hypertrophied significance. Its status and its relation to the power of other countries are used to explain many events in the world and even the development of the history of whole peoples and countries, as has been done by U.S. naval theoreticians. Their current followers, seeking from the standpoint of "sea power," "sea force," "naval power" to explain those most highly complicated events and processes which occur on the world scene, inevitably arrive at the contrived conclusion that it is necessary to step up still further the naval arms race.[41]

Gorshkov spoke not just from the vantage point of new military technologies that revolutionized the warfare—namely and above all, nuclear weapons—but also from the immense Russian experience of continental industrial war in which the Soviet Union defeated Hitler and his allied forces. It was a war which was fought by the USSR primarily on the ground and in the air on a scale never seen before and not repeated since in world history.

Mahan's ideas grew concurrently with U.S. dismay at the Chilean Navy taking delivery in 1884 of the protected cruiser *Esmeralda,* whose guns outranged anything the U.S. had at shore batteries defending San Francisco at that time. The whole idea that South American navies could ravage the U.S. coast while the U.S. had no means to defend its shores was unacceptable for the United States, thus spurring naval expansion, with the 1890 Naval Act, which envisioned construction of the U.S. Navy's battleships.[42] But these developments took place within the naval gunnery paradigm which would see a slow growth of the range of naval guns from a few kilometers, ranging anywhere between 4,000 and 14,000 yards in 1900s to around 40 kilometers for main caliber guns of Iowa-class battleships in the 1940s.[43]

Sixteen-inch main caliber guns with the range of 40+ kilometers could certainly wreak havoc on coastal cities anywhere in the world, but here was the problem—nobody could bypass a

simple fact that the seat of government was always on land, with
most of those proverbial seats being well outside the range of those
guns. Undoubtedly, aircraft carriers changed this paradigm during
World War Two, but even their ability to reach much further into
the continental mass was immediately arrested by the development
of increasingly efficient air defense means and, in case of major
powers, the deterrent effect of nuclear weapons and means of their
delivery, which relegated aircraft carriers primarily to the function
of power projection against weak nations. Even desperate attempts
of the U.S. Navy at developing a rationale for the existence of
increasingly vulnerable aircraft carriers as auxiliary backups
for strategic (a euphemism for nuclear) retaliation in the 1950s
couldn't stop the inexorable march of technology and with it, of
strategic thought.[44]

Throughout the 1950s and 1960s Mahan's ideas have
been in the process of becoming obsolete due to a revolutionary
technological paradigm shift which relegated his and other
navalists' dicta of autonomy and decisive fleet engagements, based
on the moribund idea that navies existed to fight other navies, to
irrelevance.[45] Already in 1946 Admiral Chester Nimitz, possibly
inadvertently, challenged Mahan's strategy with his contention
at Senate hearings that historically navies acted in support of
actions on land.[46] That was the idea behind Gorshkov's strategy,
which was grounded in the experience of continental warfare on
a gargantuan scale. It was Gorshkov who initiated unprecedented
development of submarine and missile technology for the Soviet
Navy, starting around the same time in 1960 when none other
than Chester Nimitz himself concluded in his fundamental treatise
predictably titled *Sea Power*, co-authored with E.B. Potter and
with other contributors, that the most revolutionary weapon in
America's New Navy—possibly the capital ship of the future—
was the missile firing submarine, combining to unparalleled
degree a potentiality for secrecy and surprise.[47]

As was the case with Douhet's ideas, Mahan's ideas endured
only for as long as the industrial and technological paradigm
which birthed them lasted. In historical terms they didn't last
long—those who had their enthusiastic strategic thinking affected

by Douhet or Mahan's writing at a relatively young age would see those ideas dissipate given the strategic reality of nuclear weapons, space flight and intercontinental ballistic missiles within their lifetime. Moreover, how then could one reconcile Svechin's ideas that each war is a "separate case," while simultaneously following a widely accepted dictum that one must learn from history? It is a contradiction which needs to be resolved. Any military academy in the world and war college or its equivalent has a department of Military History or the History of Military Art. There is no denying that studying military history is a must not only for any officer but also for anyone who gets to the levers of political power in any state, let alone a state which is militarily a major or a superpower.

Svechin lays out general requirements for those people, statesmen or, generally, politicians of high level, which are as crucial and important today as they have been 100 years ago.

> The first duty of the art of politics with respect to strategy is to formulate the political goal of a war. Any goal should be strictly coordinated with the resources available to achieve it. The political goal should be appropriate to one's war-waging capabilities. To meet this requirement, a politician must have a correct conception of the relations of friendly to hostile forces, which requires extremely mature and profound judgment; a knowledge of the history, politics and statistics of both hostile states; and a certain amount of competence in basic military matters. The final statement of the goal would be made by the politician after an appropriate exchange of views with strategists, and it should help rather than hinder strategic decisions.[48]

This is crucial, because it allows us to look at the root of the Americans' catastrophic strategic miscalculation in regard to Ukraine and consequently Russia, and Washington's formulation of the strategic goal of war in Ukraine. At this time of writing, the

military outcome of what Russia calls a Special Military Operation
(SMO) in Ukraine is not in any doubt, even by those in the Biden
Administration who sincerely believed that their political goal was
formulated correctly and was achievable. Neither their military nor
political goal turned out to be achievable in the slightest, and the
major contributing factor in this catastrophic miscalculation was
the complete atrophy (albeit always weak) of America's ability to
think and operate strategically. Or as popular Russian economist
and geopolitical observer Alexander Rogers noted sarcastically,
the United States cannot do strategy, because it only knows how to
make business plans.[49] If someone thinks that this characterization
is tongue in cheek, they would be wrong, because the situation
with America's strategic planning, both on the state and military
levels, is even worse than business planning applied to the matters
of state—it is delusional.

In fact, the problem is old and was noted by none other than
late Richard Pipes who was considered a specialist in Russia in
the U.S. Pipes lamented in 1977:

> We have no general staff; we grant no higher degrees
> in "military science"; and, except for Admiral Mahan,
> we have produced no strategist of international
> repute.[50]

Pipes' frustration is best understood when one considers
several critical factors which define what passes in the U.S. for
strategic thinking and planning. Yet, one would be hard pressed
to mount any sensible counterargument to what amounts to
Svechin's short list of requirements for political leaders insofar as
the strategy goes.

The United States, indeed, doesn't have general staff. One
may reasonably ask what the difference is between general staff
and the main U.S. organ of strategic planning known as the Joint
Chiefs of Staff (JCS). The difference is dramatic, and it becomes
simply startling when one compares Russia's General Staff and
the U.S. JCS. This difference was underscored, and not for the first
time, by Grau and Bartles, who identify them:

One of the most interesting differences between the armies of the post-Soviet Union and the West is the presence of Prussian-style General Staffs. These general staff systems provide far more than just a planning apparatus; they also function as doctrine and capability developers. The U.S. Joint Chiefs of Staff is often equated with the Russian General Staff, but this is a great understatement of the Russian General Staff's importance. The Russian Chief of the General Staff has far more authority than any flag grade officer in the U.S. military. In terms of equivalency, the Russian General Staff has the same responsibilities for long-term planning duties conducted by the U.S. Office of the Secretary of Defense and unified combatant commanders; elements of strategic transportation performed by USTRANSCOM; doctrinal and capabilities development, as well as equipment procurement for all branches of the Ministry of Defense. It even has an inspector general-like function for ensuring that its standards and regulations are adhered to.[51]

This difference in institutional purposing between Russia's General Staff and U.S. JCS was underscored by none other than then Chairman of the JCS General Mark Milley, who before his retirement penned a remarkable piece in *Joint Force Quarterly* where he expressed his desire to see a structure which, in its functionality, was remarkably reminiscent of a softer and gentler version of Russian General Staff. Milley didn't mince words and proposed a Joint Futures organization, which:

...would drive future Joint Force Design. It would be responsible for characterizing the future joint operating environment, looking beyond the current Future Years Defense Program. Building on the success of the JWC and JP 1, this organization would develop and iterate on future joint warfighting concepts. It would ensure capability development is threat informed and concept driven. This organization would not monopolize joint concept development but rather serve as a lead agency that is responsible for collaborating with the Services and combatant commands to identify and help prioritize future operational problems while synchronizing development of warfighting solutions. This future-focused organization would prioritize joint experimentation to ensure joint concepts are validated through rigorous wargaming, modeling, simulations, and other experimentation. This would strengthen Joint Force Design through competition of ideas, leveraging Service, industry, and academic innovation efforts. It would create experimentation venues to evaluate innovative tactical and operational solutions to inherently joint problems.[52]

Herein lies the problem. Any serious student of warfare would have been immediately taken aback by Milley's claims of the success of JWC (Joint Warfighting Concept) and JP 1 (Joint Publication of U.S. Army doctrine). As the Clausewitzian dictum went: "it is legitimate to judge an event by its outcome for it is the soundest criterion."[53] Why such claims have been made by Milley when the outcomes, indeed, provided the soundest criterion for judging America's military exploits in the 20th and 21st centuries as wholesale failures, is not so much for military strategists to judge, but for psychologists. As the SMO so vividly demonstrated, much of the U.S. top political and military brass simply suffered and continue to suffer from serious cases of professional envy.

Grossly overblown in its military significance, the defeat of Saddam's incompetent and backward army was the only bright spot on the U.S. post–WW II military record, and if one could still challenge, however feebly, Lieutenant General Klokotov's prescient assertions about the anomalous character of the Gulf War on the grounds of professional envy, the conclusions of Anthony Cordesman could not be dismissed as such:

Attacking with total air supremacy and carrying out
a one-side air campaign for weeks, and then fighting
an AirLand battle of only "100 hours" is scarcely
likely to be typical of future wars. It is also difficult
to generalize about the future role of many aspects of
joint warfare and combined operations.[54]

Thus, the inevitable question must be raised: where is the
success Mark Milley is talking about? A lost war in Iraq and a
humiliating debacle in Afghanistan can hardly qualify as successes,
or any sort of proof of the viability of the JWC or, in layman's
lingo, of its combination of strategic, operational and even tactical
approaches to modern war, which the American military continued
to claim is the best fighting military in the world. Surely one can
provide a long elaboration on the reasons of why the United States
cannot show anything tangible to support such a hefty claim, but
it is clear now that, as an example, a comparison between the U.S.
effort in Afghanistan and the Russian effort in Syria is not only
warranted, but irresistible. The Taliban victory over NATO forces
in Afghanistan was total, while the government of Bashar Assad
not only survived but with serious Russian military assistance
defeated ISIS forces and reclaimed much of a country.

Now, with Russia conducting a SMO in what remains of
Ukraine, some voices from the American side have started to be
heard regarding both American claims about modern warfare and
the way Russia prosecutes the operation against what amounts to
the best American (NATO) proxy in history, Ukraine, which was
designed and shaped as NATO's military ram against Russia since
2014. Speaking to a defense forum in Sweden in January of 2023,
U.S. Army General Christopher Cavoli, NATO's Supreme Allied
Commander Europe, was uncharacteristically candid:

Scale, scale, scale. The magnitude of this war is
incredible. The Ukrainians have 37 frontline brigades,
plus dozens more territorial brigades. The Russians
have lost almost 2,000 tanks. If we average out since
the beginning of the war, the slow days and fast days,

the Russians have expended on average well over
20,000 artillery rounds per day. The scale of this war
is out of proportion with all of our recent thinking.
But it is real and we must contend with it.[55]

Cavoli is not the only American military ranking officer of
note who spoke about Russia's SMO as this Svechin's proverbial
"separate case" of war, which effectively overturned previous
military doctrines. Colonel Douglas McGregor, speaking at
Natalie Brunell's podcast, termed the SMO war in Ukraine in
general a "paradigm shift in warfare."[56] But this paradigm shift is
not just in warfare, per se. For any competent military observer in
the West the effect of the interplay between the political state of
Russia and its Armed Forces as a unified organism with a clear set
of goals and methods required for their achievement did create a
sense of unease. This is no proverbial Washington Foreign Policy
consensus which has undeniably played a critically damaging role
in America's decline. The actions of Russia have been guided by
the extremely well-articulated political objectives of the SMO, as
well as sound strategy both on a geopolitical level and militarily,
not least through a set of mobilizational actions politically,
economically and militarily. Most importantly, Russia approached
the SMO with a force capable to conduct combined arms multi-
domain operations on a massive scale and adapt and improve
same throughout the whole duration of the SMO. This wouldn't
have been possible without the Russian General Staff.

To underscore this important difference, the Chief of General
Staff Army General Valery Gerasimov is not just the First Deputy
Minister of Defense of Russia, he is a non-permanent member of
Russia's Security Council, appointed to it by Vladimir Putin, with
Russian Defense Minister Sergei Shoigu also being a permanent
member of this security policy-developing organ of Russia. Thus,
Russia's highest security organ has two, one voting and another
advisory, military representatives in it.[57] It is somewhat similar
to the structure of America's National Security Council with the
U.S. Secretary of Defense being a Statutory Member while the
Chairman of Joint Chiefs of Staff serves as a Statutory Adviser.

But this similarity is skin deep because the Russian Chief of General Staff advises from the position of the chief strategist of nation's Armed Forces. This is not the case in the U.S., not to mention the fact that the Russian General Staff is the Main Organ of operational control of Russia's Armed Forces.[58] Mark Milley wasn't simply letting off steam when he continued, in his parting article about the Joint Force, with:

> Finally, and most importantly, we would designate the leader of this organization as the senior advocate solely dedicated to focus on the future joint operating environment, concepts, force design, requirements, and doctrine. He or she would represent the future joint warfighter in decision forums. This leader and organization would maintain a persistent focus on the fundamental evolution required for our future Joint Force.[59]

Milley, a few days away from retirement, didn't risk much when in effect admitting the failure of America's strategic planning and shaping of the U.S. Forces and suggesting the creation of a rudimentary general staff. But the reaction from many political corners in the U.S. was vicious, to put it mildly. Seth Cropsey, a devout neocon and a man with zero military background despite managing to occupy some positions within the Pentagon, fired a startling argument in his *The Hill* piece:

> Milley's argument, in the just-published issue of *Joint Force Quarterly*, demonstrates the U.S. military's direction—one that undermines the power of the services and centralizes strategic, operational and technological development within a pseudo general staff. This will create a military organization incapable of adapting to future conflict and reacting to unexpected technological change. Milley's proposals, in short, will lose the U.S. its next war.[60]

This retort by Cropsey was a classic American military argument since it continued to assume that America's consistently losing all its wars since Korea was somehow a good indication of America winning the next war, despite the obvious fact that a major part of America losing its grossly overstated military supremacy was precisely due to what Cropsey extolled as a virtue—the power of services who didn't win a single war in 60 plus years—precisely because neither the American political leadership nor America's National Security Council and its tentacles could come up with a proper strategy and policy which would ensure America's survival as a great nation, but rather paraded itself as an impotent military power incapable not only to fight a peer, but exposing its political and military top brass as people who wouldn't meet even rudimentary requirements for political and military leadership as formulated by Svechin.

Cropsey's retort was even more remarkable against the background of a SMO which by July 2023 was producing some shocking military developments, of which the U.S. couldn't even conceive, having learned nothing from history or about Russia. Cropsey lamented:

> Centralizing force design through a "future jointness czar" is not strategic wisdom—it is hubristic, bureaucratic policymaking. The danger is that the next chairman of the Joint Chiefs, and the next Secretary of Defense, are too blinded by their conviction in the arc of technological change that they commit the U.S. military to the wrong transformational program. Jointness is useful in creating a military force whose cooperation in training multiplies effectiveness in combat. But as the author of force design and doctrine for all the military services, it would be a disaster to trade experience for "harmonization."[61]

The audacity with which Cropsey defended the indefensible was startling and typical of the neocons who even in July 2023 continued to maintain their increasingly laughable position entertaining the idea that with NATO's help Ukraine still could defeat Russia, especially with Ukraine's suicidal "counter-offensive" which completely exposed the American establishment as geopolitically, economically and militarily illiterate and strategically inept, which led the United States into the strategic dead-end where it was handed a geopolitical defeat of historic proportions and ramifications. Moreover, the reality of which I tried to warn for many years became obvious—the United States and combined West in general have lost the arms race to Russia precisely because of Russia's General Staff and the way in which it develops strategies, plans operations and coordinates those with Russia's political leadership and influences its decision and policy-making.

CHAPTER 3.

THE DISASTROUS U.S. PREWAR CALCULATIONS

THE EVENTS LEADING TO Russia's starting her Special Military Operation (SMO) on February 24, 2022 will be recounted by real historians as a blunder of epic historic proportions by the United States and her allies, and drawing a parallel with the Axis forces launching Operation Barbarossa on June 22, 1941 is not only warranted but irresistible. As Hitler famously stated prior to the invasion of the Soviet Union: "We have only to kick in the door and the whole rotten structure will come crashing down."[62] Obviously Hitler was wrong, as was his staff in assessing the military, economic and cultural potential of the Soviet Union, but this rested at least on some foundation—Nazi Germany could show a record of accomplishments:

> ...the reasons for his [Hitler's] confidence are obvious. Germany deployed the most powerful military forces in the world. They had conquered Denmark and Norway, then the Netherlands, Belgium and France in 1940 and, in the same year, had driven the British from continental Europe. Only the Royal Air Force had saved the United Kingdom from invasion. Two months before the invasion of Russia, German armies—preceded by mass bombing—had overrun Yugoslavia and Greece.[63]

But therein also lies the problem with this analogy. The Wehrmacht by the time of Barbarossa could show a military record of defeating all leading military powers of the time, USSR excluded, and subjugating most of Europe, as well as having a vast military-economic potential. The U.S. war record is not even in the same league in the post-WW II period—it is primarily a record of losses to third-rate militaries or insurgencies—and it surely never matched the lofty rhetoric about being, as self-proclaimed, the "finest fighting force in history."[64] The finest fighting force it never was, nor did the United States as a nation ever know what real war and real costs of it were, as espoused by President Obama.[65] All nations do tend to pat themselves on the back over their military achievements but, not to take away anything from the American victory in the Pacific in WW II, or America's entering the European continent in 1944, the American case was and is a special one, primarily because of the wholesale illiteracy of the American political and military class of the military history of the 20th century projected against the background of a rather tame record of military accomplishments.

As Alexander Svechin elucidated in his magnum opus, some acquaintance with military affairs, the knowledge of history and of statistics, among many other things, of the enemy are indeed a must for political class.[66] This, however, doesn't apply to the American political class whatsoever—it is utterly illiterate in matters of international relations and military affairs. As General Robert Latiff noted, most of what the U.S. public and political class know about war is primarily from the utterly incompetent and malicious media and entertainment industry.[67] Moreover, America's views on Russia and her military history, especially the crucial events of WW II, have been influenced to a large degree by Wehrmacht commanders who provided a baneful influence on the way the history of WW II has been written in the United States, while the latter may not have borne in mind that, in the end, the Wehrmacht lost the war to Russians.

As David Glantz pointed out, not on only one occasion, the history of the Eastern Front and the role the Soviet Union played in defeating Axis forces was written largely based on a German perspective and German sources and driven by ethnic biases and political ideologies.[68] This view is so skewed that even America's respectable foremost military thinker, Colonel Douglas Macgregor, continues to articulate a grossly inaccurate, bordering on grotesque, myth about Russia's NKVD shooting in the backs of retreating Red Army soldiers and even claims that about a million soldiers died this way.[69] Rather than exemplifying his knowledge of military history, this is something from the echo chamber of America's Cold War myth-making. When even people of Macgregor's stature and high public profile continue to operate with pseudo-historical fairy tales and absolutely ridiculous mathematics, such as using claims that Stalin didn't care about casualties or that the GULAG consumed 17 million lives and stayed operational until 1989, one has to ask questions about the professional qualifications of even the best of the U.S. military.[70]

If Macgregor couldn't see the pro-Polish agenda in the at best second-rate writing of Norman Davies, on whose fantasies Macgregor based his claims, he should have paid attention to *The Guardian,* which couldn't take Davies' book seriously and published a devastating review of it, including sardonic reference to Davies' Polish nationalism.[71] But here we have a former colonel of the U.S. Army, going against a fundamental strategic and operational principle existing since antiquity, expressed in Sun Tzu's famous truism:

> Know the enemy and know yourself in a hundred battles you will never be in peril. When you are ignorant of the enemy but know yourself, your chances of winning or losing are equal. If ignorant both of your enemy and of yourself, you are certain in every battle to be in peril.[72]

Expecting any better from the American military-political establishment in what amounts to basic understanding of America's enemies is a very tall order—America remains profoundly provincial and unsophisticated in her view of the outside world and never knew or studied her enemies, real and perceived, on the level required for developing sensible strategies for interacting with them or, for that matter, fighting them to some military-political outcome favorable for the United States. American lack of knowledge of Russia, however, has an additional drawback—

large portions of American political and military class suffer from various degrees of Russophobia, while a class of America's neoconservatives suffers from a fanatical hatred of Russia and Russians. This fanaticism never was and is not conducive for the development of a serious understanding of Russia, especially given the neoconservatives' lack of military comprehension, as was exposed by the utterly amateurish and wishful thinking "forecasts" by the Kagan family "think-tank," the Institute for the Study of War.

To be sure, America's intellectual class does love to publish books on all kinds of matters ranging from geopolitics to military doctrines and strategies, but in the last 30 years the field of American strategic forecasting turned out to be at best second-rate, at worst—a hack job. The field of Russian Studies in the contemporary U.S. is absent altogether as a viable academic subject, and among the latest Russia "experts" who continue to carry the torch of offering an allegedly insider view on USSR/Russia we find Yuri Bezmenov or people of a caliber of Anatoly Golitsyn. Golitsyn was the mid-level KGB operative who defected to the U.S. and took the role of Rasputin to James Angleton, then chief of CIA's counterintelligence, selling him a cornucopia of conspiracy theories on Soviet activities and intentions.[73] But at least Golitsyn, unlike Bezmenov, was the real deal, a bona fide cadre KGB officer who did initially provide some valuable for CIA information.

However, the events of the Maidan Coup of 2014 in Kiev, organized and financed by the U.S., and Russia's reacquiring Crimea in 2014 as a consequence of it gave birth to the absolute domination in the American media of "Russia experts," who are primarily, albeit non-exclusively, of Russian Jewish descent having a strong Russophobic streak and of neoconservative leaning. Many of them such as Masha Gessen, Max Boot or Julia Ioffe do not even hide their hatred for Russia, sometimes so extreme that even Western-leaning Russian outlets had to react to Ioffe's piece in *The Atlantic* titled *What Putin Really Wants,* one of many selling a non-existent Russia to American readers. This massive opus by Ioffe was deconstructed by Anton Kurilkin on Medium,

and following a highly professional and devastating criticism led
to a conclusion that was in essence a diagnosis.

> The saddest thing about this article is that Ioffe
> will now consolidate her authority in the States as
> a specialist on Russia, and people will turn to her
> for assessments and comments, she will be called
> to the expert councils at the White House (Obama
> already called her to such a council in 2014), she will
> be quoted. Because of such experts (and, judging
> by the lack of reaction to Ioffe's opuses, there are
> not many others in the United States), Russia will
> continue to be treated in the same bad and clichéd
> way. Any attempt to improve relations will be met
> with misunderstanding by the Americans—it's just
> that instead of Russian communists they will now
> hunt for Russian computer geniuses from FSB and
> GRU, and when they hear the word "Russia" they
> will now imagine not bears in earflaps with a red star,
> but hackers with vodka.[74]

But if Max Boot or Julia Ioffe, or, for that matter, a collection
of "experts" from the Institute for the Study of War, most of whom
have zero military background and have degrees in anything but
military science or STEM, are traditional, highly neoconservative
personalities and institutions, the appearance of Rebekah Koffler
was something of a novelty. She introduced herself in her book
Putin's Playbook: Russia's Secret Plan to Defeat America as a
Russian-born intelligence expert who had briefed the Pentagon,
the White House, and NATO on Russian affairs.[75] One may have
been impressed with Koffler's career inside the U.S. intelligence
community, but there were immediately questions regarding her
Russian/Soviet background, especially points stressed at her
author page at Amazon, points she stressed repeatedly in her
many appearances at Fox News as their "expert." The Amazon
page reads:

Koffler's analysis is enriched by her deeply personal account of her life in the Soviet Union. Devoted to her adopted homeland but concerned about the complacency of her fellow citizens, she appreciates American freedoms as only a survivor of totalitarianism can. An opportunity to view ourselves and the world through the eyes of our adversary, *Putin's Playbook* is a rare and compelling testimony that we ignore at our peril.[76]

Here is the problem from the get-go with Koffler and her personal accounts. In Russia, after her earlier life in Kazakhstan, Koffler managed to enter and graduate from Moscow State Pedagogical University *with a degree in English*, or, in layman's lingo, she is an English Teacher by education. Koffler's wildest claims about her understanding of the Russian mindset and her C.V. rife with many hot-button words such as "strategic," "briefings," "analysis," et al., can certainly impress a simpleton, but reality behind Koffler's claims is much more prosaic. Koffler was born into a purely civilian Soviet family and has absolutely zero experience or grasp of Russian strategic thinking because she never served in the Soviet/Russian Armed Forces, never graduated from any military academy and, consequently, has never been a bearer of any serious clearance which would have allowed her to have a glimpse of, much less professional education in, the crucial tactical, operational and strategic documents which define this very Russian thinking. Obviously, she never was a part of Soviet/Russian military-academic and intelligence environment, which outright disqualifies her from having any serious professional opinion on any serious strategic or operational matter as related to Russia, be that military-intelligence, let alone state apparatus levels.

In this respect Koffler is a classic U.S. intelligence product and her book reflected it perfectly through its non-stop sequence of conspiracy theories, gas-lighting and gaffes, not least through claims that the United States could rely in case of war on "advanced" military technology such as Littoral Combat Ships.[77]

It was shocking to read such "revelations" from the person who actually did serve in the Defense Intelligence Agency yet didn't know that the United States Navy was decommissioning Littoral Combat Ships (LCS) at an alarming rate precisely because they were deemed militarily useless and ridden with technical problems—even though this debate about the decommissioning of these ships lasted for a number of years until yet another batch was ready to be retired:

> The House Armed Services Committee will allow the Navy to move ahead with plans to decommission the troubled Littoral Combat Ships and wants to shutter the Pentagon's Cost Assessment and Program Evaluation office.
>
> In its mark of the Fiscal Year 2024 defense policy bill, the HASC seapower and projection forces subcommittee prevents the Navy from retiring three Whidbey Island-class dock landing ships and two Ticonderoga-class guided-missile cruisers but did not include the same provision for the two Littoral Combat Ships the Navy wants to decommission.[78]

For a military analyst and Russia "expert" Koffler revealed herself to be a credentialed amateur who not only had huge issues with understanding what modern Russia is, but also an appalling lack of technical expertise as related to actual warfare. Yet, again, Koffler is symptomatic of the American lack of expertise on Russia and the way Russians formulate their strategies, plan operations and unify this into a single organism of the state, which has clearly formulated goals and ways of their achievement. United States simply has no similar such experience or political, economic and military mechanisms in place. Or, as the old saying goes, with experts like that....

And such have been the American "experts" from academe, to the Pentagon, to the State Department, to the intelligence community who, based on their echo-chamber delusions, developed a strategy for Ukraine as a ram against Russia. The foundation of this strategy was not based on knowledge but on the Russophobic delusion of Zbigniew Brzezinski, who spent most of his white board geopolitical theories development life in search for ways to defeat and break up Russia. His main contribution to his own version of reality, which also influenced the Obama Administration, was a tenet that Russia without Ukraine would never become an empire again—in Brzezinski lingo, would never again be a superpower.[79]

So, in such a context, the choice of deploying Ukraine was only natural—as was the strategy, reflected throughout a number of the American documents and publications, both public and classified, obfuscated by euphemisms, such as "rules-based order" and promotion of "human rights" among many others. Such a strategy could only have been born from ignorance of both Russia and warfare. Brzezinski's dictum went: deny Russia the possession of Ukraine and Russia will remain eternally weak. After that, the logic went, use Ukraine as a battering ram against Russia for a possible, even if not very likely military defeat and thereby, highly likely in the minds of those who concocted this strategy, tie Russia's resources in a second Afghanistan-type quagmire until a fifth column inside Russia, based on predicted deteriorating economic conditions from a "shock and awe" sanctions regime, precipitates the overthrow of Vladimir Putin and his "regime." After that, those who helped to overthrow Vladimir Putin would fill all important government posts and help the United States and its vassals to break up Russia and surrender its resources to the West's transnational corporations. It was a classic color revolution "strategy" designed for small and weak states.

There is no need to elaborate on this strategy in depth because the level of strategic planning which went into this contrived hare-brained scheme was based on perceptions of the Russia of the 1990s and on neoliberal economic modelling, which is solely based on financial legerdemain and overlooks practically all critical economic and military indicators which do separate a failed state from a nuclear superpower. This is how Washington overlooked the obvious fact of Russia largely returning itself to the status of superpower by 2014. But it was, yet again, this echo chamber which played a cruel trick with Washington's establishment: while declaring America's Gross Domestic Product (GDP) as the largest in the world—a fake economic index which doesn't reflect the real economy of a nation—American court "strategists" have convinced themselves that with the U.S. GDP of around $16.84 trillion it would be easy to deal with the Russian economic midget whose GDP was measured in 2013 at $2.29 trillion.[80]

This misperception was possible, paradoxically, through the workings of the American-dominated global economic and financial institutions who play with economic statistics any way they want, including the introduction of purely virtual indices, such as "capitalization," not to mention the credit rating system, whose only purpose is to maintain America's credit rating as a shining example of free enterprise and as, inevitably, a tool for punishing those who dare to disobey the rules-based order by means such as assigning healthy economies deliberately low credit ratings.[81] The kind of currency manipulation the United States engaged in, including its increasing at an alarming rate its public debt, was something the objects of Pax Americana were not supposed to notice. But Russia certainly did notice that U.S. public debt for March 2013 was already $16.77 trillion and growing.[82] Russia's own was around 5 trillion Rubles.[83] Russia reported her GDP for 2013 as 66.7 trillion Rubles.[84] The trend was obvious—the United States was beginning to sink in debt with the Debt to GDP Ratio for the U.S. approaching 100% while that for Russia was hovering around 10–12%.

But here was the crucial strategic question: What U.S. GDP? Based on what statistics, on what economic data? If, as the American neoliberal economists and establishment insisted, the U.S. GDP was around $17 trillion in 2013, what was the structure of this GDP? The answer was obvious—the United States has been in the deindustrialization mode since the Reagan Administration and pushed the pedal to the metal after passing the fateful legislation *House Resolution 4444 China Trade Bill* in May of 2000, which opened a floodgate to America's deindustrialization. This was in great contrast to Russia's reindustrialization, which had already started to pick up tempo by 2010, but after the overthrow of the Yanukovich government in Kiev, went into overdrive. The West, meanwhile, was still residing in its echo chamber, continuing to feed its ego, gorged to the limit, with self-congratulatory statements about the combined West being superior in every single facet of human activity to Russia. So much so that even before the start of Russia's SMO, amidst increasing and well-orchestrated hysteria in the Western media, Germany's new Defense minister Christine Lambrecht in her interview to Bild, responding to the question of whether NATO should destroy Nord Stream 2 pipeline, responded:

> We have to use the entire toolbox we have. We currently have to target Putin and his environment. Those responsible for the aggression must feel personal consequences, for example that they can no longer travel to the Champs Elysées in Paris for shopping.[85]

Naturally, Lambrecht's interview elicited a wave of a Homeric laughter across most of Russia's media and social networks. Most Russians couldn't grasp such a lack of self-awareness and level of ignorance about Russia from a politician of her rank. The popular Russian newspaper *Komsomolskaya Pravda* went on to openly mock Lambrecht, as did many other major Russian news outlets:

> Why such hellish sanctions? New Year is coming soon! Christmas, again. And no shopping! And how cunning, she proposes to ban Paris, but not a word about Berlin. This is, of course, very funny. Wisecrack of the year, one might say. But how sad this is! I want to cry, to be honest. When a person with such a level of thinking is in such a position, determining to some extent world and, for the most part, European defense policy, when the Minister of Defense of the second most powerful NATO member argues at such a level and uses such "powerful" argumentation. Bismarck

and the entire corps of Wehrmacht generals are now spinning in their graves with shame.[86]

But no matter how one views the sheer grotesqueness of Lambrecht's statement, it disclosed the simple fact that many Western politicians were still stuck in the Cold War perceptions of Russia and would have suffered serious cognitive dissonance upon visiting Moscow, St. Petersburg, Kazan or Sochi and comparing them, including their shopping, to rat- and bedbug-infested Paris, not to speak of other major Western capitals, few of which could rival the glitz, wealth, cleanness, safety and scale of Moscow. Lambrecht, as well as most Brussels and Washington bureaucrats, would have been very unpleasantly surprised by the fact that the Russian economy of 2021 was much larger than that of Germany. Even a brief comparison of Russia's and Germany's main economic indices for 2020–2021 revealed an astonishing disparity in real economy drivers.

Category	Germany	Russia
Energy Production/Consumption MTOE*	102/288	1,522/826[87]
Electricity Production/Consumption TWh**	588/490	1,158/979[88]
Steel Production Million Tons	40	76[89]
Aluminum Production Million Tons	0.52 estimate	3.64[90]
Agriculture	Importer	Exporter
Military-Industrial Complex, full cycle production.	40–45% est.	100% est.
STEM graduates. UNESCO 2018 Data.	101, 819	497, 243[91]
Pig Iron Production Million Tons	25.7	53.6[92]

*MTOE—Million Ton Oil Equivalent
**TWh—Terawatt-Hour

The fact that Germany's Defense Minister thought that "Putin's environment" really cared about shopping for grossly overpriced and useless brand names in Europe was also a great indicator of pettiness of the Western political class, which hasn't produced a real statesman for decades. As further events have shown, the combined West approached its Ukrainian debacle with Louis Vuitton mentality, ignoring practically all indicators which truly define the power of a nation when a state is addressing serious matters of war and peace. As Hungary's President Victor Orban would admit recently, 20 months into Russia's SMO in Ukraine:

> What was the strategy of the West in that war? I'm simplifying it a little bit, but this is the fact. Our strategy was that the Ukrainians will fight and will win on the front line. The Russians will lose . . . and that loss will create a change in Moscow. That was the strategy: We finance, the Ukrainians fight and die, where we are now, it is obvious that the Ukrainians will not win on the front line. There is no solution on the battleground. The Russians will not lose. There will be no political change in Moscow. This is the reality, Russia will not lose, and nothing will change in its policy. Therefore, we must face reality. We must switch to Plan B.[93]

But there was something more to Lambrecht's statement and it was much more important. Russia knew that Armed Forces of Ukraine (AFU) had been getting ready to attack the Donbass Republics with the explicit objective of provoking the Russia's response, even in view of Russian troops conducting constant maneuvers along the border with Donetsk and Lugansk republics in anticipation of an AFU offensive. In the last-ditch attempt to avoid military confrontation with what at that time amounted to the best U.S. (and West) proxy in history—trained and equipped with many critical C4 elements—Russia presented on December 15, 2021, a draft agreement, a diplomatic euphemism for demands, with Washington on mutual security guarantees.

There was very little new in that Russian proposal—it was a reiteration of the same points which Russia had insisted upon since the 1990s, the most important of them being the non-expansion of NATO, now with the added item related to Ukraine, which since

2013 was becoming in effect NATO's forward operational base.
Russia's offering to Washington merits consideration:

1. The Parties shall be guided in their relations by the
   principles of cooperation, equal and indivisible security.
   They shall not strengthen their security individually,
   within international organizations, military alliances or
   coalitions at the expense of the security of other Parties.
   The Parties shall settle all international disputes in their
   mutual relations by peaceful means and refrain from the
   use or threat of force in any manner inconsistent with the
   purposes of the United Nations.
2. In order to address issues and settle problems, the Parties
   shall use the mechanisms of urgent bilateral or multilateral
   consultations, including the NATO-Russia Council.
   The Parties shall regularly and voluntarily exchange
   assessments of contemporary threats and security
   challenges, inform each other about military exercises and
   maneuvers, and main provisions of their military doctrines.
   All existing mechanisms and tools for confidence-building
   measures shall be used in order to ensure transparency
   and predictability of military activities. Telephone hotlines
   shall be established to maintain emergency contacts
   between the Parties.
3. The Parties reaffirm that they do not consider each other
   as adversaries. The Parties shall maintain dialogue and
   interaction on improving mechanisms to prevent incidents
   on and over the high seas (primarily in the Baltics and the
   Black Sea region).
4. The Russian Federation and all the Parties that were
   member States of the North Atlantic Treaty Organization
   as of 27 May 1997, respectively, shall not deploy military
   forces and weaponry on the territory of any of the other
   States in Europe in addition to the forces stationed on that
   territory as of 27 May 1997. With the consent of all the
   Parties such deployments can take place in exceptional

cases to eliminate a threat to security of one or more Parties.

5. The Parties shall not deploy land-based intermediate- and short-range missiles in areas allowing them to reach the territory of the other Parties.

6. All member States of the North Atlantic Treaty Organization commit themselves to refrain from any further enlargement of NATO, including the accession of Ukraine as well as other States.

7. The Parties that are member States of the North Atlantic Treaty Organization shall not conduct any military activity on the territory of Ukraine as well as other States in the Eastern Europe, in the South Caucasus and in Central Asia.

8. In order to exclude incidents, the Russian Federation and the Parties that are member States of the North Atlantic Treaty Organization shall not conduct military exercises or other military activities above the brigade level in a zone of agreed width and configuration on each side of the border line of the Russian Federation and the states in a military alliance with it, as well as Parties that are member States of the North Atlantic Treaty Organization.[94]

It was in the classic language of Russian diplomacy, which expressed Russia's intentions toward NATO so eloquently; these were also the language and intentions which have been ignored by the West since the 1990s. What hasn't been understood by the West, however, was the fact that it was the Russia of the 2020s addressing NATO, not the Russia of the 1990s or 2000s. Moreover, only a few in the West noticed the analogy with the great Frank Herbert's novel, *Dune*, in which every article of the Imperium's Great Convention started with the phrase "The Forms must be obeyed." Russia's proposal was "obeying the forms." As Steven Pifer of Brookings Institution noted on December 21, 2021:

> The unacceptable provisions in the two draft agreements, their quick publication by the Russian government, and the peremptory terms used by

Russian officials to describe Moscow's demands raise
concern that the Kremlin may want rejection. With
large forces near Ukraine, Moscow could then cite
that as another pretext for military action against its
neighbor.[95]

Peremptory this draft may have been, but it was, undoubtedly,
also an attempt to avoid a catastrophe for both Ukraine and
combined West, which Russia's military-political top could and
did forecast based on the superb intelligence and arguably the best
strategic assessment apparatus in the world—the Russian General
Staff, Service of Foreign Intelligence (SVR), FSB (Federal
Security Service) and Ministry of Foreign Affairs (MID).

To Pifer's credit he did note that Russia was talking
from a position of strength of a country possessing the world's
largest nuclear arsenal and strongest conventional military in
Europe.[96] Pifer's admission, however, was not enough. Such
rare manifestations of strategic common sense, primarily among
the narrowest of strata of informed people in the West, could
not avert a catastrophe which would reshape human civilization
and dramatically shift the balance of power in favor of Russia
and her strategic partner, China. With it, the geopolitical power
of the combined West would be greatly diminished. But this
scenario, which meant a calamity for the West, couldn't have
been comprehended, let alone acted upon, even if the captains
of the combined West had—as difficult as it is to imagine—been
competent people, because understanding alone is not enough.
Only when such knowledge is internalized and becomes a guide,
only then may one seriously consider a strategic change of course
in such matters of an immense scale as the global balance of power
and matters of war and peace. Western academic and analytical
institutions are not designed for that process or purpose.

And then, there is Statecraft as Art of Governance and
Military Art. While the meaning of craft is fairly easily understood
by anyone, the difference between Military Science, as in our
particular case here, applied to Strategy, and Military Art is not
always understood. Why art, and when do Craft and Science

become one? The fundamental principles of running a state are knowable by just about anybody with the desire to learn, they are also taught in government courses in a number of Western universities. Russia has similar courses in her universities, plus she has The Russian Presidential Academy of National Economy and Public Administration (The Presidential Academy RANEPA). But those and many other similar institutions do not guarantee that even the best students will turn out to be great state managers. "Private and public" management, a euphemism for state or government management, are not the same. Moreover, the academic tool kit for governing such a state as Russia requires a crucial creative ability to apply the appropriate tool for such a governance and that is the moment when even in the 21st century the process of such governance becomes an art. In the end, it is difficult as it is to apply existing tools, let alone create new ones. There is also the issue of finding a balance between the ever present and at work various political, economic and human interests—this is an art, very often a high one.

As its approach to the SMO demonstrated perfectly, Russia's governance turned out to be creative and manifested itself as an art, not least through great forecasting and forestalling the actions by the U.S.-led NATO block, but especially so in its military and economic preparation of the country to clash with NATO, including through the process of constant adaptation to changing external and internal conditions. This was not the case for the United States, whose governance institutions, including the very top political leadership, exhibited a shocking failure to act responsibly and competently, not just in the international arena but internally. In fact, America's political dysfunction reached such grotesque forms that even ever-restrained Vladimir Putin had to point out the chaos and cessation of functioning of the much touted American "democracy" and "rule of law" related to the historic United States attempts to persecute a former U.S. president, Donald Trump. Speaking at the Eastern Economic Forum in Vladivostok Vladimir Putin didn't mince the words. As RT reported:

The numerous criminal charges against former U.S.
President Donald Trump amount to persecution and
showcase the "rot" in the American political system,
Russian President Vladimir Putin has stated. The
U.S. in its current state *"cannot claim the right to
teach others democracy,"* . . . *"The things that are
happening to Trump are persecution of a political
competitor. . . . That is what it is. And it is done in
the full view of the U.S. public and the entire world,"*
he added. The controversy is beneficial to Russia in
the sense that it "exposes" Washington *"for what it
is,"* according to Putin. The U.S. government chose
to be hostile to Moscow and has propagandized its
population into perceiving it as such, he argued.
*"[The U.S.] demonstrates what they called in Soviet
times 'the bestial scowl of imperialism,'"* he joked.[97]

The scowl of imperialism continues to be the scowl of
America's oligarchy of which yours truly, among many others,
have tried to warn for many years. But unlike the now widely
accepted fact of the United States being run by an oligarchy,
many still had at least some, however imprecise, recognition of
this oligarchy's perceived intellectual power and influence. This
hadn't been the case. As I noted in 2021:

This oligarchy, realistically, is not very bright, despite
being rich, with many of them having Ivy league
degrees. They have proved this beyond the shadow
of a doubt. Clausewitz' dictum that it is legitimate to
judge an event by its outcome for it is the soundest
criterion remains true even after two centuries.
American politics was always tawdry, now the
whole American political system, with its allegedly
"free" media and establishment academe, have been
paraded around the world as one huge tawdry blob,
whose functionaries continue to perceive it as a global
superpower, which it no longer is.[98]

For a milieu which considers Wall Street the measure of the nation's economic development, it would have been very difficult to have a grasp of the art of governing an economic and military superpower such as Russia. While some saw Russia's security proposal in December 2021 as both a peace offer and a warning, the Washington Establishment saw it, as it usually does, as an indication of Russia's weakness and even panic in Moscow. In this respect, Washington was akin to a 19th century poor street vendor from the countryside taken off the street and brought into the theater in the capital to listen to opera or see a ballet, without having even basic understanding of the intricacies of complex forms of art reserved at that time mostly for the well off and cultured. America's overall decline hasn't been a secret since well before Russia's launching the SMO, but the final deconstruction of the American military mythology as well as its lack of a strategic thinking and knowledge of Military Art was revealed on February 24, 2022, with the first Russian Army armored columns rolling into the territory of Ukraine and what would be recognized by Russia on February 21, 2022 as the Donbass Republics. The new world order was unfolding....

CHAPTER 4.

RUSSIA'S SPECIAL MILITARY OPERATION: THE OPENING PHASE

RUSSIA LAUNCHED Special Military Operation (SMO) in Ukraine on February 24, 2022. Immediately after midnight, at 00:16 on February 24, the heads of Donetsk and Lugansk Republics, now recognized by Russia, issued an appeal to Russia for help in the face of increasing Ukraine military activity, including unrelenting shelling of civilian parts of Donetsk and surrounding areas. Three hours later the president of Ukraine tried to contact Russian president, but there was no response from the Kremlin.[99] Vladimir Putin addressed the nation at 05:52 AM. In his urgent address to the nation, he stressed that he had ordered the start of SMO and stated its political goals:

> Its goal is to protect people who have been subjected to abuse and genocide by the Kyiv regime for eight years. And for this, we will strive for the demilitarization and denazification of Ukraine, as well as bringing to justice those who committed numerous, bloody crimes against civilians, including citizens of the Russian Federation.[100]

The expected condemnations from the West and chaotic diplomatic activity and a media circus ensued. Immediately a massive, coordinated propaganda campaign was launched by the NATO countries' media—a first sign of the combined West, headed by the United States, having been prepared in advance for Russia's move. The key word in the unified choir of Western statesmen and media was "unprovoked" and "brutal." As U.S. President Biden described it:

> The Russian military has begun a brutal assault on the people of Ukraine without provocation, without justification, without necessity. This is a premeditated attack. Vladimir Putin has been planning this for months, as I've been—as we've been saying all along. He moved more than 175,000 troops, military equipment into positions along the Ukrainian border.[101]

This was pure Gulf of Tonkin, a euphemism for deliberate lying from the highest political podium in the United States all over again, with the major difference that U.S. attempts to provoke Russia into direct engagement in Ukraine had been ongoing for almost eight years, with Russia trying to dodge a military scenario just as long. All Russia's efforts to point out continuing violations of the ceasefire regime and ongoing shelling of the areas in Donetsk and Lugansk regions—even documented by the openly pro-Ukraine Organization for Security and Cooperation in Europe (OSCE)—fell on deaf ears.[102] The U.S. was hellbent on seeing Russia getting bogged down—the dominating point of view of the Biden administration—in Ukraine. Considering a mediocre at best, at worst non-existent military-engineering background of the most influential actors in Biden's administration, the difference between starting a war in Vietnam or Iraq, and starting a war on Russia's threshold, one of many differences, was lost on them. The Washington establishment continued to make this mistake on a consistent basis, elevating it thus into a systemic one: it failed to realize that Russia was a military superpower with an extremely advanced ISR (Intelligence, Surveillance and Reconnaissance) complex which allowed it to document most of Ukraine's transgressions. No one at that time in the White House, CIA, NSA or Pentagon could comprehend the significance of this fact since, as it became clear much later into the conflict, many truly believed that the Armed Forces of Ukraine (AFU) could either attack, defeat and push the Russian Army out of the Donbass region or at least make sure it would get bogged down in a quagmire. This, in the opinions of the U.S. strategists, would destabilize "Putin's regime."

Here is where the important digression must be made, especially against the background of Western media hysteria and its deliberate and well-organized misinformation campaign, focused and directed at specifically Western and Ukrainian populations. Why a Special Military Operation and not a war? A reasonable question. The answer to the "secret" of this designation is in the open. All armies in the world fight in accordance with their fighting doctrine, strategy and planned operations. They also fight wars using tactical level Combat Manuals and Operational Instructions, as the titles suggest—for operational level documents. To a layman it may come as a surprise, but these types of documents describe much more than just the organization, calculations, deployment and maneuvering for units and formations of the fighting army. Operational, strategic, and most tactical level documents, apart from being highly classified military publications, also define such numbers as estimates and thresholds of military and civilian casualties, depending on the type of battle or operation. This is crucial for understanding why Russia didn't declare war on Ukraine but declared a Special Military Operation (SMO).

In a real war between state actors, which is fought for existential reasons, driven not just by political, economic, territorial and prestige interests, but also due to ideological and even metaphysical differences, the main objective is always the complete destruction of the enemy leadership, or what today would be termed "regime change." Witness the wholesale atrocity Israel has been committing against Palestinians in Gaza since October 7, 2023, purportedly targeting Hamas leadership. No doubt, the underlying reason for mass killing of the defenseless civilian population of Gaza has a very pragmatic, land-grabbing rationale behind it, but here this is just one element of an otherwise complex interplay of religious and ideological differences between Muslim Palestinians, Arabs in general, and Israeli and Western Zionists, many of whom, like the U.S. President, are not Jews at all. But

Israel seeks a total eradication of not just Hamas but the ethnic cleansing of the entire Palestinian population from the Gaza Strip, thus pursuing a political aim by means of committing crimes against humanity.

The brutality of Israel's handling of Gaza and its civilian population, with its especially large percentage of women and children, became so outrageous that it evoked sharp criticism even from the corners where Israel usually gets an unrestricted pass—the U.S. Congress. Writing in the *Washington Post*, U.S. Democratic Senator Chris Van Hollen pointed out:

> In just eight weeks of war, we have witnessed a massive level of death, destruction and displacement. More than 16,000 Palestinians have been killed in Gaza, more than two-thirds of them women and children—10 times more children killed than in nearly two years of war in Ukraine. More than 1.8 million people in Gaza, or nearly 80 percent of the population, have been displaced.[103]

The comparison was startling but also revealing; the comparative numbers of civilian deaths also partially answered the question of why Russia had launched an SMO and not a full-blown war against Ukraine. The comparison was even more significant when one considers the scale of the SMO, which dwarfs the Israel military's "war" on Gaza both in purely military-economic and in geographic terms. But the most evident answer to the question of why Russia didn't start a war, but rather an SMO, was in the immediately noticeable fact of Russia having no intention of harming Ukraine's political leadership, including President of Ukraine Vladimir Zelensky. In other words, Russia wasn't trying initially to change the regime in Kiev. An explanation for this reluctance, for the lack of a better term, would come later in March of 2022.

The order of battle for both sides on the eve of launching the SMO looked approximately as follows. The number of active personnel of the AFU on January 1, 2022 was estimated at 261,000.

Its operational reserve accounted for 234,000 servicemen ready to be recalled for duty almost immediately.[104] The recall of the first echelon of this operational reserve of the AFU, which accounted for 148,000, began as early as February 22, 2022, with a second echelon of 86,000 getting ready to follow what amounted to the start of the first mobilization of the AFU.[105] In other words, the AFU could field roughly 550,600 active duty personnel, all of whom were in the age group under 40 years old and already had service and/or combat experience fighting in Donbas since 2014, in the opening phase of the SMO. The size of the Russian invasion force, which was estimated by the Biden administration at around 175,000, could also rely on approximately 40,000+ of the Lugansk and Donetsk Republics' militia, which would put the number of Russian forces at around 215,000. In other words, the Russian invasion force was roughly 2.6 times smaller than the Ukrainian Army. In addition, the Armed Forces of Ukraine boasted a very substantial armored force, much of it modernized prior to the start of the SMO with NATO systems, which numbered, by different estimates, 3,309 armored fighting vehicles, while the Ukrainian Air Force operated 132 combat and transport aircraft.[106] Moreover, the Air Defense Forces of Ukraine had at their disposal at least 250 long-range air defense systems of earlier versions of the S-300 family, 72 Buk-M1 systems and a number of short-range Tor-M1 and Osa air defense complexes. Ukraine even returned obsolete S-125 systems into service.[107]

It was clear from the outset that Russia had an overwhelming military-technological advantage over Ukraine, fielding a very well equipped and trained army, but that was if one considered the dyadic relation: Russia vs. Ukraine alone. Once the NATO support would factor in, however, the advantage wouldn't be as lopsided, albeit Russia would still have a dramatic edge over Ukraine. The fact that NATO had already been directly involved with Ukraine since 2014 was not a secret: NATO instructors trained many units and formations of the Ukrainian Armed Forces and NATO was modernizing and equipping the Ukrainian side.[108] The United States was also training the AFU to fight in the same manner as NATO, that is to say the U.S. Army, despite the U.S.

Army having no experience with peer-to-peer warfare, and having a losing record even against third world nations. This factor of training and configuring AFU into effectively an NATO extension force wasn't initially recognized by the Pentagon and NATO planners as not an advantage, but quite the opposite—a serious hindrance to a survival of the AFU as a fighting force against the Russian Army, which was capable to blunt, if not stop completely, the main operational and tactical tool around which the whole U.S. fighting doctrine is built—U.S. and NATO air forces and air dominance—but could wreak havoc with the U.S. C4 (Command, Control, Communications, Computers) structure strategically and operationally. It took the U.S. almost 20 months to openly admit, through U.S. war propaganda media, namely the *New York Times,* that:

> The 2023 counteroffensive was built around remaking Ukraine's army in the image of America's. It was, critics said, the approach the United States had tried in Vietnam, Iraq and Afghanistan, largely unsuccessfully.[109]

But in February 2022 nobody in Washington really cared about the fundamentals of national and military strategies, operations and military art. In fact, most people in the Washington establishment and its media wouldn't know the difference between them, and that, combined with its sheer ignorance of Russia and its reliance on Kiev's "intelligence" which yet again was prodding the U.S. along the same path toward a Chalabi Moment reminiscent of the U.S. attack on Iraq and so many earlier instances—with the difference being that the United States was dealing now with a military and economic superpower of which they knew nothing—predetermined the outcome of the SMO from the very start. This created what the *New York Times* would later define as "kind of a collective expectation inflation."[110] This inflation was not a momentary lapse of reason among Washington's strategists, it was not a bug—it was a feature which defined America's failure at strategic planning and Command and Control incompetence in a war in which the U.S. Army didn't have a decisive edge over enemy but, in fact, was an underdog.

At this stage it is important to explain my numerous uses of the word "art" whenever speaking about operational art or, generally, about military art. One may reasonably ask, even though many serious military academies, with the exception of American ones, bestow degrees in military science on their graduates, which is a legitimate and not an easy science to master, whether they award degrees in military art. This term is not an oxymoron— military art is a direct relative of art, which concerns humanity's creative activity rooted to a large degree in the imagination. An instance of military art in real life could be the ability of military leaders, based on their military academic and service experience, to confuse the enemy and, through operational art, shape the battlefield to the operational and strategic advantage of their own forces. Operational art, in turn, is the artful use of formations in such a way as to deny the opponent the path to victory or stalemate. This is done to a very large degree through art, not just via the hard sciences upon which it is based, such as Operational Research, Planning, War Gaming, military technology, its combat use and physics and mathematics principles.

Operation Bagration by the Red Army, which started on June 22, 1944, is an ultimate example of not just outstanding strategic and operational planning, but of military art applied by the authors of this operation, namely Josef Stalin, Georgi Zhukov, Vasilevsky and Antonov, a handful of people who knew the true scope and scale of the plan, and who had to juggle a myriad of economic, military, strategic and operational inputs—which in itself is an art—to arrive at decisions which spelled doom for the Wehrmacht's Army Group Center and had far reaching not just military-strategic but also political ramifications.[111] In the end, even such a dry and strictly professional document such as the U.S. Army Field Manual on *Staff Organization and Operations* defines terms fairly well-known to most people such as Command and Control (C2) as: "an essential element of the art and science of warfare."[112] But it is the U.S. Joint Doctrine which gives a broad definition of Operational Art as: "The application of creative imagination by commanders and staffs—supported by their skill, knowledge, and experience—to design strategies, campaigns, and major operations and organize and employ military forces. Operational art integrates ends, ways, and means across the levels of war."[113]

It is quite obvious that Russian and Western militaries' many protocols and procedures for operational planning have much in common. They surely have the same mathematics, which is in the foundation of most of military affairs, but it in HOW those methods are applied which sets Russian and American (NATO in general) views on war dramatically apart and it is in this difference that the military art, the art of warfare, takes place and decides the outcome of war, that is having a strategic influence. One can easily understand some tactical-technical paraments of one or another weapon system, and real professionals will generally understand what the enemy can do with that, but HOW the enemy can do it on tactical, operational and strategic levels—that's an entire other story. And that is why it is prudent to state that any staff officer of the brigade level and higher who ever took part in operational planning could immediately recognize that the Russian force which invaded Ukraine was designed for achieving limited objectives and was not initially designed either for the occupation of Ukraine or for the destruction of Ukraine as a state. Most likely the Pentagon understood that, but for the U.S. Armed Forces, whose only MO for decades was "regime change" with a further subjugation of the unlucky third world country and priming it for serving U.S. interests, the non-PR driven and measured application of force specifically tailored to certain contingencies is an unknown in war. The American wars' media circus, also known as "war porn," and the election cycle in the U.S. create imperatives which prevent the United States Armed Forces from internalizing a simple fact that military victories are won not by relentlessly blowing things up with impunity and showing it on TV, but on the operational and strategic levels.[114] Those victory-bearing levels impose a completely different set of requirements for prosecuting the war.

Russians have been aware for a long time that U.S. military operational thinking lacked the depth and serious considerations of a state's military and strategic strength and depth. The entire American view of war, its "creative" and its "imaginative" parts, have been built around airpower, which, in its turn, as represented by the U.S. Air Force, viewed the war as a sequence of (relentless) bombing and missiles runs with impunity against the enemy, exhausting it and thus allowing the U.S. Army to move in and defeat the enemy's army.[115] It is a great plan in appropriate circumstances, but in real war with a peer or better than peer power it cannot work because, as much as America is infatuated with the air power, it is always a joint force which fights real wars and either wins or loses them. The last time the United States conducted anything remotely reminiscent of the peer-to-peer war was in Korea in 1950–53. That ended in a stalemate, and it was in many respects a replay of WW II, with the difference that there, the U.S. Air Force had to fight not just the North Korean but the Soviet Air Force as well. Its experience of such a fight was not rewarding. The debacle of Vietnam followed twelve years later.

As I pointed out in my very first book, the Pattonesque, that is to say Hollywoodized, view of war was and is not just the prerogative of lay people. As Rick Atkinson observed, Patton exhibited:

> The creeping arrogance, the hubris, which would cost the American Army so dearly in Vietnam. Summing up the achievements of his troops in crushing the German counterattack of December 1944, Patton with pardonable pride claims to have "moved farther and faster and engaged more divisions in less time than any other army in the history of the United States— possibly in the history of the world. . . . No country can stand against such an Army." These memoirs are valuable not least in showing, however unwittingly, that a disastrous presumption of invincibility took root in the ranks of officers who led the American military after World War II.[116]

Nothing changed for the U.S. military ever since and creeping arrogance remains one of the main engines behind America's non-stop military debacles, and, to a very large degree, inability to view 21st century warfare for what it is and what it is evolving into. Thus, being unable to recognize the military and economic potential of Russia and being constantly constrained by a myopic vision of fast, crushing warfare against an utterly incompetent enemy in both Gulf wars, the Pentagon and its political, primarily neocon, curators failed to grasp the scale of Russia's escalation dominance not just over Ukraine and its army but over the combined military capability of NATO.

The key to understanding the SMO and its dynamics was the traditional measured and calm explanation of the approach to operations by the Russian Armed Forces top brass. Colonel-General Sergei Rudskoi, First Deputy of the Chief of General Staff and the Chief of GOU-Main Operational Directorate, explained to media on March 25, 2022, that Russia had developed two plans for the SMO. The initial plan was to limit Russia's military operation to the territory of the Donetsk and Lugansk Republics, which the Russian state Duma had recognized as independent states on February 21, 2022. But then, Rudskoi elaborated, this brought about constant attempts by Ukrainian forces to destabilize the situation in the two new federal subjects of the Russian Federation, thus the decision was made to proceed with the plan of operations on all Ukrainian territory with the SMO's objectives now being the demilitarization and denazification of Ukraine.[117] The Pentagon and Western media assumed, as many initially did, yours truly included, that Russia's campaign would be a sequence of fast penetrating strikes reminiscent of the great offensive operations of WW II, encircling large portions of AFU and isolating cities along the way which the AFU would use as fortresses and in which they would try to hide. This started to happen almost immediately behind the backs of the civilian population of Ukraine.

But as the events of March and April 2022 have demonstrated, the Kremlin knew better and relied on contingency planning, which was once summarized by the fictional character, ably played by Senator Fred Thompson, in the fictional movie based on late Tom Clancy's novel *The Hunt For Red October:* "Russians don't take a dump, son, without a plan." The Russians had a plan, and it was based on an initial demonstration of (invasion-level) force, which it hoped would convince the Kiev regime of the seriousness of Russia's intentions that Ukraine remain neutral, outside any military block, especially NATO, and accept the realities on the ground, which by the end of March saw Lugansk, Donetsk and Crimea lost by Ukraine to Russia. After a few rounds of negotiations starting in Belarus and later via video link, Russian and Ukrainian delegations came face-to-face again in Istanbul. The expectations for an agreement were high. Turkiye President Recep Erdogan, who hosted the meeting, sounded upbeat when addressing both delegations: "As the members of the delegations, you have shouldered a historic responsibility. All the world is expecting good news from you."[118]

But there would be no good news. As would be revealed later, Russian forces, which by mid-March had not only captured but solidified their hold over Gostomel Airfield, located 25 kilometers from Kiev's city center, had been conducting a classic feint operation. All of the activity by the Russian Army to demonstrate a threat to Ukraine's capital was tied to the negotiations initially in Belarus and Istanbul. There was no Russian intent to capture Kiev, an effort which would lead to huge civilian and military losses on both sides, given it would have entailed storming a huge 3 million population urban center. Vladimir Putin himself later would explain the withdrawal of Russian troops from Kiev, which commenced early April 2022, as an act of a good will upon the signing of the draft agreement with Ukraine in Istanbul. Moreover, Putin's words were later corroborated by the chief negotiator of the Ukrainian delegation to Istanbul, David Arakhmia, as reported by RT:

> Russia was ready to stop the fighting had Ukraine agreed to remain neutral, but the West advised Kiev to keep going, the head of President Vladimir Zelensky's parliamentary faction—and the chief negotiator at the peace talks in Istanbul—David

Arakhamia admitted. . . . Earlier this year, Russian President Vladimir Putin revealed to African leaders that Moscow and Kiev had signed a draft agreement "on permanent neutrality and security guarantees for Ukraine" at the talks hosted by Türkiye. As soon as Russia pulled back its troops from the vicinity of Kiev, as a gesture of good will, Ukraine reneged on the deal, Putin said. The Russian withdrawal was presented by Western governments and media as a Ukrainian military victory and they began sending heavy weapons and equipment to Zelensky's government, fueling the conflict for the next 18 months.[119]

An understanding of this event is key to understanding what transpired in Washington and globally, and how this affected the Special Military Operation and the subsequent dramatic descent of the United States from the pedestal of self-proclaimed military hegemony. The reason why Ukraine reneged on the deal with Russia was simple. Then UK Prime Minister Boris Johnson played a tragic role in sabotaging the Russian-Ukrainian agreement when he appeared in Kiev without warning on April 9th and brought with him two messages: Putin was a war criminal and he will cheat anyway, so there was no point of signing anything with Moscow and the war should continue.[120]

It is clear now that Johnson, a major in Classics from Oxford and a clownish figure with zero grasp of military art, let alone science, was merely a messenger for the Biden administration which, being staffed with neocons and war hawks with law and political science degrees, was hellbent on harming Russia and Russian people. Three days after Johnson's visit to Kiev, on April 12th, Reuters reported:

British Prime Minister Boris Johnson and U.S. President Joe Biden discussed boosting military and economic support to Ukraine on Tuesday as well as the need to end Western reliance on Russian oil and gas, a spokeswoman for Johnson's office said. "The leaders discussed the need to accelerate assistance to Ukraine, including bolstering military and economic support, as the Ukrainian forces prepare for another Russian onslaught in the east of the country," a Downing Street spokeswoman said. The pair also agreed to continue joint efforts to ratchet up the economic pressure on (Russian President Vladimir) Putin and decisively end Western reliance on Russian oil and gas.[121]

This date can be marked as the official start of the slip of the combined West, headed by the U.S., from its 500-year long supremacy toward a long descent into global obscurity. As with any large landslide, it starts initially with tremors and a few rocks rolling down the steep slope, but eventually the number of rocks increases dramatically, and it becomes a deafening stream of rocks, trees and dust until the whole slope yields and rushes down where once a peaceful and undisturbed foothill lay. The level of malice, military and political incompetence, economic backwardness and degeneracy of its political and military class which the Special Military Operation revealed would astonish the world and will preclude the combined West and its captain, the United States, from continuing to order the world around. The shift in the power balance provided by Special Military Operation would become so dramatic that it has already changed history.

CHAPTER 5.

CRITICAL ISSUES I: THE TECHNOLOGY OF WAR—MISSILES

WHEN ON JUNE 17, 2022, the Royal United Services Institute (RUSI) published Lieutenant Colonel Alex Vershinin's piece *The Return of Industrial Warfare*, the article received a wide exposure in Anglo-American media. It revealed the level of strategic and operational incompetence of Western militaries, as well as the utter failure of their intelligence organizations. Even the title, which used the term "the return," was in itself a revelation of the strategic and operational delusion on the part of the Pentagon, not to mention the UK's Defense Ministry. The major point of this revelation lay in the fact that industrial warfare never returned because it had never left. This pretty mundane fact, known to just about any young lieutenant fresh from graduation from any military academy in Russia, was presented as an insight of utter import. Insight it was not—it was a self-evident reality of modern warfare; I wrote three books describing it and have been explaining this for 10 years, ever since the inception of my blog and in the many interviews I gave over the years.

Vershinin noted:

> The war in Ukraine has proven that the age of industrial warfare is still here. The massive consumption of equipment, vehicles and ammunition requires a large-scale industrial base for resupply—quantity still has a quality of its own. The mass scale combat has pitted 250,000 Ukrainian soldiers, together with 450,000 recently mobilized citizen soldiers against about

200,000 Russian and separatist troops. The effort to arm, feed and supply these armies is a monumental task. Ammunition resupply is particularly onerous. For Ukraine, compounding this task are Russian deep fires capabilities, which target Ukrainian military industry and transportation networks throughout the depth of the country. The Russian army has also suffered from Ukrainian cross-border attacks and acts of sabotage, but at a smaller scale. The rate of ammunition and equipment consumption in Ukraine can only be sustained by a large-scale industrial base.[122]

Vershinin's rather unsurprising conclusions on the need for a developed industrial base added absolutely nothing new to Russian fighting doctrine but they certainly force observers to go a few years back.[123] At issue, yet again, is the Western political, military and technological echo chamber. One American officer's tactical and operational epiphany is of most interest here and I referred to it more than once, previously. This epiphany came to light in the form of an article in the *Marine Corps Gazette* (scrubbed from it since then) by U.S. Marine Corps captain Joshua Waddell, a veteran of American wars, and it preceded Vershinin's conclusions by more than five years. As Waddell noted:

> Judging military capability by the metric of defense expenditures is a false equivalency. All that matters are raw, quantifiable capabilities and measures of effectiveness. For example: a multi-billion dollar aircraft carrier that can be bested by a few million dollars in the form of a swarming missile barrage or a small unmanned aircraft system (UAS) capable of rendering its flight deck unusable does not retain its dollar value in real terms. Neither does the M1A1 tank, which is defeated by $20 worth of household items and scrap metal rendered into an explosively-formed projectile. The Joint Improvised Threat Defeat

Organization has a library full of examples like these, and that is without touching the weaponized return on investment in terms of industrial output and capability development currently being employed by our conventional adversaries.[124]

Waddell wrote his piece before Vladimir Putin's historic address to the Russian Federal Assembly on March 3, 2018, where he revealed Russia's possession of weapon systems which redefined warfare and shifted the military balance decisively in Russia's favor. Putin's revelations of the existence of those systems was a classic example of what Waddell defined as "the weaponized return on investment in terms of industrial output and capability development." Common sense prompts us to directly connect industrial output and capability development and discard what at last, in 2024 has finally been revealed as nothing more than the financial legerdemain of Wall Street and America's financial industry which for decades has faked the numbers of real economic development of the world. Wall Street and structures connected to it such as the IMF or World Bank have been wielding Money Power.[125]

It was this power which was equated with military power merely on the basis of the metric of defense expenditure, compounded by the cooked books on the capitalization and credit ratings of the defense companies. This could have been expected from the Western community of economists, most of whom have never worked a day in their lives on the manufacturing floor and continue to view the world through the prism of financial indices, most of which are useless in serious matters of strategic intelligence, analysis and military planning. Here, we have to view war as it was always viewed and is still viewed by Russian military—war is the war of economies. Real ones. Modern war is the war of steel, iron, energy and manufacturing capacity as a foundation of military power.

For many people from the Western world, as was already demonstrated in earlier chapters, the fact that Russia is a bona fide economic superpower, apart from being a military one, often comes as a shocking surprise. Yet, the data speaks volumes. By November 2023 the United States produced 73.9 million tons of steel, while Russia produced 70.2 million tons, with Russia increasing steel production by 6.4% while United States' production fell 0.5% relative to November 2022.[126] The other critical material for military and civilian production is pig iron, from whose different iterations are manufactured such things as foundations for machining centers, piping and even motors. In 2022 the United States produced 21 million tons of pig iron, Russia—50 million tons.[127] Thus, the total of metal which the U.S. could use in military production, ranging from artillery shells to tanks and guns, was roughly 73.9 + 21= 94.9 million tons of metal. For Russia it was 70.2 + 50 = 120.2 million tons.

This, of course, doesn't mean that all of this metal goes into military production, but what it does mean is that the larger portion of this metal was available to be directed to military production, if so desired. It also reveals the scale of the manufacturing base. Remarkably, Russia's metal production shows also a growth trend, which cannot be said about that of the United States, not to mention such NATO countries as UK, Italy or France who do not even register in Top 10 steel and iron producing countries, while Germany sees all of its metal production in precipitous decline.[128] When combined with aluminum production—a material critical for aerospace in general and combat aviation in particular—the United States relies primarily on Canada for its aluminum, while Russia outproduces the United States by a factor of four—3.7 million tons.[129]

These are the numbers, among very many other ones, that serious military analysts, not to mention general staff officers, consider when planning military campaigns. They are certainly not interested in the capitalization of Apple or Facebook, nor in how stocks of Boeing or Walmart perform on Wall Street. Those indices are as irrelevant for warfare as they are for practical geopolitics and its main driver—the balance of military power, which defines the trends shaping our world. In other words, Russia had enough strategic natural and economic resources to fight a major war in Europe without experiencing any serious strain on her civilian industries and consumer market. A legitimate counterargument could be made, of course, that production of energy, steel, titanium or even some machinery, while extremely important and, in fact, fundamental for any military industry, is not sufficient for the warfare of the 21st century. One of many counterarguments concerns the design and manufacturing of microelectronics components and microchips.

While this is a legitimate counterargument, its application by the U.S. mainstream media exhibited a level of ignorance and incompetence that stunned serious observers. There is little doubt that the sanctions on Russia had been prepared in Washington long before the commencement of the SMO. Rushing to report on the "success" of these sanctions against Russia, high ranking officials from the Biden Administration engaged in a public demonstration of utter cluelessness and outright lies, such as was reported by CBS in May of 2022:

> U.S. sanctions and export controls imposed at the outset of Russia's invasion of Ukraine and aimed at crippling its economy are starting to have an impact on Russian battlefield operations. Commerce Secretary Gina Raimondo in a pair of congressional hearings this week told lawmakers that Russia has been using semiconductors from dishwashers and refrigerators for its military equipment. "Our approach was to deny Russia technology, technology that would cripple their ability to continue a military operation. And that is exactly what we are doing," Raimondo said on Wednesday. She said she has heard anecdotes from the Ukrainian prime minister that some of the Russian equipment left behind contains semiconductors from kitchen appliances because the defense industrial base is having a hard time producing more chips on its own and is facing export controls that limit its ability to import the technology from other countries.[130]

These statements by Raimondo were initially met in Russia
with a sense of disbelief at the sheer absurdity if not outright
stupidity of such claims, and then it inspired such wholesale
Homeric laughter in the media and among the regular public
that it became a meme ridiculing America's political elite.
Russians using Raimondo's claims (taken seriously and echoed
by European Commission President Ursula von der Leyen) as yet
another absurdity issued by officials from the West as a butt of
jokes reflects the intersection of two trends in Western social and
political life—the precipitous intellectual degeneration of their
elites and the slide, at least of American education, especially
college-level, to the level of many underdeveloped countries.

Gina Raimondo, like most people in the latest U.S.
administrations, has no idea of the state of Russia's modern
economy and technology. Raimondo, whose educational
background is law with a Ph.D. in sociology (doctoral thesis on
single motherhood) and a Juris Doctor degree from Yale, managed
to run some venture capital firms until becoming governor of the
state of Rhode Island.[131] This is hardly a background permitting
her to comment on the circuit design of modern weapon systems.
Apparently, the Ukrainians who advised her were similarly
incompetent—or at least believed that she would know no better
than to fall for such an absurdity.

It is worth noting that not only has Raimondo zero military
and engineering background, but also, Rhode Island, the state she
ran as a governor, by population barely measures up to one out of
many boroughs of Moscow or St. Petersburg. It was only natural
for her to parrot other such propaganda from Kiev and the White
House, such as that Russia has shut down two of its tank plants.
In other words, Raimondo, like most of U.S. politicians, lacks the
intellectual and professional tool kit enabling her to separate reality
from wishful thinking, especially in everything related to military
technology. Before making such statements she should have learned
that most military and aerospace applications require microchip
topology ranging anywhere from between 350 to 65 nanometers.
Russia produces these microchips on its own and does not need
imported semiconductors for military applications.[132] Moreover,

Russia is one of the world leaders in maskless lithography and had already developed its own maskless lithography equipment which is much more cost-efficient than Western analogues.[133] In the end, Russia and China have very mutually beneficial relations precisely in the military-technological field and China has a lot to offer if the necessity arises, including in microelectronics.

But if Raimondo's statement hasn't been embarrassing enough for the Biden Administration, another utterly ignorant claim came from a former official of the UK military, and it became another narrative which Western media and intelligence services started to push incessantly, starting in 2022. This one concerned Russia running out of missiles and trying to present the misfires of malfunctioning Ukrainian S-300 missiles as ... Russian attempts to repurpose air defense missiles as stand-off weapons. As was reported by BBC:

> Some experts say Russia is repurposing these munitions because they are running low on more precise missiles. "I'm sure they've got through their stocks, looked at their ability to manufacture more ... and realized the next best way to have that effect is to repurpose things like S-300 missiles," says Louise Jones at McKenzie Intelligence Services.[134]

It is also worth noting that Louise Jones, while claiming a seven-year long tenure in British Army Intelligence Corps, can hardly qualify for expert analysis of Russian military and industrial capabilities either, having a humanities degree in Chinese Studies and a commissioning course on Leadership from Military Academy in Sandhurst.[135]

It remains utterly mysterious what kind of commissioned officers can be prepared in a 44-week long course at the UK Military Academy at Sandhurst, even considering fairly basic tactical level skills, such as post-battle assessment or handling of tactical level intelligence. But then, Sandhurst is not an engineering school, and one cannot get the kind of serious military-engineering education there that is imperative for even a tactical level modern officer capable of operating on the 21st century battlefield. Surely, even a Ph.D. in Chinese studies and a career in investigative journalism are not sufficient to enable an understanding of the intricacies of Russia's military-economic and military-technological developments. Even if her role was only that of a spokesperson, what about the presumed experts who have been giving her such advice?

As NATO militaries proved again and again in the late 20th–early 21st centuries, they were only good at fighting third rate enemies and losing even to them, having primarily developed PR skills and media manipulation through narratives. For the British military, which can barely field a single combat-ready maneuver brigade by 2025,[136] it remains especially difficult to come to terms with being a rather inconsequential military player among military superpowers—a serious downgrade from its position in the mid 20th century when Great Britain still mattered as a military force.

These facts, some of them utterly embarrassing for the political and military leadership of the West, should not obscure the fact that the Russian Army which entered Ukraine on February 24, 2022 was still a peacetime army. And like any peacetime force it inevitably encountered some problems inescapable even for a campaign of such scale and scope, especially in its opening phase, and with clearly visible dynamics pointing towards expansion of the conflict. There is no doubt that its highly successful campaign in defeating ISIS in Syria played a very important role in not just validating a number of decisions on the technological development of the Russian Armed Forces but also on its development of some operational concepts. Here is yet another good occasion to remind and reiterate why warfare is both a military science and an art. Similar to a potter who uses different tools to shape a clay vessel on the potter's wheel, serious military organizations make conscious choices when fighting the war in regard to which military instruments, from combat hardware to tactical and operational techniques (in Russian: приёмы) they use to achieve their objectives. This turns the military craft into military art.

It goes without saying, however, that tactical and operational techniques in modern 21st century warfare are largely based not just on the quantity of the military hardware which warring states provide for their respective armed forces, but on its qualitative characteristics which constitute military capability. Thus, it is time to make two major statements:

1. The U.S. operational views and procurement practices are measured against the most favorable conditions of weak, if not defenseless enemies, which brings us to the second point, which is the logical consequence of the first.
2. The United States has lost the arms race to Russia.

Back in 2017 I wrote:

> American weapons are made for sale. They are made for profit as commercial items, be it commerce inside the U.S. or internationally. This was inevitable in a nation which never fought a foreign invader in its history nor, by dint of geography, had much to fear. It is very telling that a small American military-technological idiosyncrasy of using the term "sophisticated" instead of "effective" when passing the judgment on the quality of its weapons systems, took such a profound hold inside American military culture.[137]

The truth of this conclusion has been revealed in the most dramatic fashion when U.S.-made, generally Western, military hardware faced the realities of an opponent which only now is characterized as a NATO "peer," but in reality is much more technologically advanced, conjuring combat capabilities which remain beyond the reach of the West which cannot match Russia's arsenal which is designed to kill and kill with utmost efficiency.[138]

Russian Armed Forces launched the SMO when it already had a dramatic lead over NATO in missile and other technologies, both qualitatively and quantitively, and was in the process ramping up the production of state-of-the-art long range (standoff) missiles at a rate simply impossible to attain in the West. The first signs of the fallacy of the Western narrative, inspired by propaganda about Russia "running out of missiles" fed to the Western media and analytical organizations by the Kiev regime, was only noted by the *New York Times*—one of the main consumers of Ukrainian propaganda—by December of 2022:

> Some of the cruise missiles that Russia launched at Ukraine's civilian infrastructure in late November were manufactured months after the West imposed sanctions intended to deprive Moscow of the components needed to make those munitions, according to a weapons research group.... That Russia has continued to make advanced guided missiles like the Kh-101 suggests that it has found ways to acquire semiconductors and other matériel despite the sanctions or that it had significant stockpiles of the components before the war began, one of the researchers said.[139]

By then most of what was being published by the corporate, also known as legacy, media in the West was usually met in Russia with sarcastic smiles and it is worth noting that most of what these media produced as "reporting" or "analysis" was fast becoming memes both in Russia and among many westerners. Fairy tales of the Ghost of Kiev, the mythical flying ace credited with shooting down six Russian planes over Kyiv during the Kyiv offensive on February 24, 2022, once discredited, were immediately replaced with other absurd claims, such as the above-mentioned Russians extracting their microchips from home appliances, to Russia constantly running out of missiles. The discovery by Western analysts that Russia continued to produce the air-launched cruise missile Kh-101,[140] having a range of 5,500 kilometers and its later iteration Kh-BD with the range of up to 8,000 kilometers—which have no rival in the West—was one of many such "revelations."[141] No country in the world has such a capability, with the U.S. venerable Tomahawk missile having a maximum range of around 2,500 kilometers.[142] By all criteria both the Kh-101 and Kh-BD are not tactical missiles due to both having ranges comparable to strategic systems, as well as due to their ability to carry nuclear warheads, being stealthy, and being very accurate, with highly developed inertial guidance with correction (updates) using GLONASS and with optronic thermal guidance at the terminal approach for capturing the target.[143]

The operational and strategic ramifications of such weapon systems are clear to anyone, and they have been fully demonstrated during the SMO. Carried by Russian strategic bombers such as the TU-95MC and TU-160 these missiles have been launched from the safety of Russia's airspace, with the strategic bombers never nearing the theater of operations. The only advantage which the Ukrainian side had during such launches was the early warning provided by NATO's primarily U.S. ISR (Intelligence, Surveillance, Reconnaissance) assets which warned AFU of the takeoff of Russian strategic bombers from their main base at Engels. The U.S. didn't make a secret of it:

> While Western officials haven't publicly acknowledged the full extent of that aid, the *New York Times* reported that the U.S. has provided Ukraine with information on command posts, ammunition depots and other key Russian nodes. Such real-time intelligence has reportedly allowed the Ukrainians to target Russian forces, kill senior generals and force ammunition supplies to be moved farther from the Russian front lines. At the beginning of the war, the U.S. would alert Ukraine whenever cruise missiles were incoming, according to Hecker. Alarms would sound nationwide, and Ukrainians would hunker down wherever they could find protection. "Obviously, this happened a lot, so they weren't able to fight the war," he said. "As we matured through this, we could give them a better idea of where it might be going."[144]

Noteworthy, of course, are those upbeat and very often confabulated reports about the effectiveness of U.S.-made weapon systems, as translated into alleged and grotesquely inflated Russian losses, and intel revealed something peculiar about the U.S. military. As even General James Hecker, the head of U.S. Air Forces in Europe, has demonstrated by lying in the above reported conversation about the effectiveness or rather lack thereof of U.S. weaponry and support, the U.S. top brass has demonstrated its operational and strategic incompetence and its inferiority complex, growing exponentially with the progress of SMO both in the technological and military senses. The U.S. simply had nothing comparable to Kh-101 and Kh-BD. In fact, the U.S. military didn't have a single weapon system which compared favorably with Russian analogues. To make life worse for the Western media's initially grossly talked-up West-supplied Ukrainian Air Defense, updated versions of Kh-101s started to use flares, which complicated detection and tracking of low flying missiles even more.[145]

Moreover, even though it was able to alert Kiev about impending launches of Kh-101s and their predecessors Kh-555 (NATO "Kent"), the Russian Black Sea Fleet continued its strikes against Ukrainian targets using both land attack missiles of the Kalibr 3M14 and 3M14M family, with 3M14M being a further development of the original Kalibr with its improved targeting and an astonishing range for ship-based missiles of 4,500+ kilometers. The work on this version of 3M14 had started long before the SMO commenced.[146] Kavkaz-2020 strategic maneuvers saw the first use of this new missile, which was launched by the SSK *Kolpino* of the Black Sea Fleet.[147] For a layperson reading these numbers it may not sound like much, but what must be stressed here is that just these two families of cruise missiles gave Russia an unprecedented ability not only to attack targets in Ukraine with ease—about this there was very little doubt in the real professional environment—but also demonstrated to NATO its capacity to easily reach the whole of Europe with its military installations, thereby further awakening them to the serious conventional (non-nuclear) and nuclear consequences for the United States proper, insofar as both seaboards, the Atlantic and Pacific, were now exposed to Russian Navy ships and submarines capable of delivering strikes by launching Kalibr-M missiles while remaining well beyond the reach of U.S. forces. That is, Russian Strategic Aviation's capability to strike targets in the U.S. proper without leaving the safety of Russian air space.

These capabilities, among very many others that have been demonstrated by Russia, didn't remain unnoticed. Even before the SMO commenced, exactly a year before to be precise, the Congressional Budget Office (CBO) released a report titled *National Cruise Missile Defense: Issues and Alternatives*. It drew a grim picture of the state of the U.S. missile defense, in which the radar field of the U.S. missile defense was at an elevation of 300 feet—the exact elevation or even lower at which cruise missiles fly—and was shown as a polka dot space incapable of detecting modern cruise missiles with a complex flight profile, not to mention the ability to shoot off decoy flares.[148]

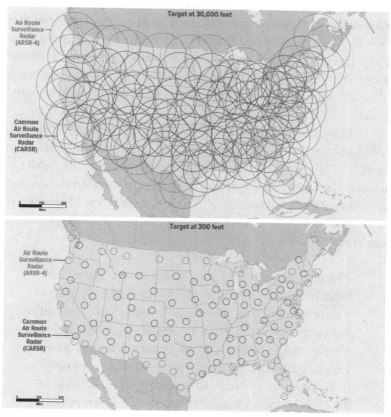

Data source: Congressional Budget Office.

In other words, the self-proclaimed hegemon with the "finest fighting force in history" was completely defenseless in the case of a conventional war against a power such as Russia. Moreover, the report asserted, the United States Navy whose main task was a theoretical defense of America's shores, even when employing Cooperative Engagement Capability (CEC) and some of the remaining coverage from a satellite constellation which would be either completely eliminated or dramatically degraded in the event of such a war by Russian anti-satellite capabilities, would have huge difficulty in detecting or tracking salvos of such missiles at the U.S. proper, which would require an immense search effort of vast areas of the Pacific and Atlantic Oceans.[149] This, of course, is discounting the ability of modern Russian ships and submarines to launch hypersonic missiles such as the serially produced and already deployed 3M22 Zircon with its range of 1,500 kilometers. This missile allows its carriers, such as frigates of the Admiral Gorshkov-class (project 22350M), corvettes of the Gremyaschii-class (project 20385) and nuclear-powered submarines of the Yasen-M class (Project 885M SSGN) to stay beyond the reach of recon and strike assets of even the U.S. Navy's carrier battle groups.

What visibly has shaken the Western military establishment, however, was the use by Russia of high supersonic missiles such as Kh-32 and hypersonic Kinzhal missiles during the SMO. I warned for years that the appearance of very high supersonic, let alone hypersonic missiles in the Russian arsenal would render any of NATO's air defense useless in any serious conflict. In 2018 I warned:

> The real revolution in military affairs starts with modern hypersonic fully shoot-and-forget weaponry whose capabilities trump completely any kind of net-centricity by virtue of those weapons being simply un-interceptible by any existent means. Enter Russia's latest missile, a hypersonic Mach=10 aero-ballistic Kinzhal. No existing anti-missile defense in the U.S. Navy is capable of shooting it down even in

the case of the detection of this missile, which flies in a hot plasma cloud while maneuvering at the terminal approach to the target. Kinzhal's astonishing range of 2000 kilometers makes the carriers of such a missile, MiG-31K and TU-22M3M aircraft, invulnerable to the only defense a U.S. Carrier Battle Group, a main pillar of U.S. naval power, can mount—carrier fighter aircraft at their stations around CBG. Carrier aviation simply doesn't have the range.[150]

The combat use of both Mach=4.2 Kh-32 cruise missile and Mach=10 Kinzhal against American-made Air Defense Complex Patriot PAC3, as well as others of NATO AD systems transferred to AFU, and most likely manned in part by U.S. Army personnel, had a very rude awakening to the realities of the modern 21st century battlefield. The delusion of the infallibility of U.S. military technology was so great that even the professional U.S. military bought into Ukrainian and U.S. propaganda about it "shooting down" Russia's hypersonic weapons. Writing for the Modern War Institute at West Point, Captain Peter Mitchell penned a remarkably unprofessional note, which claimed that the Patriot managed to shoot down one of the Kinzhals and that, generally, hypersonic missiles have been overhyped. Mitchell, exhibiting good command of English language dramatic descriptive tools, noted:

The May 4 interception of a Russian Kinzhal hypersonic missile by one of Ukraine's Patriot air defense systems in Kyiv has caused a significant stir in the international missile defense community. The ensuing saturation attack against Kyiv on May 16, which according to Russian sources was specifically aimed at knocking out a Patriot system, has only further underscored the significance of advanced missile defense systems in today's evolving security landscape. This dramatic first-ever engagement between modern Western air defense systems and the

hypersonic weapons specifically designed to defeat
them was marked by contrails streaking the skies
over Ukraine, literally and figurately underlining the
significance of this latest technological revolution.[151]

One can probably attribute Mitchell's excitement to a
complete insulation from the realities of modern missile warfare,
but this occasion was neither the first nor the last embarrassing
demonstration of a lack of professionalism by some of the U.S.
Armed Forces officers when discussing modern warfare. The
May 16, 2023 incident to which Mitchell referred at that time was
the first occasion on which Russian forces decided to end their
toleration of Patriots in Ukraine, a restraint due, inter alia, to the
presence of U.S. personnel manning those complexes.

The May 16 attack resulted in mass hysteria in the American
corporate media and in serial denials until the reality started to
set in, with U.S. "officials" telling Reuters that the system was
most likely damaged, but "doesn't appear to be destroyed."[152]
While the low professional level and lack of integrity of the U.S.
and Western corporate media and their "sources" and "officials"
is nothing new, the news of "only damage" made such claims a
meme all around the world, including the "damage assessment"
for this particular battery of Patriots which started on May 16,
2023 and has continued ever since without any revelations about
the extent of said "damage." Remarkably, should the U.S. legacy
media and Captain Mitchell have done their due diligence, they
would have discovered that earlier, the Patriot PAC3 batteries
manned by U.S. personnel had already performed dismally in
Saudi Arabia while "defending" Saudi Aramco's facilities against
the Houthis' low-tech slow drones and missiles on September
14, 2019. The failures of Patriots against the Houthis' primitive
arsenal would continue.[153] Two weeks after destroying the first
Patriot, Russia struck again, with Russia's Defense Minister
Sergei Shoigu reporting another Patriot destroyed by Kinzhal on
May 31, 2023.[154]

There was another "lesson" from the annihilation of the
first of at least five more Patriot systems transferred to Ukraine,

possibly more. Apart from the impossibility of intercepting hypersonic maneuvering targets by legacy systems such as the Patriot or any other Western air defense complex, there was a huge issue with detecting and tracking such targets. No Western AD complex is suited to do this. As the Congressional Report stated, current U.S. sensors are either incapable of tracking Russian and Chinese hypersonic missiles or only begin to track them when they are about to strike.[155] If that wasn't enough, instead of collapsing from sanctions and running out of kitchen appliances to extract microchips from, Russia dramatically ramped up production across the whole spectrum of its missile arsenal, be that strategic missiles systems such as RS-28 Sarmat, capable of carrying strategic hypersonic Avangard blocks, to tactical-operational Iskanders, to P-800 Oniks, hypersonic 3M22 Zircons, 3M14(M) ship and submarine based cruise missiles, to quintupling by May 2023 its production of Kinzhal missiles.[156] A hint as to Russia's immense hi-tech industrial capability was given by the Kiev regime's primary propaganda outlet, *The New Voice of Ukraine,* which reported the day after the first Patriot was annihilated on May 16, 2023 that Russia had launched about 8,000 missiles against Ukraine since the start of the invasion.[157]

At the time of writing in January 2024, Russia continues to ramp up its missile production, including hypersonic missiles. The situation also became dire for the NATO ISR complex, which once could warn Kiev on the time of takeoff of MiG-31K fighters, the main carriers of the Kinzhal. Now, it is virtually impossible because the Kinzhal can now be carried by Su-34 fighter bombers, which makes the work of identifying which ones are Kinzhal carriers very difficult and leaves no time for warning.[158] Realists in the U.S. military, who preferred to follow their professional intuition and face facts, recognized the immense operational-strategic implications of the Russian missiles arsenal and its ability to obtain accurate targeting and strike with almost impunity within an extremely short time from detection, identification and developing of targeting for a launch. As the U.S. Army War College *Parameters Magazine* noted:

The Russia-Ukraine War makes it clear that the electromagnetic signature emitted from the command posts of the past 20 years cannot survive against the pace and precision of an adversary who possesses sensor-based technologies, electronic warfare, and unmanned aerial systems or has access to satellite imagery; this includes nearly every state or nonstate actor the United States might find itself fighting in the near future. The Army must focus on developing command-and-control systems and mobile command posts that enable continuous movement, allow distributed collaboration, and synchronize across all warfighting functions to minimize electronic signature. Ukrainian battalion command posts reportedly consist of seven soldiers who dig in and jump twice daily; while that standard will be hard for the U.S. Army to achieve, it points in a very different direction than the one we have been following for two decades of hardened command posts.[159]

For decades, the United States continued to ignore the ever-evolving warfare and real technological progress and industrial development. As a result of American Ukrainian adventurism, the U.S. has found itself in unfamiliar territory—having no answers posed by my book, *The (Real) Revolution in Military Affairs,* which came about through the development of revolutionary weapons systems. Here, especially in missiles, the United States lags behind Russia not by years, but by generations. In some sense it is a logical result for a system which operated and continues to operate on self-aggrandizing mythmaking while facing a precipitous decline in the technological and military expertise of its elites.

CHAPTER 6.

CRITICAL ISSUES II: THE TECHNOLOGY OF WAR— COMBAT AVIATION

FEW WAR PROPAGANDA MYTHS have ever been embraced so uncritically, so enthusiastically and so incompetently by the United States corporate and social media and "expert community" as was the story of the Ghost of Kiev. In accordance with Kiev's crude lie, immediately picked up by the Washington and NATO propaganda machine at the start of the SMO, the Ghost of Kiev was an extraordinary Ukrainian combat pilot who, flying an outdated Soviet MiG-29, managed to shoot down numerous Russian Air Force combat aircraft, including the most advanced Russian fighters such as the SU-35. Inevitably, Kiev's ludicrous lie and sympathetic social media claims reached such a grotesque scale that even one of the major purveyors of anti-Russian propaganda, the BBC, was forced to report on the Ukrainian side's walking back its own fantastical claims:

> This hero is said to have downed as many as 40 enemy planes—an incredible feat in an arena where Russia controls the skies. But now the Ukraine Air Force Command has warned on Facebook that the "Ghost of Kyiv is a superhero-legend whose character was created by Ukrainians!" "We ask the Ukrainian community not to neglect the basic rules of information hygiene," the message said, urging people to "check the sources of information, before spreading it." Earlier reports had named the ace as Major Stepan Tarabalka, 29. The authorities confirmed that he was

killed in combat on 13 March and honoured with a
Hero of Ukraine medal posthumously.... It describes
the "Ghost of Kyiv" as "a collective image of pilots
of the Air Force's 40th tactical aviation brigade, who
defend the sky over the capital," rather than a single
man's combat record.[160]

Eventually the BBC had to speak to those whom it regards
as experts, who forced it to acknowledge the reality of modern air
combat and questioned whether one pilot could have downed as
many as 40 Russian planes.[161] This preposterous Ghost of Kiev
story would be neither the first nor the last time the Western media
would be left with egg on its collective face, having been ready
to spread any news, most of it fake, that enabled it to gloat over
Russian military and civilian deaths and other types of losses,
exposing a level of Western Russophobia that barely concealed
an inferiority complex of some magnitude. Yet, this story was
instructional.

Russian technological superiority over AFU, especially in
the air, was absolutely overwhelming. This, however, should not
lead to the conclusion of the Russian Air Force (VVS) having a
stroll in the park in its route to achieving, initially, air superiority
and later, air preponderance. Russian VVS did sustain some
losses. For once, NATO ensured that Ukrainian Air Force would
be supplied with all available remnants of former Warsaw Pact
combat air assets. The AFU received an astonishing number of
Western-made air defense complexes, supported by NATO-
provided Intel and Recon information which created the most
hostile anti-air environment of the modern era, including even the
war on Vietnam.

That said, it is worth noting that by January 2024 the
Russian Defense Ministry reported the destruction of 567 fixed
wing aircraft, 265 helicopters and 450 air defense complexes of
the AFU.[162] These numbers have been shocking for real Western
military experts, because the Russian air force has been responsible
for a lion's share of AFU's eliminated combat aircraft, comprising
all aircraft of all types deployed within all branches of the AFU,

including its Navy and Army, a rough equivalent of the French Armed Forces.[163] In other words, the Russian VVS was flying in the kind of extremely hostile environment that no NATO air forces in general nor its pilots in particular had ever experienced, heretofore. This factor alone was considered a sufficiently serious reason for many air force specialists in the West to conclude that Russian Air Power would experience serious difficulties when operating in Ukraine's skies. This also was one of the major reasons that led many air force professionals in NATO countries to experience, as would most services in the Western militaries, an acute case of professional envy, after all their predictions on the dynamics of Russian VKS operations would fail. After all, as pilot-astronaut-senator Mark Kelly had professed: ". . . I flew with Russian pilots, fighter pilots who couldn't fly formation."[164] Of course, Kelly neglected to mention when and under what circumstances he could have flown with Russian pilots. The only occasion on which he could have flown with them would have been a very long time ago, leaving this former U.S. Navy pilot with next to no clue about the modern Russian Air Space Forces (VKS) of the 2020s and their Table of Organization and Equipment (TOE).

But there was no deficit in doom and gloom predictions for Russia in the Western so-called "expert" community, with some young Ph.Ds. from the Royal United Service Institute (RUSI) such as Norway's own Justin Bronk, a professor in the Royal Norwegian Air Force Academy, havng already on the fifth day of the SMO concluded that the Russian Air Force was missing in action while Russia sustained costly loses.[165] Predictably, he based his analysis on Kiev's propaganda and by doing so, paraded himself as a military amateur—as would be the case with most of the "experts" from Western think-tanks and Defense Ministries, including many with high officer ranking. The publications of RUSI, an outgrowth of the British military, contributed to the astounding exposure of NATO militaries as having an extremely low operational literacy and zero experience in 21st century warfare across all domains. Colonel Douglas Macgregor mercilessly characterized the British Armed Forces as lilliputian,[166] underscoring the overall lack of serious combat experience and scale of the British military and, as an inevitable consequence, the weakness of their professional military education, whether through the Military Academy in Sandhurst or any other military related educational program such as Defense Studies in King's College in London. One cannot learn much by studying the turkey shoot in Iraq and flying in a low to no risk environment.

The unavoidable reality is the U.S. experience with real air combat and SEAD (Suppression of Enemy's Air Defense)—to say nothing of that of its militarily insignificant European allies—is very limited, confined to a set of missions flown against the either grossly outdated or altogether absent air forces or air defenses of Iraq, let alone those of Afghanistan, which has neither. The extent of operational planning in those cases merely required launching standoff weapons (e.g., TLAMs) at identified and largely electronically suppressed air defense installations, with U.S. and NATO combat aviation flying after that, essentially with impunity. This anomalous approach to and "experience" of air warfare was neither applicable in Ukraine nor produced any insights into modern air combat operations. As Cordesman notes in describing Iraq's air defense at the time of the Operation Desert Storm:

> Problems in land-based air defense: Most Third World states must borrow or adapt air defense battle management capabilities from supplier states, and have limited independent capability for systems integration—particularly at the software level. They lacked the mix of heavy surface-to-air missile systems to cover broad areas, or must rely on obsolete systems which can be killed, countered by EW, and/or bypassed. Most Third World short-range air defense systems do not protect against attacks with stand-off precision weapons or using stealth.[167]

Cordesman's description of the already largely obsolete by 1990 Iraqi Air Defense is telling.

As has been discussed in chapter Three, Iraq had approximately 129–130 surface-to-air missile sites and complexes, and 18 major surface-to-air missile support facilities. These included 20–30 operational SA-2 batteries with 160 launch units, 25–50 SA-3 batteries with 140 launch units, and 36–55 SA-6 batteries with well over 100 fire units. Baghdad had more dense air defenses at the start of the Gulf War than any city in Eastern Europe, and more than seven times the total surface-to-air missile launcher strength deployed in Hanoi during the height of the Vietnam War.[168]

Of course, what Cordesman forgets to mention is that Iraqi air defense in 1990 was, in fact, the same air defense used in Vietnam in late 1960s-early 1970s and by that time it was largely two generations behind modern combat aircraft, air defense and standoff weapon systems development. The most modern Iraqi air defense complex SA-6, 2K12 "Kub" system, designed in the 1960s and supplied to Iraq during the Iran-Iraq war was obsolete by the start of Operation Desert Storm. This system was, however, actively augmented in the Soviet Air Defense Troops with much more advanced Buk-M1 in the 1980s. Not surprisingly these much more capable mobile AD systems were in the possession of the AFU prior to the SMO, not to mention earlier versions of the S-300 AD systems, most of which had been integrated through Polyana AD C3 systems. Per density of air defense (the number of AD complexes per square unit) Ukraine in the 1990s occupied the first place in the world.[169] In other words no NATO air force had any comparable experience with operating in the air defense environment as Ukraine, as was the case from the start of the SMO. Most of what was written and spoken by numerous "experts" in the West about air combat in Ukraine was astonishingly ignorant if not altogether a manifestation of sour grapes, especially, as many predicted, yours truly included, even the provision of the newest NATO air defense complexes such as Patriot PAC3, SAMP-T or NASAMS would not make much of a difference.

However, Western air forces had at least some comprehension of how the Russian VKS conducts its operations via Russia's VKS' operations in Syria in support of Syrian Arab Army and Russian ground troops, which played a crucial role in defeat of the Islamic State (ISIS). Russian VKS operational tempo was high, so much so that some publications in the U.S. noted in 2015. This did enable the West to draw some conclusions before the commencement of the SMO:

> Compared to the 2008 Georgia War, which was the last time the Russian Air Force operated in a combat environment, the Russian military appears to have made great strides in increasing operational tempo and improving inter-service integration. It has also made significant advances in its ability to carry out expeditionary operations and showcased its recently developed stand-off strike capability. ... The operational tempo of Russian air operations in Syria has been quite high, with an average of 45 sorties per day in October carried out by a total of 34 fixed-wing aircraft and 16 helicopters. Furthermore, the pace of the operations increased over time, rising from approximately 20 sorties per day at the start of the operation to around 60 per day at its peak later in October.[170]

Russian high operational tempo has been achieved through improvement in its logistical and maintenance support of operating aircraft and the overall robust design of Russian aircraft, including highly advanced combat aircraft such as the SU-30SM, SU-35 and even the SU-57 which saw its first combat use in Syria. A comparison with the statistics from 1990 through 2017 for annual depot-coded hours per flying hour for such USAF and NAVY mainstay combat aircraft as F-16 C/D, F-15 C/D and F/A-18 C/D as reported by the U.S. Congressional Budget is dramatic.[171]

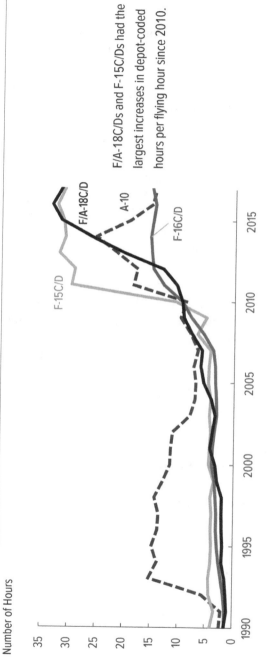

Annual Depot-Coded Hours per Flying Hour for Selected Combat Aircraft, 1990 to 2017

Number of Hours

F/A-18C/Ds and F-15C/Ds had the largest increases in depot-coded hours per flying hour since 2010.

F/A-18C/D

A-10

F-16C/D

F-15C/D

Source: Congressional Budget Office, using data from the Department of Defense.

Depot-coded hours reflect the amount of time that aircraft are considered to be under depot-level maintenance and unavailable to military commanders. An aircraft can be in depot-coded status without being physically located in a depot.

Verified depot-hours per flying hour for such aircraft as Russia's SU-35C are difficult to find; especially since the start of the SMO Russia has been keeping a very tight lid on information which may provide some operational insights for NATO. What is known is that the data concerning the first batches of SU-35s indicated a resource (service life) of 6,000 flying hours, while the resource of its main engines Saturn AL-41F1S (aka, 117S) is 4,000 hours, with servicing required after 1,000 of flight hours.[172] It is easy to conclude that pretty much any Russian-made modern weapons system is much cheaper to sustain in terms of maintenance than any Western analogues. Comparing the cost of flight between a U.S. F-35 fighter and Russia's latest offering, the SU-75 Checkmate stealth fighter, Sergei Chemezov, the CEO of the Rostec corporation which includes United Aircraft Corporation, stressed that the cost of a flight hour of SU-75 will be seven times less than an hour of flight of the F-35.[173]

This is an astonishing ratio, and it underscores the difference between the industrial DNA of Russia with that of the U.S. It also underscores a dramatic difference in the design of the hardware and procurement policies. The latest versions of the venerable F-15 in service with the USAF continued to undergo service life extensions from original 4,000 hours to 8,000 hours in 1990s; now they are being extended to 12,000 hours, as was declared in 2011 through the SLEP (Service Life Extension Program).[174] There is nothing unusual in extension programs for any kind of machinery, after appropriate testing and assessment are completed, but in the case of the United States combat aviation, all this reflects the massive boondoggle that the F-35 program has become, with the U.S. now producing aircraft which is hardly suited for the modern battlefield of the 21st century with its presence on any airfield and in hangars on any theater providing an easily identified target indefensible by NATO—indefensible due to the grossly overstated capabilities of all NATO air defense complexes against modern Russian standoff weapons and an extremely hostile Electronic Warfare environment. The alarm already sounded in 2021 on the highest political level:

The F-35 fighter jet may not be as "survivable" as originally expected, according to Chairman of the House Armed Services Committee Rep. Adam Smith. He bases this belief on the many recent innovations in missile technology. As reported by Air Force Magazine, Smith during a virtual event on Tuesday urged the force to invest more in smaller, unmanned systems as he believes the F-35 may not remain as cutting edge and seemingly invulnerable as once thought. However, he did not suggest that the F-35 is nearing obsolescence or no longer viable. The department chief also noted that the F-35 remains more survivable than other fighters "by quite a bit," citing the F-16 fleet as a comparison. Still, Smith said that the F-35 system "also got some environments that it's not going to be able to get into because of how much missile technology has improved since we started building the thing."[175]

This explains in part the reluctance of NATO "experts" to look beyond Kiev's propaganda or, as would be prudent to assume, refer to some rather unpleasant comparative data on the performance of the Russian VKS in the SMO with any air and SEAD campaign by the USAF, which was and is undeniably circulating in the community of former American military and intelligence professionals with connections in the Washington Establishment such as Colonel Douglas Macgregor, CIA analysts Larry Johnson and Ray McGovern, or DIA professional Scott Ritter, among many others who time after time have gone on record through many media channels ranging from Tucker Carlson or Judge Andrew Napolitano's programs to other types of alternative media, debunking the "official" numbers cooked up inside the Kiev and Washington war propaganda machine. The fact that this information gets around and is being emphasized at least in some strata of the Washington establishment is best proven through the fact that Representative Adam Smith was raising concerns about

actual capabilities of F-35 in real combat even before the start of
the SMO.

The United States combat aviation community has
developed a condescending attitude towards foreign combat
aviation primarily through the experience of flying against
enemies who literally couldn't shoot back. This attitude remained
largely intact throughout the initial phase of the SMO until the
reality of Russian VKS operations started to become difficult if
not impossible to ignore. Military aviation-dedicated publications
such as *Airforces Monthly* or *Combat Aircraft* are indicative of
this change. The early phases of the SMO saw such publications
enjoying minutiae of Ukraine-Russia War in the air until it became
clear that the Ukrainian Air Force had lost all of its experienced
pilots and the new crop of combat aviators was not prepared to face
Russia's world class air force. While Western media continued to
spread propaganda from Kiev, already by August 2022 the Russian
Defense Ministry was reporting damning statistics which were
widely reported in Russian media. As one popular outlet stressed:

> Since the beginning of the special military operation,
> the Armed Forces of Ukraine have lost 267 aircraft
> and 148 helicopters. But it's not just about aircraft,
> which are now in terrible short supply in Kyiv. The
> best personnel of the Ukrainian Air Force are dying
> along with the aircraft, and it is impossible to replace
> them with anyone in the near future. Experienced
> Ukrainian pilots began to die almost immediately
> after the start of Operation Z. On the second day after
> the start of the SMO, pilot Alexander Oksanchenko
> died in an air battle. On March 3, the Ukrainian
> online publication "Dumska" reported the death of
> Oksanchenko's partner, Major Stepan Chobanu. ... On
> March 13, Major Stepan Tarabalka died. He became
> part of the myth about the invincible Ukrainian Air
> Force, and through unscrupulous writing of The
> Times journalists, he was called the "ghost of Kyiv."
> Let us remind you that, according to legend, the

"ghost" shot down 40 Russian planes while flying a MiG-29, and all this supposedly at the very beginning of the special operation. However, the command of the Ukrainian Air Force itself denied this version, calling it an uplifting lie. And no one shot down 40 Russian aircraft.[176]

There was an inherent shortage of good pilots in Ukrainian Air Force even before SMO, but with the start of the SMO, the Ukrainian Air Force had to contend not only with the superior Russian VKS but additionally with what the U.S. Air Force never before experienced—high precision standoff weapons and Russia's ISR complex. For instance: when many high-ranking officers of Ukrainian Air Force met with their NATO supplier in Vinnitsa on July 14, 2022, a salvo of 3M14 Kalibr cruise missiles targeted the Vinnitsa Officer Club where this meeting was held, and killed a large number of Ukrainian pilots and its superiors.[177] This pattern of Russia's gathering human and signal intelligence on meetings taking place between Ukraine (and NATO) high-ranking officers and then developing targeting and striking such gatherings has been and will be repeated on many occasions, and not only with Ukrainian Air Force personnel. It is not very difficult to get the approximate range of the kill ratio of Russian pilots compared to those of the Ukrainian Air Force, but if one singles out purely air-to-air combat, without counting Ukrainian aircraft shot down by air defense, it could be anywhere between 1 to 20, if not 1 to 30 and possibly higher. The appropriate term for this would be a slaughter of the Ukrainian Air Force in the air.

The situation became so bad for the Ukrainian Air Force that already by March 2023—a year after the start of SMO—Ukraine was begging for Western combat aircraft such as the F-16. As a sappy sentimental report by *The Times*, full of false accusations against Russia, stated about the fate of the Ukrainian Air Force quoting General Serhii Holubtsov:

My best pilots are dying while we wait for F-16s.... The Russians have much longer-range radars and

munitions on newer jets. They use a missile with a
200km range to take out our S300 air defences, which
have a range of 150km, then 1,500kg guided bombs
to attack front line towns like Vuhledar, Bakhmut and
Maryinka. If we had F-16s with AIM 120 missiles
and a range of 180km, we could push the Russian
planes much further back.[178]

The dramatic and rather delusional tone of Holubtsov's
interview was understandable because by that time most of what
the Pentagon could collect in terms of combat aircraft from former
Warsaw Pact (now new NATO) members' militaries had already
been sent to Ukraine and was either shot down or annihilated on
the ground in hangars. This is an unpleasant reality NATO forces
have been forced to face. In a rare instance of lucidity, RAND's
senior defense analyst David Ochmanek warned in 2019 about
NATO war with Russia and China:

"We lose a lot of people. We lose a lot of equipment.
We usually fail to achieve our objective of preventing
aggression by the adversary," RAND analyst David
Ochmanek told a security conference on Thursday.
"In our games, when we fight Russia and China, blue
gets its ass handed to it."[179]

A former Pentagon top bureaucrat, however, wanted to cool
things down, and stated that:

"In every case I know of, the F-35 rules the sky
when it's in the sky," Robert Work, a former deputy
secretary of defense, told the panel on Thursday. "But
it gets killed on the ground in large numbers."[180]

The data on which Robert Work was basing such assertions
remains a complete mystery. It is especially true today in regard
to the F-35 fighter which has never seen any real combat, let alone
operated within an environment where it would be seen by modern

radar and have to face weapons which are not only combat proven but have performed paradigm shifting air-to-air kills. The R-37 (aka RVV-BD) is an air-to-air missile which is a standard issue for most Russian combat aircraft ranging from the MiG-31BM to the SU-35S and SU-57. As was reported in October 2022:

> Russian Su-57 fifth-generation fighter plane appears to have achieved its "first kill" by firing a new long-range air-to-air missile to bring down a Ukrainian Su-27 fighter, local media claimed. The report claimed a Ukrainian fighter jet was shot out of the sky with an R-37M missile. The report says that the Ukrainian Su-27 had barely moved above the safe height to intercept the Geran-2 kamikaze drone when it was shot down.[181]

The characteristics of the R-37 are, indeed, paradigm-shifting for air-to-air combat and completely overturn American views on air operations. The R-37 has a range in excess of 300 kilometers, state of the art active homing device and is a genuinely hypersonic (M=6) missile, which only needs initial targeting— it is a "shoot and forget" system, which has shown the highest probability kill ratio over other air-to-air systems.[182] [183] Presently, no Western country has anything comparable to it, let alone having a well-established record of extremely long-range hits against aerial targets.

This is Beyond Visual Range (BVR) on steroids, not an idea the USAF, or any NATO air force for that matter, can easily accept. The whole notion that the Russian VKS have a whole generation of real combat aces, let alone many of whom hold world records for the longest air-to-air kill is, in fact, anathema to the USAF whose mythology has been carefully constructed by the U.S. media and Hollywood. In fact, neither the USAF or the U.S. Navy air wings have anything which compares favorably with the arsenal Russia's VKS use, both as air-to-air and ground attack missiles. As impressive as the R-37M is, the emergence of the Russian anti-radiation missile Kh-31PD (a rough equivalent of the USAF AGM-88 HARM missile) is also a major development, especially when one considers its range, which is 250 kilometers at roughly M=3.23 with a 110-kilogram warhead.[184] The transition of the Russian VKS to fully combat-proven hypersonic missilery is already having massive tactical and operational ramifications for the USAF. U.S. combat aviation's most potent serially produced air-to-air weapon is the AIM-120 AMRAAM medium-range missile. While its maximum range and speed are officially classified, it is undeniably not a hypersonic missile.[185] It is dramatically outranged by the R-37M and in a BVR duel from the distance of 150 kilometers it would take the AIM-120 AMRAAM at least one and a half times, possibly twice, as long to reach the intended target than for the M=6 R-37M, which will cover this distance in about 63 seconds. The implications are clear since any carrier of the R-37M will have enough time to maneuver out of the kill envelope of the AMRAAM.

This comparison, however, is not enough to provide a comprehensive view of modern air combat without considering what Russian Armed Forces bring to the table in terms of arguably the best air defense in the world. On October 16, 2022, Russian major media reported the Russian air defense complex S-300V4's shooting down of the Ukrainian Air Force's SU-24 and SU-27 at a distance of 217 kilometers, thus setting a new world record. The previous one was set by the S-400 in March of 2022 when it shot down a Ukrainian SU-27.[186] The initial targeting for a significant number of such kills was provided by Russian Early Warning aircraft (AWACS) such as the A-50U (NATO: Mainstay).[187] By the time the Pentagon recognized that these kills were becoming a routine occurrence and that the Russian VKS had been conducting fully developed network centric operations, the condescending tone, even among most illiterate Western propagandists, changed—reality started to dawn on many who for some reason thought that the USAF was the best in the world. The June 2023 issue of the popular magazine *Combat Aircraft Journal* came out with what was for many USAF buffs a rather stunning headline on the cover: *Keeping Up With Russia And China*.[188] In John Lake's article about the fate of the modern USAF, some stunning revelations have confirmed the forecast by yours truly made in 2018, in what I presented as a set of Q&As about the future of U.S. combat powers possible operations against a peer power, based on David Ochmanek and RAND's view of combat operations by the USAF against Russia. It is worth revisiting it here, again:

Q. When was the last time the USAF fought in a highly dense EW environment with AD systems whose capabilities covered ALL challenges which are presented by the latest in U.S. technology, itself?

A. Never. In fact, the USAF may not even have internalized it yet, that it *will* (not may) fight blind with its Command, Control and Communications (C3) either seriously challenged or completely disrupted.

Q. When was the last time the USAF fought a world-class adversary AF which can approach or match the USAF on the theater both in the quality of its pilots and aircraft, and in their quantity?

A. Never, since Korea.

Q. When was the last time the USAF deployed to the front-line, or even rear, airbases which were subjected to major attacks by both an adversary's AF and salvos of cruise and tactical operational high precision stand-off weapons, which led to a severe disruption of that adversary's air operations, massive casualties of personnel and significant loss of its aircraft?

A. Never. After observing a rather unimpressive performance (OK, failure) of the Patriot anti-missile systems against obsolete 1970s Yemeni Scud knock-offs recently, one is forced to ask: what will this AD do against a state-of-the-art, stealthy, AI-driven and EW-resistant missiles salvo, say of 40 or 60 missiles? How about several such salvos?

Q. Does Mr. Ochmanek understand that the myth of Stealth has been completely dispelled and that modern AD complexes and advanced radar systems of modern aircraft such as the *SU-30SM, SU-35C* or *MiG-31BM* can see, track and shoot down any "Stealth" target?

A. Maybe.

Q. Does this RAND group calculate U.S. attrition rates in such conflict correctly?

A. No. Anyone who thinks that a force of around 800 good but fairly conventional (or really bad) combat aircraft can go up against Russian Air-Space Forces in Russia's vicinity and win is either disingenuous or incompetent. The USAF will not be able to suppress Russia's AD system to start with; the opposite, degrading of USAF EW and kinetic capabilities, most likely will be true.[189]

The reason this review of my forecasts is provided here is not to tickle my pride but to underscore the importance of a serious study of not just technical and tactical trends in modern warfare, however immensely important, but of operations based on reality and not Hollywood fantasies. Four years after my warnings, John Lake went on to accept at least some tactical and operational realities of 2023:

> In the age of rapid technological change—accompanied by increasing uncertainty and complexity—the U.S. military advantage is being eroded and the nation can no longer take for granted the unchallenged military dominance it has enjoyed for the last three decades. Now that the USAF is facing the growing possibility of having to fight a peer-level opponent, the balance is shifting back in favor of low-observable (LO) F-35....[190]

But as I have stated for years, low observable aircraft are neither a panacea nor a magic wand in the context of having zero experience with developing and conducting operations even against such an opponent as the Ukrainian forces at the peak of their form both on the eve of SMO and then prior to AFU's amateurishly planned and executed catastrophic "counter-offensive" of 2023. The U.S. combat aviation problem lies in the fact that it simply fell behind modern warfare developments, still believing that beating weak and incompetent enemies somehow adds to doctrinal development and hence to a development of force. Any force. It does not. As General Mark Kelly, Commander of the USAF Air Combat Command, admitted:

> We have to focus our fighter force to face the realities of a new threat environment.... Our fighter force was designed for a Soviet force. We are behind and our current incremental rate of change is insufficient.[191]

Kelly is correct here, albeit without acknowledging his useless and misleading classification of "peer," i.e. the U.S., itself. Kelly talks about the USAF's rate of "incremental change," but one can continue to change, even if not incrementally. But the United States military as a whole, and the USAF in particular, have no resources or means to close the ever widening gap in capability between American and Russian Air Defenses insofar as such systems as the S-500 are already being produced serially in Russia with their immense range of more than 500 kilometers against aerial targets, not to mention their full integration with Russia's Air Force and Air Defense. The air space of Russia is becoming increasingly prohibitive to penetration by any combination of USAF and NATO forces. The United States' overall military doctrine, which states that U.S. ground forces *must* have USAF air superiority, is simply not designed for modern war with a "peer" opponent which will deny it any combination of force air superiority and through this, deny it freedom of maneuver for ground troops. With the U.S. air defense systems such as the Patriot PAC3 and other systems such as the NASAMS among many others, including the French-made SAMP-T, performing dismally on the modern battlefield, one has to follow Scott Ritter's lead when he defined NATO as a "paper tiger."[192]

As at this writing, Russia has dramatically ramped up the production of the now fully combat tested 5th generation SU-57 stealth fighter in 2023, with production to increase even more in 2024.[193] Considering the constantly evolving and dazzling array of Russia's air defense systems and of its constantly expanding satellite constellation and other means of ISR, the never-ending talk of NATO supplying U.S.-made F-16 fighters to Ukraine as any kind of a game changer amounts to nothing more than propaganda. No NATO combat aircraft ranging from the obsolescence-nearing F-16 to the problems-ridden F-35, to strategic bombers, including the B-2, can penetrate Russian airspace without being detected, tracked and shot down. The only use Ukraine may have from Western aircraft is as platforms for launching NATO's standoff weapons such as the British-French Storm shadow/SCALP land attack missiles, which demonstrated a very high probability of being shot down during the first sortie, which for very many Ukrainian pilots has been their last.

Russian VKS combat operations are a bitter pill for many in NATO's air forces to swallow, especially so for the USAF, which suffers from low readiness levels and is even defined as "very weak."[194] Seeing, in contrast, the extremely high operational tempo of Russian VKS is for the United States—being the land where flight and aviation was born, and having for many decades been a culture of glorification of combat aviation in literature, movies and television, now on YouTube—a paradigm shift of which I warned for many years. Today, after Ukrainian air force has been utterly destroyed together with most of Ukraine's West-supplied air defense complexes, the only type of operations it can conduct are PR actions such as shooting down a defenseless Russian IL-76 transport plane carrying 65 AFU POWs to be exchanged for Russian ones, despite the fact that, as it demonstrates, the flight path and flight plan of this aircraft had been coordinated with the Ukrainian side.[195] This is the modus operandi of a defeated power, whose only remaining capability is to conduct terrorist acts in a futile attempt to convince their bosses in Washington that they can still fight, despite the obvious fact that Washington simply has neither the resources nor the technology which would make any difference to the outcome of the SMO, during which Russian air power has demonstrated to the world what air warfare of the 21st century is.

CHAPTER 7.

CRITICAL ISSUES III: OPERATIONS—THE AFU "COUNTEROFFENSIVE"

ASK ANY MILITARY HISTORY BUFF in the United States what *Operation "Bodyguard"* was, and they will immediately reply that this operation was an elaborate deception plot to confuse Nazi Germany on the date and place of the Western Allies' landing in western Europe.[196] The Red Army had developed a fully fleshed concept of *Maskirovka*, which provided an example, playing a crucial role in preparation of *Operation Bagration*:

> Operation Bagration won the war in the east, and that victory can be attributed to a practice at which the Red Army excelled—deception. The Soviet practice of maskirovka literally translates to "camouflage," but in the context of military doctrine has a wide variety of definitions covering everything from strategic disinformation to the effective masking of an individual soldier's foxhole. . . . The Soviets invented the art of maskirovka, and perfected it over the course of World War II. By the summer of 1944, it was second nature, and the operational planning reflected this. In absolute secrecy, the Soviet High Command (Stavka) managed to position over 2.3 million men and the necessary supplies, all the while deceiving the Wehrmacht as to the actual objectives of the offensive.[197]

In the end, one can hardly disagree with what one of the U.S. Army's military professionals concludes:

> Throughout the recorded history of warfare, military planners and commanders have sought to deceive their adversary as to the size, timing, or location of an attack in order to gain a decisive advantage. From the famous Trojan Horse to modern efforts to use the electromagnetic spectrum to "spoof" or jam sensors, deception in some form remains an essential component of military operations.[198]

When talking about Military Art one must keep in mind that deception is a crucial part of this very art precisely because it introduces stochastic, i.e. random, variables into planning and operations. But in what has become a historic first, the events of Summer 2023 in Ukraine absolutely overturned and demolished a number of critical assumptions about warfare in general and the professional qualifications of the military-political establishment in Washington D.C. in particular. The AFU offensive against Russian forces in Summer 2023 was not only announced in advance but was spun by Biden Administration and its planners and promoted as what was essentially a doomsday scenario for Russian forces. Granted, not everyone bought this, even among many of Biden's supporters. As the *Washington Post* noted in Spring 2023:

> Ukraine's challenges in massing troops, ammunition and equipment could cause its military to fall "well short" of Kyiv's original goals for an anticipated counteroffensive aimed at retaking Russian-occupied areas this spring, according to U.S. intelligence assessments contained in a growing leak of classified documents revealing Washington's misgivings about the state of the war. Labeled "top secret," the bleak assessment from early February warns of significant "force generation and sustainment shortfalls," and the

likelihood that such an operation will result in only "modest territorial gains." It's a marked departure from the Biden administration's public statements about the vitality of Ukraine's military and is likely to embolden critics who feel the United States and NATO should do more to push for a negotiated settlement to the conflict.[199]

The most stunning factor in this whole situation was the fact of *not* classifying the so-called "counter-offensive" by AFU, while classifying the assessment which, correctly, forecasted some serious issues for the AFU. This assessment was definitely driven by a common military sense and basic understanding of what is called the Correlation of Forces and Means (COFM). Of course, the problem for the West was that the Russian side was preparing to turn those "shortfalls" into unmitigated military catastrophe for Ukraine and the Biden Administration, who had pushed for this amateurishly planned adventure. But even this "classified" assessment—a marked departure from the Biden administration's public pronouncements about the vitality of Ukraine's army—should have given the planners in the White House, State Department and Pentagon a serious pause.[200] But it didn't. The reason it didn't lies in both the U.S. military's lack of expertise with real modern warfare of the 21st century across the board and in a precipitous intellectual decline of the fully "echo-chambered" Washington elite, whose insulation from reality and lack of serious competencies in any matters of military strategies and national governance reached grotesque and deadly proportions for both the remnants of Ukraine and for the United States itself.

As the events would show, even the so-called military expert community in the West had very little grasp of the Russian military and the way it approaches the battle. As Colonel Jacques Baud pointed out:

> Knowledge of the Russian system by our so-called "military experts" is extremely fragmentary and tinged with prejudice. From the Russian side, this is

a considerable advantage, as these "experts" tend to constantly underestimate Russian capabilities.[201]

Baud touches here on the profound difference between information and knowledge. Information about Russian Armed Forces, the NATO staffs have aplenty; it is the knowledge that they lacked and continued to lack while planning the operation for what, in the minds of Washington's establishment, should have been a triumph for the Biden Administration one year before the presidential election, given Donald Trump increasingly looking like a possible contestant for the Oval Office. Nothing could have been more beneficial for Biden as being able to declare himself a true war time president and a banisher of the universally hated in Washington Vladimir Putin and the Russian people.

It is too early to arrive at a definite conclusion on the genesis of the AFU's counteroffensive which was planned in Washington D.C., where the AFU were viewed merely as cannon fodder.[202] One of the clues, however, for this military adventurism could probably be found in what, in the West, was called "The Battle for Kiev" as well as "The Battle for Kharkiv" where Russian forces evacuated the city of Kherson leaving a huge portion of its population to the left bank of Dnieper River. Obviously, calling both of these "battles" was a complete misnomer because in both instances there was no Russian intention of taking either city, nor of fighting any real battles around those cities, nor of holding on to the operationally insignificant flatlands and settlements around Kharkov. But the urge to report AFU military "accomplishments" was so strong that triumphalist rhetoric based on military fantasies prevailed and the Washington establishment convinced itself of the reality of operations they couldn't see beyond the tactical level. Operational withdrawals by Russian forces operating in economy of force mode and not risking the lives of their soldiers have been presented as strategic level successes of the AFU and by extension, of NATO planners. At that time there still had not been understanding of what Russian strategy was, despite the fact that by Winter 2023 it was becoming patently clear that Russian forces were already settling into strategic defense in pursuit of only one objective—the physical annihilation of the AFU and all the support it was being afforded by NATO. There was no need to rush to conquer territory when the enemy was feeding its forces into the meatgrinder with a kill ratio by Winter 2023 ranging from between 1 to 8, to 1 to 10 in favor of Russian forces, reiterating a number already mentioned by Vladimir Putin in June of 2023 at the start of the ill-fated "counteroffensive."[203] In other words, despite Russian forces inevitably sustaining losses too, the so-called "operations" by the AFU throughout the entire duration of the SMO can only be characterized as a slaughter of Ukrainian manpower on the scale no serving U.S. or NATO military leader has ever encountered or grasped.

This slaughter, however, was not characteristic just of the so-called AFU "counter-offensive." Before it, in what many characterize the initial period of the SMO as "phase one" of the hostilities, Russian forces managed to essentially wipe out the core of the first iteration of the AFU by the end of April 2022 by inflicting more than 40,000 confirmed casualties and annihilating 2,678 tanks and IFV (Infantry Fighting Vehicles).[204] As a demonstration of the KIA losses ratio which would continuously manifest itself throughout the duration of the SMO, with the trend of growth in favor of Russia, it is worth noting that the first week of SMO—from February 24, 2022 through March 2, 2022—saw AFU casualties at 6,570 (2,870 KIAs and 3,700 wounded), while Russian casualties amounted to 498 KIAs and 1,597 wounded. The ratio in KIAs in the first week amounted to 6,570/498 or roughly 1 to 13 in favor of Russia.[205] In plain language, the preservation of the AFU personnel was not the first thing on the minds of Washington and Kiev planners, who operated entirely within the framework of the United States' internal political and media dynamics, which in turn was built, as has been the case with most U.S. wars, around the narrative to be imprinted into the minds of the American electorate. Such an approach has very little to do with real military art but a lot to do with careers and financial rewards (a euphemism for corruption) for America's military-political class. Under such conditions it is very difficult to expect the emergence of solid professionals, who should have completely discounted the grossly misinterpreted AFU "successes" during non-existent battles in which the Ukrainian side had been sustaining catastrophic losses since the start of the SMO. In such a case, it would have come as a surprise to many "military experts" in the West that Russian forces had never lost the operational initiative.[206] This point has been reiterated throughout the whole duration of the SMO by operational level officers of the Russian Defense Ministry, but was hardly heard amidst the triumphalist bragging in the Western media by Ukrainian officials, who even went as far as to declare, as Ukraine's' Deputy Defense Minister Havrylov put it, that:

> "We will launch our counteroffensive—when and where it doesn't matter now," he said. "[And when that happens] Russia will be in panic; you will see a lot of panic. They still don't understand that [their] propaganda is demonstrating a false picture of what is actually happening on the ground. This war will be won on the ground, not on the TV screens, not on the internet."[207]

Many in the West bought it, especially political and media "elites"—insofar as strategic defense is an unknown entity in those circles whose knowledge of warfare comes primarily through the entertainment industry, which means that an average Western politician views victory not in terms of achieving political goals of the war, or achieving military objectives leading to the achievement of those political goals, but primarily through the pictures of explosions, devastation and square milage of captured territory. This is the very definition of the military incompetence and illiteracy which took hold in the American political discourse, and it cannot be helped since no American servicemen, let alone policy maker, died in the last 100 plus years defending United States proper and the lives and well-being of their families. Russians have done so for millennia. But the desire to see Russia militarily humiliated was so irresistible that all common military sense has been lost.

One of the key features of NATO's training of the AFU was the psychological tuning of AFU soldiers to the idea that Russian forces had been primarily manned by unwilling conscripts with low morale and combat cohesion, who would run the moment they see Ukrainian armor and infantry. This premise was destroyed from the very start of the SMO, but NATO trainers continued to use this fantasy even in 2024. As one of the POWs taken by Russians in January 2024, Fyodor Dybits, testified, the soldiers of the AFU are very depressed and do not want to fight. He said that he was forcefully mobilized and then sent for training in Spain to some training center which had a sign "The Royal Academy" hanging at the entrance. But the level of training, as Dybits characterized it, was far from royal. Spanish psychologists, however, have been conditioning trainees from the AFU that victory over Russia is at hand, and that AFU soldiers will have advantage over Russians once the training is concluded. Dybits pointed out, however, that this training provided no advantages.[208]

Far from being unique, Dybits' story is a typical one for the AFU which, even before the start of "counter-offensive," was starved of motivated and well-trained soldiers. But on paper, at least, the AFU seemed to have a chance. A number of the up to 30,000 AFU troops trained abroad and equipped with primarily Western-made armor brigades have been concentrated at the South-Donetsk axis, with some sectors having concentration of more than others, who had immediate task of breaking through the Orekhovo-Tokmak line in the hope of gaining operational freedom in order to take Melitopol and reach the Azov Sea, thus cutting the land corridor to Crimea, while a second strike was planned towards Energodar with the objective of capturing the Zaporozhe Nuclear Power Station.[209] The overall number of identified AFU troops engaged in the so-called "counter-offensive" reached 80,000, with around 500 main battle tanks, by the end of May, 2023.[210] It didn't matter in the operational and strategic senses for a simple reason—even before General Surovikin's order in November 2022 to evacuate Kherson, Russian engineering forces had been busy in constructing what would be erroneously called Surovikin's Line. In reality it was Stavitsky's or, broadly speaking, the Russian Army Engineering Troops' defense line, who Stavistsky commands, which had been constructed in anticipation of the so-called counter-offensive.

The term "line," of course, is a misnomer. It is a deeply echeloned combination of defensive positions consisting of three zones of defense with a total depth of up to 60 kilometers. Each zone is a combination of fortified positions, anti-tank "dragon teeth," and a system of trenches and minefields. As one popular Russian news outlet characterized this line:

> In the last months our army was able to erect the most
> formidable line of defense since the end of WW II. In
> its effectiveness it surpasses both the French Maginot
> and Finnish Mannerheim Lines.[211]

Of course, comparisons to the Maginot or Mannerheim lines are somewhat erroneous, albeit easily understood by lay people. The main mistake here is comparing effectiveness of the static engineering systems of WW II, with that of the 21st century revolutionary development of ISR (Intelligence, Surveillance, Reconnaissance) of the Russian Armed Forces, which starts from space, moving through airspace down to the ground with ISR means ranging from satellite constellations to air assets down to signal intelligence and classic operations by scouts which allow for 24/7 awareness—let alone when one knows about the impending offensive for months. In this case any movement of sufficiently large units of the enemy is easily detected and plans are adjusted accordingly. Once one adds total air dominance, a much higher weight of artillery salvo and the overwhelming advantage of the Russian side in standoff weapons, not to mention in the morale and training of Russian troops, one must, indeed, agree with this assessment of the "Surovikin Line." The first week of the so-called counter-offensive proved it beyond the shadow of a doubt.

As Colonel (Ret.) Anatoly Matveichuk commented to *Rossiiskaya Gazeta* on June 7, 2023, at the very start of this "counter-offensive":

It could be stated confidently that the Ukrainian Army fights strictly by U.S. Army standards. At first, they throw company or battalion tactical groups to recon defenses, and if they feel that defense yields they throw strike armor formations into the breakthrough. Our military understood these tactics and it didn't surprise. It can be stated that if this continues the same way, they risk losing several brigades they trained abroad for this counter-offensive. These allegedly elite formations equipped with NATO's hardware are getting stuck in our defenses, namely at the first line of defense.[212]

Matveichuk's forecast, as well as that of many other Russian military professionals, was precise. The rule of thumb for such offensive operations is that if the breakthrough is not achieved within the first week or two, the outcome of this offensive operation becomes uncertain at best. At worst, the operation should be considered a failure. The immediate historical analogy which, indeed, fits is *Operation Zitadelle* by the Wehrmacht in July 1943, commonly known as the Battle of Kursk. The concept of this operation was to break through the flanks of the base of a large salient, thus pinching it off, which would mean the encircling of two Red Army Fronts (Army Groups). The Red Army got ready by erecting an echeloned defense. The Wehrmacht launched the operation on July 5, 1943, and reached some penetration on both flanks until July 12, 1943, with the Battle of Prokhorovka, which stopped the Wehrmacht's advance on the most exposed southern flank of the salient. A confabulated Anglo-American military history of WW II states that Hitler stopped the operation due to the Western Allies landing on Sicily and started to transfer forces to Italy—allegedly in accordance with some obscure statement by Erich von Mainstein, which was heard by somebody who, obviously, wanted to grossly embellish the Allied influence on the cataclysmic events on the Eastern Front. Reality, of course, was different, which explains the depth of Western militaries deliberate ignorance of the Eastern Front. As I pointed out in my first book: what was omitted in Western WW II historiography was the fact that the only German division which actually made it to Italy, completely without its heavy equipment, was the *Leibstandarte SS Adolf Hitler* Division. Both *Das Reich* and *Totenkopf* Panzer Divisions were never transferred to Italy and were redeployed to the so-called Mius-Front, a heavily fortified German defensive line along the Mius River in Southern Russia. There they would face another Red Army offensive. Moreover, the *Leibstandarte SS Adolf Hitler* Division was deployed to, and then remained stationed in, northern Italy, mostly for garrison and punitive functions, which could hardly be called combat tasks. This Division would meet its end on the Eastern Front, with some remnants of this once crack unit surrendering to the U.S. Army in the West.[213]

The fact of falsifying the military history here is secondary to the main strategic consideration that Hitler abandoned *Zitadelle* for two major reasons: the lack of the meaningful breakthrough within first week and the increasing threat of the Red Army's offensive in Southern Russia. With the power of hindsight it is easy today to conclude that the AFU counter-offensive was driven not by sound military judgement and professional operational planning but strictly by U.S. internal political dynamics and Kiev's desperate desire to show any success, even if it was merely a propaganda one, with a complete disregard of the tactical, operational and strategic experience, and, of course, the lives of the personnel of the AFU. The U.S. Army and AFU share of responsibility for what has happened since June 2023 is irrelevant here; these were NATO generals who approved of and participated in the suicide of the AFU. It matters greatly that throughout the Summer of 2023 the AFU haven't been able to approach, let alone penetrate, the first line of Russian defense, being confined by the Russian Armed Forces to what is known as *Polosa Obespecheniya, also known as Zona Prikrytiya* (*Support Strip* or *Zone of Cover* respectively), also known in Russian as *Predpolie* which means literally a *Forefield*—a strip of land, the part of the zone of combat operations used for the cover of the main grouping of defensive forces from the enemy's probable offensive before the first line of defense.[214,215] The U.S. Army has a similar concept of the cover zone, whose task is to conceal the first line of defense and force the attacking enemy to deploy its main forces. Field Manual (F.M.)-3.0, the latest version published in 2022, speaks about the *Security Area*.[216] Ironically, this Field Manual was published at exactly the same time when the Russian Forces were beginning to construct the so-called Surovikin Line, seemingly against all logic of U.S. Army wars, which are usually fought against weak opponents and whose offensive operations have a rough timespan of 40–50 days, within which the enemy is bombed into submission. Somewhere in the middle of this operational term regime change occurs, which helps to remove the hostile government and break the control of the resisting forces completely. One such example, albeit through the use of numerous U.S. proxies such as Syria's Kurds and Islamic anti-government groups, was attempted in Syria until Russia entered the fray in 2015. In general, the growth and use of the "opposition" political forces and anti-regime propaganda and sabotage have been a part of U.S. operations throughout history. This brings us to a separate issue of both AFU offensive planning and the mutiny by the Wagner group.

Yours truly doesn't pretend to know all of the military and intelligence aspects, a euphemism for regime change, of the West's war against Russia—they will not be known for decades—but the Wagner group mutiny, also known as the Prigozhin mutiny, started on June 23, 2023. The hallmark of a U.S. "regime change" sabotage operation was recognized immediately—it was coordinated with the start of the AFU's offensive, which commenced on June 4, 2023. The Wagner group's mutiny started 19 days later and was framed by the CEO of Wagner, Evgeniy Prigozhin, as a response to an alleged bombing of the Wagner group's positions by ... the Russian Army ... because of which "a huge number of Wagner fighters has died."[217] Obviously, Prigozhin's so-called "March for Justice" on Moscow was doomed under any circumstances but the mutiny was tied to what, under the ideal execution of the plan by the AFU, would have been a breakthrough of Russian defensive lines creating a threat to Melitopol, while simultaneously attacking towards Berdyansk and Bakhmut.[218] These "successes" by the

AFU were supposed, in the minds of NATO and AFU planners, to create political instability in Moscow and the Wagner mutiny was supposed to be the straw that broke Putin's camel's back, with Prigozhin and his "troops" emerging as an alternative political power in Russia.

There could be no 100% confirmation or otherwise of the association of Prigozhin and Wagner, which operated mostly as a totalitarian sect through the Council of Commanders, with the intelligence services of Ukraine in NATO, but this seems a reasonable assumption, especially when one considers the psychological profile of Evgeniy Prigozhin and many of his associates. Prigozhin, who never served a day in the armed forces, was a career criminal who at various points spent time in jail, including for one episode of robbing a defenseless woman of her possessions, including jewelry, on the street in Leningrad.[219] The real wealth of Prigozhin came, however, not through his exploits as a restaurateur but through his ownership of Wagner Group, a private military company, which earned him a fortune to the tune of one billion dollars through contracts with Russia's Defense Ministry.[220] The myth of Prigozhin and Wagner was being continuously fanned through Prigozhin-owned media. He also was known for his unrestrained ambitions and cruelty among the rank and file of the Wagner Group. In all, Prigozhin's psychological portrait is that of a psychopath with a megalomaniac element—a precise type well fitted for manipulation, given his ambitions and detachment from reality. In plain language—Prigozhin was a perfect target for intel organizations such as the CIA. Viewed from this point a piece in the *Washington Post* in May 2023 titled "Wagner chief offered to give Russian troop locations to Ukraine, leak says" is revealing.[221] Obviously, the Kremlin immediately dismissed the notion that Prigozhin could have discussed giving Russian positions to the Ukrainian side.[222] But the Kremlin might have made a PR mistake here because a month later Wagner's mutiny would change everything and be called out in Russia in no uncertain terms, one of which was "back stabbing." In light of that and some other details which started to emerge after the mutiny fizzled out, it becomes not only possible but highly probable to conclude that Prigozhin and some of his people did have contacts—but not with Ukrainian, but rather with either American or British intelligence organizations. That aspect of AFU's offensive can be left for future generations of the intelligence services historians to ponder.

Yet, when taken in its totality—the planning of the AFU offensive revealed professional incompetence on both operational and strategic levels by the U.S. and Ukrainian military, especially insofar as the assessment of both morale and combat cohesion of Russian forces went. It remains a complete mystery how such an offensive could have been conceived even if the AFU would have followed its Pentagon's version insofar as:

> U.S. and Ukrainian officials sharply disagreed at times over strategy, tactics and timing. The Pentagon wanted the assault to begin in mid-April to prevent Russia from continuing to strengthen its lines. The Ukrainians hesitated, insisting they weren't ready without additional weapons and training. U.S. military officials were confident that a mechanized frontal attack on Russian lines was feasible with the troops and weapons that Ukraine had. The simulations concluded that Kyiv's forces, in the best case, could reach the Sea of Azov and cut off Russian troops in the south in 60 to 90 days. The United States advocated a focused assault along that southern axis.[223]

If ever there was a military delusion, operational and strategic rigidity, template thinking, and incompetence on a global scale—the Charge of the Light Brigade times a thousand—this was U.S. military's "plan." It amounted to the slaughter of the AFU on a scale surpassing U.S. Army losses in Europe after D-Day. It remains unclear how—not just having no reliable numbers of Russian forces or the Russian Armed Forces TOE (Table of Organization and Equipment), but also being generally ignorant of Russian tactics—such a plan could have been put in motion. In the end, the issue was not a matter of the Russians erecting the so-called Surovikin Line; in the end it wasn't needed because practically the entire momentum of the AFU's "offensive" was extinguished in the Zone of Cover with no formation of the AFU ever even reaching the first of three lines of defense. But by the time the combined West was forced to face the grim reality of the catastrophic failure of this "offensive," the butcher's bill for the AFU amounted, even by ever conservative Russian assessments, to a staggering 159,000 AFU casualties, the annihilation of 766 tanks, including 37 Leopards and 121 aircraft.[224] This was annihilation of the third "edition" of the AFU, with the first one having already been finished off by May 2022.[225]

There is a certain psychological peculiarity in the AFU counteroffensive which was willing to endure such a scale of destruction within the 5-month period. It manifests itself in numbers: Russian Ministry of Defense counts only losses of the AFU it can actually identify, primarily by means of objective control such as drones and by the reports of tactical level units, which can also count and document the bodies of the AFU personnel firsthand, that is, when conducting post-battle assessment. In other words, such a count happens only to a tactical depth, which, depending on the configuration of the opposing forces, can range anywhere from between 10 to 30 kilometers. What is absolutely not included in this count are bodies which are simply evaporated or pulverized as the result of the use of heavy bombs, short range ballistic missiles, or thermobaric weapons such as the MLRS system Tornado, among others, which belong to the class of weapons known in the U.S. Field Manuals as "long range fires" and are capable of striking to operational depth with deadly results. The same goes for even longer-range standoff weapons such as cruise missiles. The number of casualties these weapons inflict could be equal if not larger than the casualties sustained by the AFU in the immediate combat zone. Hiding their own casualties while grossly exaggerating those of the Russian Army has become a trademark of the Kiev regime and the U.S. media and cabal of so-called "military experts." Thus, it is very peculiar that no high ranking U.S. Army officer voiced any objections, knowing what had happened to the first two "editions" of the

AFU, to what, indeed, amounted to a meat grinder of the 21st century. Could this reluctance to speak their mind, let alone risk their careers, for purely military-humanitarian reasons actually be an expression of deeply seated racism and hatred of Russia and Russians, that they saw no problem with sending hundreds of thousands of people to their ultimate end? Or could it be the fact that for most of these Western military people the gruesome realities of real war have never been comprehensible? The answer most likely is a combination of both.

No U.S. servicemen have ever operated in a combat environment even remotely comparable to the realities of the SMO, let alone comparable to the realities of AFU as it faces the Russian Army, which becomes stronger with each passing week, precisely because it is supported by arguably the most efficient and largest military industrial complex in the world. It is absolutely unclear how the average Pentagon planner relates to these realities, especially when operating on the basis of a largely confabulated American military history in which Russians are always backward people, who can fight only by attacking the enemy in human waves and using rusty and obsolete weapons.[226] This view persists in Washington, despite the rather grim calculus as expressed by U.S. officers themselves. Writing in the Autumn 2023 issue of the U.S. Army War College *Parameters*, Crombe and Nagl of the U.S. Army TRADOC (Training and Doctrine Command) admit:

> The Russia-Ukraine War is exposing significant vulnerabilities in the Army's strategic personnel depth and ability to withstand and replace casualties. Army theater medical planners may anticipate a sustained rate of roughly 3,600 casualties per day, ranging from those killed in action to those wounded in action or suffering disease or other non-battle injuries. With a 25 percent predicted replacement rate, the personnel system will require 800 new personnel each day. For context, the United States sustained about 50,000 casualties in two decades of fighting in Iraq and

Afghanistan. In large-scale combat operations, the United States could experience that same number of casualties in two weeks.[227]

Reality, of course, is even grimmer. As has been stated and written by yours truly for years, neither American society nor the U.S. Army are designed to fight while sustaining 3,600 casualties daily, let alone under conditions which overturn most of the U.S. Army field manuals in which the U.S. Army relies on air dominance and advantage in long range or deep strike fires—this advantage is no longer there. It hasn't been for a while. The Russian arsenal employed in the SMO completely outranges and outperforms not only the American but all NATO systems, ranging from self-propelled artillery with the newest paradigm-shifting 2S35 Koalitsiya-SV self-propelled artillery system reaching sustained serial production and arriving to the front-line units, to the steady growth of Russia's satellite constellation, improving its ISR capability. This is just one of many examples of the Russian Armed Forces fielding the newest combat systems which not only outrange anything in the U.S. arsenal but also other systems which are produced in industrial quantities—such as loitering munitions e.g. Zala's Concern Lancet—that have played a crucial role in defeating what was supposed to be the end of "Putin's Regime," but in reality was hoped to be the end of Russia.

But most importantly, which has been completely lost on NATO's planners and advisers, was the spirit of Russia's soldiers and officers who again and again demonstrated not only tactical and operational finesse but heroism and self-sacrifice for their country—no U.S. field manual accounts for this in the enemy while Russian COFM (Correlation of Forces and Means) accounts for this in its enemy and introduces even value α—a factor of moral superiority of one side over another. Part of this parameter is a ratio of the losses of both sides (and) after which they can still conduct a battle. Thus $\alpha =$, this parameter is used in modelling of the combat actions.[228] So in the end, it was the dexterity of Russian operational and strategic planning and advanced technology which amplified the effect of Russian overall superiority to the point of its crushing defeat of the offensive by the best U.S. proxy in history. This undermined America's regime change plan for Russia in its entirety, parading NATO militaries as utterly unprepared for modern warfare and dealing a catastrophic blow to the main pillar of America's self-proclaimed hegemony—the myth of American military power. Throughout its history, Russia has done this time after time after time, fighting for the preservation of Russian civilization. Be those battles against Teutonic knights or Mongol-Tatar invasions or on the battlefields of the Eastern Front in WW II, the outcome was always determined, as explained by the Russian genius, Leo Tolstoy, in his immortal prose:

> But all the generals and soldiers of [Napoleon's] army … experienced a similar feeling of terror before an enemy who, after losing half his men, stood as threateningly at the end as at the beginning of the battle. The moral force of the attacking French army was exhausted. Not that sort of victory which is defined by the capture of pieces of material fastened to sticks, called standards, and of the ground on which the troops had stood and were standing, but a moral victory that convinces the enemy of the moral superiority of his opponent and of his own impotence was gained by the Russians at Borodino….The direct consequence of the battle of Borodino was Napoleon's senseless flight from Moscow … and the downfall of Napoleonic France, on which at Borodino for the first time the hand of an opponent of stronger spirit had been laid.[229]

CHAPTER 8.

MEDIA AND STRATEGY

AS STRANGE AS IT MAY SOUND it took Richard Pipes, a Washington court Russophobe and falsifier of Russian history, to identify a key problem in the American approach to strategy and doctrine development. There are many indicators that Pipes neither wanted nor intended to give a proper framework of Soviet nuclear doctrine, but nonetheless, in his tendentious writing he hit the nail on the head with regard to the American approach to formulating strategy and doctrine—strategy being a first derivative of a doctrine, albeit in the West both are often interchangeable:

> American doctrine has been and continues to be formulated and implemented by and large without reference to its Soviet counterpart. It is assumed here that there exists one and only one "rational" strategy appropriate to the age of thermonuclear weapons, and that this strategy rests on the principle of "mutual deterrence" developed in the United States some two decades ago. Evidence that the Russians do not share this doctrine which, as its name indicates, postulates reciprocal attitudes, is usually dismissed with the explanation that they are clearly lagging behind us: given time and patient "education," they will surely come around.[230]

Remove "Soviet" and "thermonuclear weapons" terms and substitute them with "Russia" and "conventional weapons" and you get a precise diagnosis of the United States when it comes to real war and why "the finest fighting force in history" has a dismal record when it comes to winning wars starting from 1950. The American side formulates and implements its doctrine—and by extension, strategy—without reference to its Russian counterpart, or for that matter any other. Pipes gives part of the reason for that, noting when describing his response to head of the Arms Control and Disarmament Agency Paul Warnke:

> On what grounds does he, a Washington lawyer, presume to "educate" the Soviet general staff composed of professional soldiers who thirty years ago defeated the Wehrmacht—and, of all things, about the "real world of strategic nuclear weapons" of which they happen to possess a considerably larger arsenal than we? Why does he consider them children who ought not to be "indulged"?[231]

Pipes wrote this in 1977 when the generation of American statesmen and officers who remembered WW II was still around and actively involved in the American political life. But by 2022 there was not a single person in America's upper political and military echelons who had a good grasp of the real military history of the 20th century and of the history of Russia. This was effectively rewritten in the U.S. along with the simultaneous rewriting of the American history, especially insofar as military history is concerned. The history of WW II was completely rewritten in the West and as a result, the post-Soviet collapse triumphalism grossly deformed American views of warfare. This U.S.-doctored history of WWII manifests itself practically daily through the narratives of many U.S. retired top brass who, before the catastrophe of the AFU offensive, completely confabulated the operational and strategic realities of the SMO by drowning them in verbose tactical minutia spiced up with copious amounts of both Kiev regime and domestic American propaganda, a euphemism for lies.

Here we reach an important juncture. It is a self-evident truth that the average person who has never had any real experience with the armed forces can, however barely, understand basic tactical concepts such as the range of artillery or being on the "defensive" or going on the "offensive." But that is as far as it goes, albeit a wider berth should be given for Americans who are on average well-acquainted with firearms and own many. This is not the case with Europeans who have, with the exception of such country as Switzerland, a very vague understanding of firearms such as the AK-12 or M-4, let alone how to use an RPG-7, let alone an ATGM Kornet unless they had gone through some military training. Most people in Europe and the U.S. have not. As a result, in such a complex combined arms conflict as the SMO, average people naturally gravitate towards the simplest of emotional images—explosions, burning hardware, missile launches et al—and to narratives which, in the Western realm, never go beyond tactical minutiae. The reason for that is simple: Western media—albeit that also applies to a majority of Russian media as well—simply have no expertise in warfare on the level higher than tactical action at best; at worst they have no grasp at all, even those very many, not all, who report from combat zones. Being illiterate militarily and having no understanding of modern warfare as it is fought and planned, Western legacy media journalists simply improvise. And these untruths are amplified by the changing of the modus operandi of news reporting in the West as was formulated by British journalist and playwrite Tom Stoppard, who posited: "I still believe that if your aim is to change the world, journalism is a more immediate short-term weapon."[232] Stoppard's definition of journalism as a weapon is profound, as profound as are the implications of a local hardware store salesperson with high school diploma performing open heart surgery on a dying patient. The implications in both instances are severe and the lack of the needed skillset becomes a double-edged sword with deadly consequences.

The notion that a person with an advanced journalism degree from an Ivy League college—who wouldn't be able to solve simplest quadratic equation or apply basic trigonometry in matters of scouting, let alone understand systems integration on newest tanks or combat aircraft, much less how operations are planned and what operational calculations go into this planning—can accurately interpret and convey what is occurring on contemporary battlefields is preposterous. Yet, following Hofstadter's notion about the complexity of modern life, ever-increasing at that, and the necessity to train one's mind, the only advancement in modern Western journalism which has been achieved is acquiring a position in what former President Richard Nixon described as the "media-elitist complex."[233] He also warned of its increasing influence based primarily on sheer arrogance and self-entitlement. This aligns extremely well with the demonstrated utter incompetence and arrogance of most Western journalists in matters of real warfare and modern military technology. This, combined with the earlier addressed ignorance of most of the cohort of Western "military experts," contaminates America's sources of knowledge across a broad spectrum. Thus, the journalist class in the West can be both manipulated and manipulate within the realm of tactical minutiae and of "stories," including personal ones, pouring forth "content" which adds no value in educating the public—or indeed American and foreign elites—about the real state of affairs. In fact, they misinform most of the time.

The only weapon this class has is a willingness to "shape the world" in accordance with their and their bosses' ignorant and extremely socially, economically and culturally damaging agendas. The results are usually reflected in catastrophic policies, ranging from the utter failure of the "green agenda" to the instigation of wars, from a gang rape of Yugoslavia by the combined NATO forces in 1999 to prodding not just Ukraine but Germany and other European countries to commit national suicide by going to war, direct or by proxy, with Russia. Many Western journalists would easily qualify for being charged as war criminals the same way as was the case with Goebbels' propagandists such as anti-UK broadcaster William Joyce (Lord Hae-Haw), hanged in the UK in 1946, among others. The average "military correspondent" from CNN, FOX or MSNBC, moreover, will be stunned to learn that the Russian Army never lost the operational initiative to the AFU and its curators from NATO throughout the whole duration of the SMO. The reason they will not be able to report that—even if we were to assume the highly unlikely proposition that the Western media is peopled with reporters having both the integrity and the will to report the real facts of a war—is that they still will not *understand* why Russian forces never lost operational initiative.

To really understand that they would need a systemic combined military and engineering education to be able to see how tactical actions translate into operational and strategic successes. This requires a serious grasp of the physical principles on which weapon systems operate and integrate with each other and how that relates to maneuvering of forces during operations. This is a serious science which requires a very good grasp of advanced mathematics, physics and weapons design and systems integration, to say nothing of understanding the tactics of large formations which conduct battles, which, in their turn, constitute operations. These tactics are the tactics of formations at the brigade and division and corps level, which depend, among many other things, on the quality of the leadership of such a formation. Needless to say, such matters are not taught in journalism or political science schools anywhere in the world, and this tactical level is the level at which most journalists in the Western world operate, leading them to get completely lost. This is, of course, in addition to not having clearance and access to intelligence, which is strictly classified.

In other words, apart from malice and pushing an agenda, the Western public is subjected to reporting and commentaries by people who do not even have the qualifications to command a squad, much less company or battalion—let alone to know why they are doing what they do. One of the brightest examples of such "journalism" was the reaction of H.I. Sutton, who passes in the U.S. for an "expert" in Russian submarines, to an attack by the AFU on the Black Sea Fleet's Kilo-class submarine *Rostov-on-Don* and a landing ship *Minsk* (of the Baltic Fleet) which have been dry-docked for repairs and maintenance in Sevastopol. Some photos of the alleged damage to the *Rostov-on-Don* submarine began to be circulated by a number of media outlets the next day. While the landing ship did, indeed, sustain very serious damage due to superstructure fire, the case of submarine's "damage" was a very different story. As the *War Zone* reported:

> Regardless, the degree of damage sustained by the submarine suggests that it will have to be written off altogether. In the very best-case scenario, it will

require a rebuild, salvaging whatever components they can, which will put it out of action for years. Furthermore, any such repairs would almost certainly have to be undertaken outside of the Black Sea, which would be a serious logistic endeavor in itself. Two different authorities on submarine warfare, undersea warfare analyst H. I. Sutton and former U.S. Navy submariner Aaron Amick, both tweeted today that they consider the *Improved Kilo* class boat damaged beyond repair.[234]

In fact, what Sutton (and Amick) had been looking at was what even a first year enlisted submariner could identify, which was the lack of deformation of the submarine's hull, which is the first indication of a limited explosive impact, which was primarily limited to the light hull of a submarine, because all Russian submarines of pr. 877 and 636, similar to the second and third generation of Russian nuclear subs, have a two hull design—light (outside hull, light-лёгкий) and hard (жёсткий), that is pressurized, hull, where all the systems and submarine crew are. The "dramatic" pictures have shown only moderate damage to the light hull, which took the brunt most likely of fragments and of the segment of the light hull immediately in front of the sail. Yet, "authorities" such as Sutton, obviously have never heard of the light hull and exposed themselves as amateurs.

Subsequently, statements by Sutton and Amick have been completely debunked by the Russian Ministry of Defense when it stated to TASS a few days later that "The submarine sustained insignificant damage which didn't affect her hard hull. Repairing this damage may insignificantly increase the time of submarine in her planned repair."[235]

How American "authorities" on submarines didn't know basic facts of Russian submarines' design remains a mystery but this example is just one out of a well-established pattern of media figures engaging in outright propaganda and/or having no clue about what they have been talking about. Some reporting from U.S. media on the situation on the ground in the SMO from its inception has been downright hilarious. David Ignatius of the *Washington Post* noted in July of 2023, when it became clear that the long-anticipated AFU offensive had begun to disintegrate into a disjoined series of local tactical actions:

> Putin's army holds its defensive positions in Ukraine, hiding behind a blanket of mines. But the Russian army's command and control is disintegrating. It is a mess that Putin seems unable to admit, let alone fix.[236]

David Ignatius, whose educational background is in politics and economics and who has never served a day in uniform in any capacity is highly unlikely to know anything about the C2 (Command and Control) of theater-wide operations.[237] He certainly wouldn't know how Combat Communications Networks—a key in C2, thus making it C3—are set up for platoon let alone battalion or brigade levels. It is especially true in regard to increased clandestine communications (in Russian, SPS) which are both highly classified and use extremely complex encryption protocols and are also used as the foundation for netcentric operations, which are dependent on data links. Ignatius would likely be surprised to learn that in Russia there is a separate Military Academy of Communications named after Marshal Budennyi, which comprises in itself a five-year long military academic program which graduates cadre officers in combat communications and up to two years-long training in what in the United States would be termed a war college. All of it is dedicated, apart from what is common for any military academy in Russian combined arms programs, to combat communications. These are advanced military-engineering programs whose specialists, in actuality, provided a very high level of reliability of communications for Russian forces in the SMO. There are only two ways Ignatius could have come up with his patently false statement, among very many other ones, either through what most "journalists" view as serious professional activity, collecting rumors and anecdotal evidence among the political and military top, or simply by making it up.

Even a brief review of the output of the Western corporate journalists throughout the whole duration of the SMO testifies to the fact that not only are most of them incompetent hacks but that many of them are, in fact, sociopaths. *Psychology Today* gives this definition for sociopathy:

> Sociopathy refers to a pattern of antisocial behaviors and attitudes, including manipulation, deceit, aggression, and a lack of empathy for others. Sociopathy is a non-diagnostic term, and it is not synonymous with "psychopathy," though the overlap leads to frequent confusion. Sociopaths may or may not break the law, but by exploiting and manipulating others, they violate the trust that the human enterprise runs on.[238]

This definition covers most high-profile journalists in the combined West. The best demonstration of such a behavior, combined with traditional Russophobia of the journalist corps in the West, is the chief editor of London's *The Economist*, Zanny Minton Beddoes, who without any compunction gladly shared her thoughts with Jon Stewart on his show, that the Ukraine proxy war was the "cheapest way for the U.S. to enhance its security" due to the fact that these were Ukrainians, not Westerners, who were "being killed."[239] This is classic behavior of a sociopath, combining in itself a complete lack of understanding of warfare and practical geopolitics with an aggressive attitude and a lack of any empathy for those who will be enduring great suffering as a result of what they advocate. For Beddoes human life demonstrably meant absolutely nothing. She shows a complete disregard for the lives of Slavik *Untermensch*. The fact that by the time of her interview the AFU had lost by different accounts between 500,000 and 1,000,000 men, more than Great Britain lost in WW II, didn't bother this representative of London's "elite." Nor did it bother another sociopath, former Prime Minister Boris Johnson—another product of the humanities degree mill of the Western system of education, holding a degree in classics. Mathematics and the grasp of numbers and scales is not Western elites' forte, albeit that would not in and of itself remold the consciences or rather lack thereof of the sociopaths of Western political class and media. It is not surprising then that the moniker *presstitutes* has stuck to the representatives of journalist profession, albeit this title sounds tame by comparison with Hunter S. Thompson's characterization of fellow journalists, when he crudely described the phenomenon thus:

> The press is a gang of cruel faggots. Journalism is not a profession or a trade. It is a cheap catch-all for fuckoffs and misfits—a false doorway to the backside of life, a filthy piss-ridden little hole nailed off by the building inspector, but just deep enough for a wino to curl up from the sidewalk and masturbate like a chimp in a zoo-cage.[240]

Thompson, the inventor of gonzo journalism—a type in which the journalist becomes a central figure of the story itself, a legitimization of narcissism—knew what he was writing about. He also was unequivocal in stating the obvious symbiosis of American journalism with the political class. The SMO merely exposed what has been known for a while and not through laborious descriptions of the low or altogether lack of morals of the Western journalism class, but through the fact that this class of misfits and illiterates never got anything right in regard to real war of which the SMO is an exhibit A. Or of Russia, of course. The informational legerdemain could not obscure the fact of the Western propaganda being constantly wrong. In the end, effective propaganda should be built around what Alexander Svechin defined as follows:

> The domestic policy of every state should also be considered from the perspective of creating a sound basis in the state for agitation and propaganda abroad. Only this basis will make the "paper war" which has

always accompanied armed operations strong and significant.[241]

Here is where Western corporate journalism, which should now be firmly considered as interchangeable with propaganda, fails miserably—while the combined West is in a precipitous decline, modern digital media allows practically anybody to look up any audio, image or video on the internet about the situation in the combined West, and compare with the official narratives. Long are gone the times when some opinion piece in *Wall Street Journal* or *The Economist* has been taken uncritically as the ultimate truth. The "sound basis" for Western propaganda is no more. The whole world knows what Detroit or Kensington Avenue in Philadelphia look like. Unlike during Soviet times, many Russian tourists travel extensively around the world and confirm the smell of urine in Paris or that, beyond some touristy routes, London is grey and bleak and unsafe. The economic collapse of the West cannot be hidden anymore, including the misery and desperation of people in the West manifesting itself through social ills and economic dislocation. The steadily unfolding totalitarian future also cannot be denied. In simple words, the two main vehicles of Western propaganda of the last 30+ years—material success and "democracy"—have become recognized as nothing but illusion, a make-believe Hollywood picture. But very few propaganda campaigns damaged the already largely tarnished Western image of a supreme military power that the United States wants to project as much as the CIA and the U.S. Army's recruitment advertisements promoting the LGBTQ+ agenda. The video about Emma, a daughter of two moms, who enlists into the U.S. Army to become one of the operators of Patriot air-defense complexes became a global phenomenon for all the wrong reasons for the United States—it was ridiculed all around the world, with Dave Rubin summarizing it very well: "We are screwed, people."[242] The most profound indicator of a decline is when one becomes a laughingstock of the world. In 2017 Patrick Buchanan noted about U.S. decline that nobody quakes in their boots from fear of the U.S. anymore.[243] Now in 2024 Washington and its crude propaganda are the laughingstock of the world.

Under such circumstances, the Western media are forced to do what they usually do—stage the news stories or report false flag operations, even if they are openly-committed atrocities by the Kiev regime. One of the more remarkable ones is the so-called Bucha Massacre, attributed in the West to Russian forces. Practically every single Western media corporate outlet reported the death of civilians in the town of Bucha as an act of mindless atrocity by Russian Army. It was a classic false flag committed for purely PR reasons, seeking to counter Russian-Ukrainian negotiations in Istanbul with a view to preventing any kind of peace deal.[244] The significance of this confluence of events was ignored by the Western corporate media who rather heralded the appearance of dead bodies on the streets of Kiev with traditional pathos and fake concern for lives of innocents. Russian Foreign Minister Lavrov commented on April 4, 2022 on this and an earlier media accusation, flatly denying Moscow's culpability:

> Two weeks ago, attempts were made to present the situation in a Mariupol maternity ward as a crime by the Russian military. It later turned out that the purpose of these efforts was openly provocative, and that fake materials had been submitted. They were later debunked. Another information attack took place the other day in the town of Bucha in the Kiev Region soon after Russian service personnel left the vicinity under specific plans and agreements. A "show" was staged there several days later, and Ukrainian representatives and their Western patrons are broadcasting it on all channels and social media networks. All Russian service personnel left the town on March 30, 2022. On March 31, 2022, the mayor of Bucha made an official statement that everything was all right there. Two days later, we saw the "show," organized on the town's streets, and they are now trying to use it for anti-Russia purposes.[245]

But this was not only the Russian foreign minister's view of these events. They were also widely debunked on the internet, with some such as Armstrong Economics calling it a false flag by the U.S. and Ukraine almost immediately after the event.[246]

Propaganda always plays a part in war on each side, but the SMO is a very special case. For the first time in the history of large armed conflicts, the largest armed conflict of the 21st century is being played out virtually in real time, sometimes with an excessive amount of imagery and videos provided by both sides advancing alternative points of view. This has led to most false flag operations of the combined West being debunked either immediately or within a very short time. In the end, the modern Western media cannot produce effective propaganda due to its being stuck in the realities of the 1990s—even though they use social media all the time—because most Western propagandists put forth a crude and simplistic narrative, ignorant of the fact that war in general and 21st century warfare in particular can call upon a wealth of military and technological tools and understandings to expose the lies in their fragile constructions.

Seymour Hersh is certainly a journalist of a very high profile and reputation, but his story breaking the U.S. sabotage of the Nord Stream 2 pipeline merely confirmed what many knew or suspected already, and simply required the formalization of a media piece to make waves. And no matter how good, and deservedly so, Seymour Hersh is in terms of investigative journalism, he waded in to comment on the subject with which he has very little understanding in another instance in a March 2023 speech at the National Press Club where, lacking serious military background, he grossly overstated the significance of plans for the deployment of a single Brigade Combat Team of the 101st and elements of the 82nd Airborne divisions to Romania, effectively creating anxiety among some circles removed from military realities.[247] The reality of those deployment plans was far more prosaic and had nothing to do with an alleged and grossly embellished desire to "confront" Russia, let alone go openly against Russian forces in Ukraine while having no depth of resources and being outgunned and outmanned by a gigantic margin. As was later disclosed by Pentagon, all that was going on was a simple rotation:

> The U.S. Army will send another infantry brigade and division headquarters to Eastern Europe in the coming months, meaning that the Pentagon is sticking with a larger force presence established after Russia's 2022 invasion of Ukraine. The 3rd Infantry Brigade Combat Team from the 101st Airborne Division at Fort Campbell, Ky., will deploy 3,400 soldiers to replace the division's 1st Infantry Brigade Combat Team this fall, the Army announced Wednesday. The units primarily will be based out of locations in Romania, but also will carry out missions stretching up to the High North, said Col. Martin O'Donnell, U.S. Army Europe and Africa spokesman. Additionally, about 200 troops from the 82nd Airborne Division headquarters at Fort Liberty, N.C., will replace a 10th Mountain Division headquarters that has been operating out of Romania. "The deployments are one-for-one unit replacements and will not change the overall U.S. force posture in the region," the Army said. [248]

Anyone even remotely acquainted with armed forces realities would know that for the United States to assemble a force which would be able to survive the modern battlefield for more than two weeks against an opposition such as Russia could mount would require many months, if not years. It would include assembling a force of roughly one million and then resolving the issue of pre-deploying it in Europe as well as solving the issue of the sustainability of such a force, unsolvable in present conditions where the existing NATO industrial capability would run out of ammo within two-three weeks.[249] This case of Sy Hersh, for all good he did, is presented here to demonstrate a classic instance of Hofstadter's complexity issue—the modern world, let alone an extremely complex field of modern warfare and military science, requires a very good grasp of such realities if it is to transcend rhetoric and supposition. This grasp comes only through an appropriate education and experience, and even that is no guarantee against exposing one's military expertise as dismal, as has been done by a whole pleiad of American military luminaries ranging from General David Petraeus to Ben Hodges, whose "forecasts" on the SMO have been so detached from reality that they have become the butt of jokes in Russia and among serious analysts such as former CIA Larry Johnson and the indomitable Scott Ritter, among others, within the United States. Media exposure does not guarantee one from destroying one's reputation. In fact, the opposite is true.

This applies equally to the journalist corps of Russia, much of which, due to military illiteracy bar some rare exceptions, has similarly reduced itself to nothing more than gonzo-journalism or relying on war "reporting" by a whole army of so-called Russian "military experts," most of whom never served a day in armed forces or had next to zero background in operations, and being in the field primarily for the personal gain, be that financial, career advancement or both. One can only imagine the horrendously atrocious level of such "reporting" and "analysis" which painted a completely distorted picture of the events to the extent that at some point the rumor started to circulate in Russia that such "correspondence" might be FSB and SVR psyops intended to completely confuse the AFU and NATO command. This also applies to the relentless media campaign by Wagner Group owner, the late Evgenii Prigozhin, who dramatically embellished the difficulties of his Wagner private military force operating near Bakhmut while practically eliminating any mentioning of the critical support being provided by regular Russian forces. Little doubt, the Western media bought it, including a preposterous Prigozhin lie about Russian troops fighting with shovels.[250] Little did they know that Prigozhin's hysteria and sick fantasies had primarily been a result of the Russian Defense Ministry terminating contracts with the Wagner group—the main source of Prigozhin's fortune. The fact that Western corporate media have been reporting informational trash as news from the SMO, de facto working as not only the propaganda arm of Washington but also of Kiev regime, cannot obscure the crucial fact of American punditry being illiterate militarily across the board.

But while these issues related to educational and experiential competence might have been enough to destroy whatever remained of the reputation of Western punditry, the more sinister aspects of activity of Western propaganda machine cannot be ignored—here we must address other players than the Western media which are complicit in propaganda worthy of Dr. Goebbels' ministry. In fact, a number of AFU's POWs testified to the fact that even such an organization as the OSCE (Organization for Security and Cooperation in Europe) is directly involved in staging Ukraine's "military successes." As one of them testified, the OSCE group arrived in the village of Temirovka in Zaporozhe oblast where they "shot" the report about how the AFU suppressed and then chased retreating Russian forces for three kilometers. A major part of the report was shot, however, in a different location, far removed from the combat zone. For entourage they even brought in an Armored Personnel Carrier. Later this "report" was circulated in most of Ukraine's social media.[251] The Ukrainian public for the most part exists in a completely imaginary world where the AFU beats Russian forces daily and is constantly on the offensive—so much so that even its catastrophic defeat at Avdeevka is transformed into providing evidence of Ukrainian military genius. As one of the leading Ukrainian pundits, Alexander Musienko, described the catastrophe of the AFU at Avdeevka, which was captured by Russian forces on February 18, 2024, thereby removing a strategic anchor of all AFU defense at Donetsk axis:

> I think we need to avoid such categories (assessments). Not everything is exclusively definite during this war. In this case, I consider it [Avdeevka] mostly as a victory.[252]

The fact that these words could have been uttered in such circumstances merely shows the degree of the delusion in which the Ukrainian public resides, due to domestic media propaganda whose modus operandi is a carbon copy of that of the Western corporate media, which has no limit to the depth of human depravity to which it is ready to lower itself in justifying any atrocity and war crime, as is the case with Ukraine and now made even more evident to the world's public with the internet enabling full view of the genocide being committed by Israel in Gaza against the Palestinians. No normal person with any remaining human decency would want to work for what was exposed first by the SMO and then by the tragedy in Gaza as such an utterly corrupt, amoral and prostitute institution as the corporate media. The role of propaganda and outright brainwashing of the Western public was on full display in Canada's parliament on September 22, 2023, when it gave a rousing standing ovation for the "veteran" of 14th Ukrainian Waffen SS Division "Galychyna," 98-year old Yaroslav Hunka, who was hailed as a "Ukrainian" and "Canadian hero," was everything one needed to know about the media-driven view of WW II in Canada and in the West.[253] No amount of the damage control which followed in Anglophone corporate media could undo that exposure. The only accidental element of this depravity was the unwitting revelation of the combination of ignorance of history and hatred for Russia that drives the Western elites and media, which see no problem with using Kiev's Nazis, such as the 3rd Assault Brigade, aka Azov Nazi formation (which was again demolished at Avdeevka after the liberation of Mariupol) or any other terrorist organization in their futile attempts to defeat Russia.

But the final blow was delivered by Tucker Carlson and his interview with Vladimir Putin on February 9th of 2024. That this was such wasn't demonstrated by the fact of a hysterical corporate western media trying to do damage control at the vision of a Russian leader easily carrying a conversation for two and a half hours energetically and without any teleprompter—in irresistible and catastrophic comparison to Joe Biden. Nor was it even the real information on the successful progress of the SMO and Russia's economic development, as well as the lesson in Russian history, that damaged the already widely compromised Western corporate media. *It was the fact that this interview by Tucker Carlson recorded across all platforms around one billion views.*[254] No

Western political leader nor any Western corporate media will ever be able to achieve such an audience, not even combined. And herein, in this well documented success and what amounts to an unprecedented event in the history of media, lies hope—hundreds of millions of people around the world wanted to hear from Putin themselves, firsthand, thus, explicitly showing their suspicion of and contempt for the Western propaganda machine which has outlived not only its purpose but lost any moral ground for being taken seriously. As the events in the SMO and then in Gaza have shown—its time has run out. The West has lost the propaganda war after losing a real one.

CHAPTER 9.

SYSTEMIC MILITARY DIFFERENCES

ON THE SECOND ANNIVERSARY of the Special Military Operation, February 24, 2024, all media around the world were abuzz. The marking and commenting on the end of the second year of SMO ranged from obscure YouTube channels to major corporate media in the U.S. The *Washington Post*, a major player in disseminating the Kiev regime's propaganda for two years published an opinion piece by Alex Horton with the bland title: "What the Pentagon has learned from two years of war in Ukraine." In a meandering piece filled with tactical and technical minutiae, Horton noted:

> The U.S. military is undertaking an expansive revision of its approach to war fighting, having largely abandoned the counterinsurgency playbook that was a hallmark of combat in Iraq and Afghanistan to focus instead on preparing for an even larger conflict with more sophisticated adversaries such as Russia or China. What's transpired in Ukraine, where this week the war enters its third year with hundreds of thousands dead or wounded on both sides and still no end in sight, has made clear to the Pentagon that battlefield calculations have fundamentally changed in the years since it last deployed forces in large numbers. Precision weapons, fleets of drones and digital surveillance can reach far beyond the front lines, posing grave risk to personnel wherever they are.[255]

And herein lies the problem for the United States and its military: tactical adjustments are relatively easy, such as rewriting field manuals for a very strict emission control (EMCON) of radio signals, including the use of cell phones in and near combat zones, or getting better at camouflage or having a better understanding of tactical formations' interaction with both ISR and strike drones, whose use was recognized as a very serious factor in modern combat. These are easily discerned lessons, give or take some. There is one huge problem with all that—wars are won on strategic and operational levels. One can lose a company or two, or even a battalion on the axis of an enemy's large force breakthrough when trying to contain it, but if such a sacrifice allows a division, a tactical-operational formation to which this battalion is attached, to maneuver and strike the flank of the attacking enemy, thus breaking enemy's offensive action, and then catching it off-balance and destroying it—such a sacrifice in purely operational terms is completely justified. The U.S. military doesn't know how to fight such wars, because it hasn't fought an enemy which could defend and maneuver in such a way. As Horton reports:

> Pettyjohn, with the Center for New American Security, acknowledged that the U.S. and Ukrainian militaries operate differently, meaning some takeaways from the war with Russia may not be applicable. But she noted that some American military leaders she has spoken to have seemed circumspect that there's much for them to learn. They underestimate, she said, how the nature of fighting has changed, holding tight to the risky assumption that the United States would simply do better in similar circumstances.[256]

Herein lies the recipe for disaster, because many in the U.S. military simply cannot recognize what is unfolding before their very eyes other than the scale of the SMO. The reason lies much deeper than mere declining educational and cognitive levels of the American military-political-media class. It is an issue of culture. One can study cultural idiosyncrasies to whatever extent one wants, but one cannot change the fact that the U.S. military is an expeditionary military, which throughout the 20th century has committed its forces when, both in WW I and WW II, most of the fighting and dying has been done by others. This simple historical fact might come as an inconvenient truth, but the essence of war was taught to the U.S. Army within less than a minute when North Vietnamese commander, Gen. Vo Nguyen Giap, responding to a U.S. general who is claimed to have told his NVA counterpart in Hanoi five days before the fall of Saigon, "You know you never beat us on the battlefield," replied: "That may be so, but it is also irrelevant."[257] Reducing all these fairly simple thoughts to an even simpler, much more fundamental cultural factor, we must stress the obvious fact that no U.S. Armed Forces person, from private to four-star general, ever fought in defense of the United States of America. The U.S. military is not just an expeditionary military, it is also an imperial military that fights imperial wars of conquest and doesn't address the concept of defense of a Mother- or Fatherland in its strategic and operational documents. Thus, it cannot fight a real conventional combined war of scale against peer or better-than-peer opponents who fight in defense of their own country. This is a fundamental cultural difference which dictates the warfare on operational and strategic levels. And this cultural and intellectual gap cannot be bridged. Thus, while the Pentagon may learn some tactical lessons or tricks—and even that is questionable due to obsolete TOE (Table of Organization and Equipment) of the NATO armies—the operational and strategic paradigms of the SMO indeed don't apply to U.S. forces, which lack moral and cultural pivot which defines the warrior of continental warfare and the way this warrior fights. The U.S. military doesn't fight in defense of America, it fights for imperial conquests only. Russian soldiers fight in defense of their homeland.

That makes the cultural, moral and spiritual imprints on Russian and American soldiers dramatically different. There are surely still competent and courageous officers and soldiers in the U.S. military, but none of them has any experience of fighting for their wives, children and relatives. An abstract statement about the U.S. "defending and advancing vital national interests" as

stated in its Introduction to the 2022 National Defense Strategy
and that of the long list identifying threats to Russia in its 2014
Military Doctrine cannot be more apart in their essences.[258] The
U.S. Defense Strategy identifies a very short list of four items of
very broad priorities such as defending the homeland from the
People's Republic of China or deterring strategic attacks against
the U.S. and Allies.[259] Moreover, U.S. National Security Strategy
regurgitates the same old postulates of U.S. hegemony. While
repeating the same general priority of "ensuring the security of
the American people" the pivot of the whole strategy lies in this
phrase: *The need for a strong and purposeful American role in
the world has never been greater*.[260] It goes without saying that
no single American scholar's justification of U.S. fighting in
Afghanistan or Iraq, let alone illegally occupying parts of Syria,
can pass the basic smell test of even second rate geopolitical and
military scholarship. Obviously, using the beaten to death and
illiterate cliché that "we must fight them over there, so we don't
fight them here" also won't do.[261] In other words, the primitivism
and bombastic tone of America's foundational defense and
security documents are such because they need to obfuscate the
rather favorable security environment of the United States, since
no competing superpower wants to conduct an amphibious assault
on the U.S. soil, or bomb Chicago or destroy Boston. Lamentations
such as these really don't make any sense, since neither China nor
Russia have any military bases near the United States. When it
comes to space-based threats, both the USSR and the U.S. had
been developing anti-satellite weapons long before China joined
in, yet the National Defense Strategy still frets that:

> The scope and scale of threats to the homeland
> have fundamentally changed. The PRC and Russia
> now pose more dangerous challenges to safety and
> security at home, even as terrorist threats persist. Both
> states are already using non-kinetic means against
> our defense industrial base and mobilization systems,
> as well as deploying counterspace capabilities that
> can target our Global Positioning System and other

space-based capabilities that support military power and daily civilian life. The PRC or Russia could use a wide array of tools in an attempt to hinder U.S. military preparation and response in a conflict, including actions aimed at undermining the will of the U.S. public, and to target our critical infrastructure and other systems.[262]

While very verbose, the statement conceals the main reason for the worry of Washington establishment—the loss of the arms race with Russia and, eventually, with China. That forebodes an interruption of the American military's real purpose, which is ensuring the existence of American imperialism, whose main beneficiaries are not Americans but primarily the transnational capitalist elites. Transnational capital cannot have national interests, it only has capital's interests and the existence of a cohesive American nation focused on its own interest is a direct threat to it and to the social and political class which services this capital. In comparison, the Russian 2014 Military Doctrine and 2015 National Security Strategy spell out the set of threats to Russia in good detail. The Russian Military Doctrine lists thirteen, from A to M, external threats, such as:

Building up the power potential of the North Atlantic Treaty Organization (NATO) and endowing it with global functions implemented in violation of international law, bringing the military infrastructure of NATO member countries closer to the borders of the Russian Federation, including through further expansion of the bloc.[263]

The conditions specified in this paragraph alone, out of 12 others, are simply beyond the American experience ever since the Cuban Missile Crisis in October of 1962, which almost resulted in nuclear confrontation when the Soviet Union deployed its ballistic missiles to Cuba—too close for the American liking. The latest American doctrinal document ATP 7-100.1, which names Russia as the enemy, identifies the role of Russian General Staff and its scientific approach to national defense, to war in general:

> 2-35. Russia uses scientific substantiation to understand the types of current and future conflicts, those most likely to occur, and the capabilities necessary to succeed in those conflicts. This understanding guides the development of its military forces. Although it creates the theory of why and how the military must evolve, the actual application depends on many other factors, including public support, economic viability, and technological advancements.
>
> 2-36. The Russian General Staff uses analysis by the military scientific community to define the conditions of modern conflicts as well as to develop and validate the forms and methods of employing its military forces. The analysis incorporates both the classical and asymmetrical means of military employment in support of strategic objectives, as well as operational and tactical actions.[264]

So the key difference between Russian way of war and that of the United States, as was stated earlier already in this book— that the Russian General Staff is the main organ of command and control of Russian Armed Forces and that as such it encompasses the whole of the development and employment of Russian Armed Forces—is now recognized and admitted by the U.S. Army. The United States doesn't have such a structure; rather it has separate services' doctrines with command and control functions delegated to each of the specific Unified Combatant Commands. This is not just an administrative difference, but a profound cultural difference. It explains both why the U.S. Armed Forces is overstretched due to the unrealistic, if not altogether ignorant and illiterate geopolitical views of America's political class and why it is losing the arms race due to the exhaustion of financial and material resources—due to their primarily being recycled within the U.S. military-industrial-congressional-media complex, which is increasingly incapable of either formulating realistic goals or sensible procurement policy because its primary concern is to secure profits, which requires instability and conflicts around the globe. The Russian military and military-industrial complex operate on completely different premises. In plain language—the Russian General Staff is simply much better at what it does because it plans for defense of the nation. So does Russia's military-industrial complex which is owned by the Russian state.

Moreover, even a brief review of the academic levels of Russia's service academies (aka Military Institutes) and U.S. service academies reveals a considerable general academic and military science gap between the two systems. The average Russian officer graduates from the academy with at least five academic years for combined arms and six academic years for naval and VKS and other military-technological academies with a full specialist engineering degree and what would amount in the Western educational framework to the "minor" in military science, obviously with services specifics. This all derives from the classic Russian/Soviet tradition in education which always emphasized strong STEM training and results in what Grau and Bartles describe as:

> The Russian education system continues to emphasize mathematics and science. Consequently, "math anxiety" is not a problem, particularly among military professionals. Mathematical determination articles are a normal part of most Russian professional military journals. Russian officers use mathematical models to aid in their planning. Nomograms and calculations quickly resolve issues such as determining pass times and march durations; duration and density of artillery fire to achieve necessary percentages of kills and equipment destruction in area fire missions; the time and place where the forces will encounter the enemy main force; the optimal march routes; the time required to move from the assembly area and

transition from battalion to platoon attack formation;
the artillery expenditure required during this
transition; or the numbers of trucks and trips required
to move tonnages of different cargo. The math does
not stop there.[265]

This has been fully demonstrated in the SMO, as an
example, with the majority of instances of AFU advancements
being nothing more than their moving into the areas from which
Russian troops had withdrawn, primarily for reasons of tactical
or operational necessity and, most of all, for saving the lives of
their own troops instead of sacrificing them in an unnecessary
slugfest for dominance of a locality with very little operational
significance. The Russian command corps, from junior officers to
operational level command, has shown itself very adept at modern
warfare and utilizing available resources in the largest military
conflict since WW II. This is a no small achievement, and here
professional military education and moral upbringing played a
decisive role. Western propaganda concentrated almost entirely on
the undeniably respectable staying power of many of AFU soldiers,
which also was recognized by Russian counterparts; however, it
almost completely ignored a massive number of instances of the
heroism of Russian soldiers and officers throughout the SMO.
CNN obliquely admitted Russian steadfastness which contradicts
claims of their nihilism:

> It is a nihilism that only amplifies a key question
> Ukrainian forces have: Why do the Russian troops
> fight so hard for these tiny settlements? As they push
> further into occupied territory, the fight remains as
> hard. The fact that Russian forces fight so persistently
> for each settlement has raised doubts about claims
> that Russia's defensive line is fierce but thin.[266]

It is Russia's shared history and culture across dozens of
Russia's ethnicities and religious confessions that has also played
a decisive role in the massive number of Russia's volunteers

applying for the SMO. By December 2023 Russian Armed forces had enrolled 486,000 volunteers and, as Vladimir Putin stated, the flow of volunteers continues unabated, averaging 1,500 volunteers a day.[267] These numbers and cultural dynamics are beyond the grasp of most U.S. military and intelligence people, who grew up on a steady diet of American military and political propaganda about the Soviet Union and Russia and who have continually failed to come to terms with the operational and strategic reality of the SMO, instead drowning in the tactical minutiae and shoddy military scholarship derived from the U.S. outlandish military mythology. The U.S. military has found itself within the Kubler-Ross model's denial phase.

This denial, combined with professional incompetence exacerbated by an acute sense of professional envy could be found in what is supposed to be a serious publication by TRADOC titled *Russian Tactics,* in which an attempt is made to assess Russia's Air Defense while making a questionable reference to the Israeli Air Force and its operations in Syria.

> While Russia's Aerospace Defense Forces contain a vast array of operational and strategic air defense assets, the bulk of short and medium range air defense resources are situated with the Air Defense Troops of the SV. Indeed, medium and short-range air defense assets can be found in dedicated SV air defense brigades while SV maneuver units contain an abundance of organic short range air defense resources. This three-tier or layered system allows for the creation of anti-access area-denial zones which could prove challenging to aggressor aircraft, cruise missiles, and UAVs. However, recent conflicts in Syria and Libya have shown that many of the exported Russian air defense systems proved ineffective in countering drones and low flying missiles. The Israeli Air Force also has been extremely successful in defeating Russian air defense systems using combinations of electromagnetic warfare

(REB), anti-radiation missiles, and precision guided munitions. These limitations for export versions are at least partly due to inadequate operator training and lack of dedicated maintenance. These limitations will have reduced impact on the effectiveness in the SV. Although Russian Aerospace Forces and the SV have certainly made great strides in building an integrated air defense system, major challenges remain in the realm of acquisitions, training, and operational viability.[268]

While the publication provides some explanations for the alleged successful operations of the Israeli Air Force, it fails to mention that the Syrian Army's latest AD complexes are some 60 Russian-made S1 Pantsir missile-gun systems, which gave a very good account of themselves, with only three of them lost throughout the duration of Israel's attacks since 2015; they are the only truly modern systems. The rest are Iranian copies of Soviet/Russian systems and legacy Soviet systems such as S-75 or Kub. Yet even this rather antiquated system achieves a very good number of hits on Israeli's standoff weapons, which are launched beyond the air space of Syria, thus prohibiting Syrian air defense from using its longer-range missiles which would violate the air space of Lebanon or Israel proper. How, then, this "success" can be meaningfully related to the unprecedented scale and scope of Russian air defense operations against all classes of targets under the extreme conditions of electronic warfare in the SMO in Ukraine remains puzzling. This is not a good way to analyze Russian Air Defense which, based on the openly available data, has performed very well against the best NATO standoff weapons such as the Scalp and Stormshadow cruise missiles and a variety of tactical ballistic missiles such as the HIMARS and ATACMS.[269]

But this is not the only gaffe from which this TRADOC publication suffers. Its assumptions provide a perfect illustration of the ignorance of those who train and develop doctrine for the U.S. Army. This publication states that Russia pursues a global strategy driven by a desire to once again be recognized as a world power.[270] This is a complete delusion which turns Russia's fundamental security concerns upside down and ignores Russia's history. Recognition of Russia as a world power is a *fait accompli*; it is not driven by a search for prestige or self-aggrandizing, as is the case with the U.S. to a large degree, but rather for its security purposes, given Russia's military history, whose scale and duration is simply beyond the grasp of the U.S. military. As even the late Richard Pipes acknowledged in 1977, when summarizing Russia's history and losses sustained from foreign invaders: "Such figures are beyond the comprehension of most Americans. But clearly ... Such a country (Russia) tends also to assess the rewards of defense in much more realistic terms."[271] It could be stated today that the present crop of U.S. politicos and military leaders are incapable of assessing modern war in any realistic terms whatsoever. This is not surprising, given the precipitous decline in the educational and intellectual levels of the American military-political elite which has been exposed as utterly incompetent and derived from its experience in bombing defenseless nations with impunity. The U.S. is simply not designed for fighting peer or better than peer power in 21st century combined arms operations of scale without resorting to nuclear weapons.[272]

This is the shocking lesson that the SMO has provided for the rest of the world, coalescing into a complete picture from a variety of pieces and bits of information, ranging from burning Abrams tanks and demolished Patriot PAC3 air defense complexes to the absolute impotence in operational planning by NATO to the parade of four-star U.S. "military experts" whose forecasts of Russia's defeat failed miserably.

But if there ever was an embodiment of a failure of American power, it is almost daily exposition of the President of the United States, Joseph Biden, obviously spiraling into senility and dementia. By accepting or failing to effect a change in such a representation of itself, the U.S., or whatever passes today for a salad of incompatible ethnicities and cultures within its borders, has no future. The destruction of the industrial base or falling behind in critical industrial outputs and technologies can be obfuscated for a little while longer, albeit with increasingly less effective propaganda and financial legerdemain, but this cannot easily hide the results of the American and West's "leadership" on the battlefields of Ukraine where the globalist elites have sacrificed the lives and well-being of millions of gullible Ukrainians to their blind hatred of Russia and Russians. They have sacrificed the integrity (both moral and physical) of Ukraine to their desperate desire to defeat Russia, without even knowing what they are dealing with. No American servicemen ever lost a member of his or her own immediate family to war, every Russian family has its "own hero," as the lyrics of famous Russian song go.

America is not exceptional militarily; it never was. The U.S. Navy gave an excellent account of itself in the War in the Pacific, but it still ended up with the U.S. dropping nuclear bombs in 1945 on Japan, which was ready to surrender.[273] The heroism and dedication of Allied soldiers and officers at Normandy beaches on June 6, 1944 deserved all the praise, but the war in Europe was already won by 1944 and the only issue facing the Allies was whether the Red Army would end up on the shores of La Manche, thus confining Great Britain to the Islands and isolating it together with the U.S. from Europe.[274] As the diplomatic efforts that preceded and even accompanied the SMO finally taught the Russians, they should never trust the West again and should expect continuous attempts from Washington on Russia and Russian people, even as the combined West descends into tyranny and new dark ages. For countering those, Russia has what the combined West lacks:

1. A much more advanced military arsenal.
2. Industrial capacity capable of sustaining and enhancing it, without sacrificing the standard of living of the general population.
3. New political and military elites which are antithetical to the globalist neo-liberal cabal in charge of the combined West.

The combined West has no answer to any of the points above.

That said, it is the issue of elites, or rather the gigantic cultural, educational and life experiences gap between the Russian and American elites which cannot be bridged, that should give the combined West serious pause. It will not. Nonetheless, we should elaborate. In his address to the Federal Assembly on February 29, 2024, the president of Russia delivered the point which is not possible to be made in the allegedly democratic and "free" West:

> In his speech, Putin suggested that the word *"elites"* had *"discredited"* itself in Russia over the years, adding that they were unworthy of the moniker. Those who *"filled their pockets in the 1990s . . . are definitely not the elites. The true elites are those who serve Russia,"* he stressed. The country's new elites are the *"workers and the warriors,"* the president insisted. They *"don't boast of their successes, but take responsibility in the key moments,"* he said, adding that they are the people who *"can be entrusted with Russia in the future."* The participants of Russia's military operation against Ukraine have proven that they *"won't retreat, won't let you down and won't betray you,"* Putin said. *"They are the ones who should be taking the leading positions"* in society, he said.[275]

His words addressed the country as a whole, which is politically united and is breathing like a unified socio-cultural and economic organism, some of Russia's problems notwithstanding. Against the background of general Western disintegration and that of the United States in particular, the issue of elites becomes crucial for the survival and prosperity of Russia. If Putin et al are seen as the elites and it is then thought that they can somehow be removed, this would nonetheless not change the situation, given that those whom Putin is characterizing as Russia's true elites will remain.

This is not the case with the United States, whose governing "elites" (as the West understands the term) have simply detached themselves from the best interests of the country and enclosed themselves in the aforementioned "echo chamber" of dubious ideologies and shoddy scholarship. As for its military elites, the problem is that they do not possess any serious governance or technical skills which are imperative for effective governance of modern complex societies.

Take current Chief of Naval Operations of the U.S. Navy Admiral Liza Franchetti, who holds degrees in journalism and in organizational management from the University of Phoenix.[276] At this stage, Franchetti's service record notwithstanding, one has to question how a person with manifest humanities degrees can run a modern nuclear missile-carrying navy such as the U.S. Navy, which requires a serious military and engineering background. Compare Franchetti's C.V. to that of her counterpart, Russian Navy Admiral Nikolai Evmenov, whose educational background (the same as yours truly) is in engineering with a strong navigation emphasis, which takes about six academic years in naval academy: in Evmenov's case VVMUPP (Higher Naval College of Submarine Navigation) with continued education at Kuznetsov's Naval Academy (2 years) and Academy of the General Staff (another 2 years).[277] This disparity in educational backgrounds cannot be starker, which brings forth irresistible question of how can one become a serious commander of a modern destroyer or nuclear submarine without having a profound understanding of the engineering complexity of all systems, including weapon systems. This understanding necessarily includes the physical principles of their operations—all aspects and applied derivatives, such as electronics and mechanics among many, of higher mathematics and physics, which translate into the science of systems integration. Yet, looking at the modern U.S. military in general and the U.S. Navy in particular one can see the legacy force stuck operationally and strategically in 1990s, with disastrous procurement policies.

The issue is not just at the level of U.S. services; it goes higher, to the political decision-making level, where most of national security and defense bureaucrats reflect the warnings of both Menken ("morons with Ph.Ds") and Schumpeter, who in 1943 in *Capitalism, Socialism, and Democracy* expressed concern over the armies of unemployable humanities-educated people, warning that "All those who are unemployed or unsatisfactorily employed or unemployable drift into the vocations in which standards are least definite or in which aptitudes and acquirements of a different order count. They swell the host of intellectuals in the strict sense of the term whose numbers hence increase disproportionately."[278]

Schumpeter's critical foreboding of the emergence of a class of Western "elites" whose preponderant educational background may enable them to know, or rather have heard about, many things but who have absolutely no skills or tool kit to seriously understand any of them is reflected today in America, and the West's intellectuals. This also is the essence of American higher education for the "elites," including to a certain degree, professional military education, service academies included. One can take a look at the background of former undersecretary of defense for policy in Obama Administration, Michel Flournoy—a brain behind the destruction of Libya—whose educational background is in social studies and international relations, courses which in the West are nothing but triumphalist fairy tales. We should not also forget Douglas Feith, the brain behind Iraq's disaster of 2003, who was characterized by General Tommy Franks as "The fucking stupidest guy on the face of the earth."[279] Of course, it would be very presumptuous to paint all U.S. elites in Douglas Feith's color, but large swaths of them do qualify.

Yet in contradiction to what should have been a strong point of such training—an understanding that in matters of serious geopolitics, the essence of real war and warfare in general is always *necessarily* a cultural act—their conduct not just of the NATO proxy war against Russia, but of the operations throughout the Middle East (Iraq, Syria, Afghanistan, Libya) has demonstrated a massive failure, the latter interpreted by some as intending to simply create chaos, in which case, mission accomplished. Recognition of this factor is completely absent in NATO militaries, who view military conflict only through the lens of the predominant narrative, based on domination through the unremitting application of force.[280] This may explain why throughout the SMO one witnessed one failure after another by U.S. top brass to provide a modicum of true expertise on Russia and her military. Nations do fashion themselves in the image of the machines they produce; nowhere is this more true than in weapons—extremely complex showpiece machines for destruction and killing.

For decades there was no better promoter of what is called military porn than the United States. The SMO changed all that, albeit the process started much earlier. The simple fact of Russian tanks having a much lower profile than any NATO tank was never a matter of image only, albeit one cannot deny a certain aesthetics of many weapon systems. Rather, it was an issue of function—the fight on the plains of Russia in defense of the country. There, the maintenance of a low profile is a must, to make acquiring and aiming at them more difficult for the gunners of NATO tanks.[281] Russian air defense systems such as Tor-M2 are highly mobile and are capable of launching at targets while moving, while the S-300+ family of air defense systems, unlike the American Patriot, facilitates the fully vertical launch of missiles without the necessity to direct the launchers. All these details, even on the aesthetic level, allow a glimpse inside the Russian military mind and how it approaches the war. But if the U.S. military cannot grasp this, how can one expect the American "intellectual" and political class to do so, when it does not know the difference between PR and substance?

This is foundational to my proposal that with the events in Ukraine, we are witnessing America's final war, insofar as the definition of a true war goes, which is the state of the hostilities between nation-states which requires a sustained and maximum exertion of effort and resources ranging from military and economic to moral and cultural ones. This is because the United States has neither the resources nor the knowledge of how to fight a real one, nor is the possibility of its acquisition of that capacity anywhere in sight. We'll try to answer this question in the next chapters.

CHAPTER 10.

HOW EMBEDDED STRUCTURAL FACTORS THWART WESTERN MILITARY DOMINANCE

FOR MANY PEOPLE of 50 years of age and younger the decades of the 1970s and 1980s mean very little in terms of military history and the balance of forces of NATO and Warsaw Pact. But some retrospective is in order, because it will give some insight into the way Russians see the West as a military opponent. The West's triumphalism of the 1990s has obfuscated the changing strategic landscape in Europe during the Cold War 1.0, and it was known even then that the Soviet Union had enough force to create a strategic calamity in the West in case of real war, to be known as WW III then, and that the combined NATO force could withstand the main thrust of a hypothetical Soviet strike for about a week or two, after which nuclear weapons would be used. Hence, the option of a nuclear response was retained by NATO:

> The alliance retained the option, however, to use nuclear weapons first if its initial response to a conventional attack did not prove adequate to containing the aggressor, and to deliberately escalate to general nuclear war, if necessary. While adoption of the flexible response policy allowed the alliance to avoid a policy of prompt and mutual suicide (as many of NATO's tactical nuclear weapons would have detonated on alliance territory), NATO still continued to rely on the first use of nuclear weapons to deter or counter a major conventional assault.[282]

It was not some kind of paranoia which drove this decision, albeit the fear factor was definitely present. It was the time of America and West's peak industrial development and of a much more competent political elite and top brass. Serious analysis went into drawing war scenarios which hadn't yet been poisoned by the triumphalist exuberance of the post-Gulf War defeat of the Iraqi Army. Even the U.S. Naval War College in the series of its Global War Games considered a scenario in which, in case of a global war, the Red Forces, i.e. the Warsaw Pact, would reach the Rhine and enter France within 35 days.[283]

MAP 4
The Central Front 1986 Game D+19 to D+42

This was a tacit admission of NATO's conventional weakness, despite the fact that, unlike today, the U.S. forces in Europe had the support of a highly trained and capable Bundeswehr, and other NATO allies, whom Soviet Command viewed as a very capable force. Of course, the Soviet Union held its massive force in Germany and other Warsaw Pact countries for deterrent purposes and had no intention of attacking NATO unless it was attacked first, with Soviet military doctrine having an explicit defensive character.[284] But this is purely the political dimension, which was also turned upside down by Western Cold War propaganda. An unclassified report on Soviet armor of that time period provided an unvarnished assessment of the prospects of the U.S. forces in Europe with an emphasis on tanks and ATGMs:

> While U.S. innovations since 1974 promise two effective new tanks for the 1980s (the M60A3 and XM-1) plus a range of potent new tank penetrants and incapacitants, Soviet measures against U.S. anti-armor weapons, which we now know have been quite effective in 1970s, could keep them well out in front of American development throughout the 1980s. In the arms likely to dominate the outcome of a future battle for Central Europe—armored fighting vehicles and counterweapons—the U.S. Army, then, probably will remain qualitatively and quantitatively inferior.[285]

This conclusion remains true today, despite the fact that the former Warsaw Pact countries have joined NATO, that Russia doesn't have troops in Germany ready to counter a NATO attack and, in fact, justifiably views the combined West as an existential enemy of both the Russian people and the Russian state—with the dramatic difference that the overwhelming majority of Russians no longer buy the stale and fraudulent rhetoric about "democracy" and "human rights," and for the first time view the combined West with open contempt. Their attitude is based partly on recognition of the dismal performance of American and European weapons systems on the real battlefield.

The fate of NATO's armor is a case in point. Combined Arms in the 21st century is not just a fancy term for ground operations with interaction of different types of forces. Rather, Russia is now requiring that this combination of forces *operate as a system*. One of the major operational and strategic shocks for NATO and its military planners is the fact that defense can be as effective in attriting the enemy as offensive operations, especially when one considers the attention given by the Soviet military planners to defense of the Soviet Army's armored forces from NATO's standoff weapons by developing a system of tactical and operational level air defense, electronic warfare and radar complexes.[286] This concept, as was addressed earlier, is not properly developed in the NATO armies, especially for the realities of a drone anti-tank warfare which saw an explosive development of counter-drone EW systems and further development of air defense such as the Tunguska-M, Tor and the Tor-M1 of Soviet times.[287] Performance of further development of such systems, such as Tor-M2, in SMO against drones was noted as very effective even by U.S. military sources.[288] Another system of note, the Pantsir S1, is also about to receive an inexpensive and mass produced missile, the Gvozd' (Nail, in English), which was developed specifically for use against such targets as drones, commonly known as UAVs; it is also capable of intercepting subsonic targets such as TLAMs.[289]

These developments, combined with the further development of anti-aircraft air defense systems, such as the Buk-M3 and the S-300 and 400 family combined with an advanced air force, guarantee the survival of Russia's main battle tanks as one of the main tools of modern war, thus preserving the Soviet/Russian tradition of maintaining a highly developed armored component of ground troops. So notably, for the foreseeable future, at least, matching Russia in terms of the development and production of tanks and attached air defense systems remains beyond the grasp of any NATO country, the United States included.

Furthermore, Russia's development of loitering munitions such as the Zala developed and manufactured Lancet and latest Scalpel loitering munitions and especially the gargantuan rate of their production makes it extremely problematic for any combination of NATO forces to be able to counter Russia's tanks. Such a NATO force, even if granted that it will be able to be prepositioned and deployed—a very doubtful proposition in itself—will be subjected to drone and loitering munitions strikes, as happened to the first Abrams tank, which was destroyed near Berdychi on February 26, 2024. This took a team of Russian Army FPV drone operators only two strikes—first into the engine compartment, thus stopping the Abrams, and second under the turret—using the FPV drones armed with the RPG-7's heads.[290] Russian drone operators were taken aback "by the arrogance with which they drove the tank in the open. They really believed in this machine."[291] This clarification is important since it exposes the level of propaganda in the West regarding what it considers as its top of the line military technology such as the Abrams, which it constantly claimed to be the best tank in the world.[292] The Russian Army, obviously, has its own opinion on that claim; the next Abrams tank was destroyed by the first shot of Russian T-72B3 tank on March 5, 2024.[293]

The destruction of Abrams tanks shouldn't be taken in isolation, though the severe reputational damage dealt specifically to American-made hardware is undeniable. The destroyed Abrams tanks are just one component of NATO tanks overall, including the Leopard-2s and Challengers, which have met their ultimate demise on the battlefield of the 21st century as they tried to reproduce the first Gulf War against what is now arguably the best army in the world. A moderately persuasive argument can be made that, should those tanks be driven by NATO personnel, they might have fared better, but this argument goes only so far. For starters, some AFU tank drivers—those who survived—could likely give lessons in armor maneuvers to any NATO tank commander insofar as NATO has no experience of fighting in the European theater in highly adverse climate conditions and terrain. But ultimately, while many Western pundits rushed to claim, yet again, the end of the era of tank formations or tried to apply utterly inapplicable lessons of the Yom Kippur or Gulf wars, no amount of trying to fit primarily false Russian armor losses fed to Washington by Kiev regime could explain away the evident outcomes. Their conclusions, even those by professionals, inevitably failed to grasp the essence of the matter. Take the classic GIGO (Garbage In-Garbage Out) "analysis" by Michael Losacco, an armor officer who based his conclusions on the fantastical reportage of battlefield events by the U.S. media and accordingly noted:

> Russian tanks are having a bad time of it in Ukraine, suffering high casualties as Ukrainian troops, equipped with antitank guided missiles and armed drones, frequently ambush Russian armored formations unaware of their surroundings and lacking

dismounted ground support. Observers in search of
lessons are watching the war play out, interpreting the
incredible attrition rate imposed on Russia's tanks as
validation of the widely held assumption that armored
formations cannot successfully operate alone—an
assumption that was similarly solidified fifty years
ago, when Egyptian and Syrian forces destroyed
Israeli tanks en masse during the 1973 Yom Kippur
War.[294]

The uncritical acceptance of what are Kiev regime
propaganda claims as it concerns Russian losses is in itself
a serious reason for doubting the grounding in reality of many
NATO officers who apparently couldn't recognize the grotesque
confabulations by Ukraine swallowed by the gullible and illiterate
U.S. legacy media. This also brings into question the professional
competence of people like Losacco who, when writing about self-
evident tactical and technical measures required for survival of the
tank as a weapons system, e.g. counter-drone measures, not only
based his conclusion on false Russian losses and the fantasies of
such "military experts" as *Forbes*'s David Axe, but on a very small
sample size. Should he have done a proper assessment, including
of the sources he used, he would have recognized the crucial
factor of the tactical level air defense configuration of Russian
forces and of their aggressive EW on the theater. In the end, antidrone screens appeared on Russian tanks almost immediately with
the start of the SMO. Moreover, Russians pointed out the very low
effectiveness of the American-made FGM 148F Javelin against
tanks, and especially so in a complex urban environment.[295] This
is a combat environment that is unknown to any NATO officer,
including those NATO military "advisers" in Ukraine who man
the air defense complexes and program the flight plans for cruise
missiles—primarily tactical or operational rear positions.

Once all very numerous circumstances of armor operations
by Russian forces are considered, it becomes patently clear that
the tank as a weapon system not only has a future, but continues to
evolve, increasingly becoming one of the key nodes in netcentric

operations tested by the Russian Army in actual serious combat conditions. Both T-90M Proryv and T-14 Armata, several of which saw limited action both in direct combat and in a self-propelled gun mode from defended positions to test Armata in real combat, are fully netcentric capable.[296] This fact changes the battlefield dramatically once the T-14 Armata's impressive electronic and optronic reconnaissance capabilities are incorporated into what has already proved its deadly effectiveness—the "ROK/RUK" concept, the English acronym for Recon-Fire-Complex (Razvedyvatel'no Ognevoi Komplex) and Recon-Strike-Complex (Razvedyvatel'no Udarnyi Komplex). Colonel Jacques Baud provides a good summary for both in the table below.[297]

Summary of the Differences between ROK and RUK

	ROK	RUK
Driving level	Tactics	Operational
Driving systems	KRUS STRELETS	AKATSIYA-M SOZVEZDIYE-M2 ANDROMEDA-D
Means of recognition	Razvedchiki Light drones: KUB ORLAN-10/30	Spetsnaz Medium and heavy UAVs: ORION
Means of action (examples)	Artillery (122/152 mm) Suicide drones: GERAN-2 LANCET-3 KUB-BLA	Artillery (152/203 mm) Aviation Missiles: ISKANDER KINJAL ZIRKON Electronic warfare systems (REB)

One of the latest demonstrations of the effectiveness of both was yet another destruction of the Patriot air defense complex PAC2 version on March 9, 2024, when the movement of the complex about 50 kilometers from the front-line near Sergeevka was spotted by a Russian reconnaissance drone. Targeting was provided for the Iskander missile complex which then launched on very short notice and destroyed both the vehicle and all missiles in a spectacular explosion.[298] This scenario repeated itself time after time throughout the SMO with the effectiveness of Russian ROK/RUK improving as time passed and with its increased incorporation of hypersonic weapons to strike high value targets.

Evidently many in the NATO militaries still cannot grasp the extent of the real revolution in military affairs, of which I have written non-stop for many years, which came about with the development and combat use of hypersonic weapons and Russia's increasingly sophisticated and evolving ISR complex. When considering launching a salvo of TLAMs against Russia from Devesulu Aegis Ashore facility able to house not just anti-ballistic missiles but TLAMs in its MK-41 VLS, planners should have taken into account the fact that, in case of 3M22 hypersonic Zircon missiles whose speed is Mach=9+, Russian missiles would arrive at the facility at Deveselu, when launched from Bastion missile complex somewhere around Sevastopol, in about 4 minutes from the time of launch. The distance from Deveselu to Sevastopol is about 750 kilometers. TLAMs would, at this time, still be flying over Romania's territory. Any U.S. Navy carrier battle group operating in the Eastern Mediterranean is always tracked by the Russian recon complex, including by constantly increasing satellite constellations ranging from the fully functional purely military *Liana* constellation, capable of providing targeting against surface targets, to other recon satellites operating in the interests of Russia's Ministry of Defense.

Private companies are also developing their own satellite constellations such as the SITRO-AIS vessel tracking mini-satellites by the Sputnix corporation. An additional 100 satellites of different types are planned to be launched in 2024 by the Sputnix corporation alone.[299] By 2025 Russia plans to produce 250 satellites a year; by the year 2030 the minimal number of the Russian satellite constellation should be up to 2,000 satellites.[300] This makes the global battlefield transparent for the force with advanced RUK, which allows it to strike not just on the operational but in strategic depth, as would be the case in the unlikely event of NATO deciding to fight Russia in Europe. Let me underline this point: no locality in Europe is safe, as is the case with U.S. territory.

These developments give the tactical-operational truism "if you can be seen, you can be hit" a whole new dimension. Such is the case with the use by the United Kingdom "on behalf" of Ukraine of the unmanned surface vehicles (USVs), or surface drones, against some of the ships of Russia's Black Sea Fleet. This was possible due to American and British recon assets, including such as P-8 Poseidon or RC-135 planes, operating with impunity in the international air space over the Black Sea, thus providing targeting against surface assets of the Russian fleet. This was the case with the damage to the minesweeper *Ivan Golubets* and patrol ship *Sergei Kotov* which was sunk after battling a swarm of British USVs in early March 2024. The problem is not new given the confined framework of the SMO—if the war were to be with NATO itself, those planes would have been shot down and NATO satellite constellations dramatically impeded.

The Russian Navy recognized and addressed the problem, including through the implementation of a program for countering such a threat by ships of the Russian Navy. This program includes additional optronic means of surveillance and reconnaissance, additional 14.5-mm mounts for machine guns, additional EW means, installed on the ships of the Russian Navy.[301] However, hypersonic weapons cannot be countered by merely adding more sensors and more air defense missiles. This would be like polishing a cannonball in a futile attempt to make it fly farther. Currently there are no means at NATO's disposal which can stop hypersonic weapons. Considering the very long range and increasing speed of such weapons, with Russia working at increasing the speed of both the Kinzhal and Zircon beyond Mach=10, one can reasonably assume that no surface ship of any NATO Navy could survive in a war with Russia.[302] It also means, as has been pointed out in this book a number of times—the very low survivability of NATO's C4 infrastructure in case of real war. Five years ago, I posited:

> . . . this time around, new technical and operational properties of hypersonic weapons are such that they

do provide a technological leap ahead which rewrites the warfare book radically—this is a definition of a revolution in military affairs. It is, of course, very premature to talk about complete obsolescence of modern surface fleets but it certainly spells doom for carrier-centric navies as fleets designed to fight for sea control against peers or near-peers. As a carrier-centric navy the U.S. Navy is not a force which can fight and win against Russia and China in their littorals.[303]

It is no longer premature to talk about the complete obsolescence of carrier-centric navies which are now facing impossible odds—not only in the littorals but in the open ocean and even in their own naval bases. Combined with the explosive development in submarine technology and underwater drones ranging from recon to strike drones—consider the immensely powerful Russian Poseidon, capable to not only devastate shores but hunt down any carrier battle group with impunity—the real revolution in military affairs has taken place. It is a *fait accompli.* In the end, the speed of this development decided the issue. Never in the history of warfare has the gap between the capacity of the tools of destruction of opposing forces been as massive as it is today between NATO and Russia. Moreover, this gap concerns not just technology of Russia and NATO, but the operational concepts that gave birth to those weapon systems. It is the latter which features so heavily in any assessment of whether Western forces will ever be able to catch up. The carrier-centric navies are in their final days of existence as a viable force on the 21st century global battlefield.

Let us then address the issue of the global face-off between Russia and the combined West, headed by the United States. This stand-off is indeed global and is not limited to the geographic locality, however large, of Ukraine. This stand-off spreads into all domains from the world ocean to space, and encompasses not just military but also related economic, financial and industrial capacities. This has played a crucial role in providing the framework for Russia's initial SMO, which was immensely important but, as Russia now moves on to view its actions in Ukraine as now a war rather than only an SMO, it was only one part of many in this global stand-off, which some call now the Cold War 2.0. The simple truth is, this is not a cold war; it is very much a hot one. The only reason the hot part is still confined to the Ukraine is given by Colonel Kostenko and Major-General Vatrushev in their article in *Voennaya Mysl*:

> The Russian Federation has become the first power to openly stand up to defend her own geopolitical and national interests and went to an open confrontation with the Western world, which personifies the hegemony of the global empire represented by the USA. The United States is unwilling to enter into open military confrontation with Russia, which has powerful military potential and forces of strategic deterrence; to maintain imperial ambitions they transfer interstate confrontation to other sites. They use the territories of national states, so that, on the one hand side, they can demonstrate their military power, and on the other hand, to eliminate any leader of the country, who at least indirectly opposes their interests or supports Russia's position.[304]

The heart of the matter is simple: it is the fact that the much-propagandized U.S. conventional military supremacy is nothing but a bluff. This is not to say that U.S. Armed Forces cannot create devastation and turn some geographic localities into rubble; they certainly can. But they cannot fight a peer or better than peer opponent and win such a fight. Apart from many economic, cultural, and social reasons for that, there is this increasingly obvious fact that the United States (and NATO) is losing the arms race with Russia. It would seem, despite their demonstrable ignorance with regard to Russia's military capacities which we have addressed at length, they nonetheless recognize this fact—and this explains their unwillingness to enter into open confrontation with Russia.

Any combination of NATO forces fighting conventional war in Russia's immediate geographic vicinity is bound to lose it, with catastrophic losses in their personnel and war materiel—and even more, should such a war expand to impact their homelands.

Short of all out nuclear war, American conventional military might is primarily a hologram which has been demonstrated to the world through its fighting manifestly incompetent and backward opponents—and losing. As the saying goes the proof is in the pudding, or to quote the late Senator Fulbright: "It is simply not necessary for us to go around forever proclaiming: 'I am the greatest!' The more one does this sort of thing, in fact, the more people doubt it. . . . "[305] At this stage of its history, the United States simply went over its military credit limit and did so in the most dramatic fashion, because it couldn't recognize the limitations of its power—a first sign of immaturity of American military-political elites. U.S. military-industrial-congressional-media complex could be very proficient in unleashing wars in distant lands and profiting from them, but it is not very good at designing and producing weapons that work, nor in developing military science with data sets.

Recognizing this could be very hurtful for American military pride and self-esteem, but it is the only way the U.S. can both come to grips with its own limitations and develop strategies with a view to not repeating over and over same mistake of grossly underestimating its opponents. It takes integrity, honor and courage to face the facts—a test which most American military "experts" have miserably failed. How likely is this in the near future, or within any time period which could make a difference to the relative standing of American military power in the world?

Part of this failure can certainly be attributed to the obvious decline of American (and NATO) military education, which follows largely the same degenerative path of the European Bologna Process, which effectively killed European education. The shortcomings of this Process is indicated by the fact that Russia exited the Bologna Process and completely overhauled its system of higher education by returning to the best practices of Russian/ Soviet classic higher education.[306] This is a strategic decision, returning Russia's higher education to the classic formula of 5–6 years long study for the degree of Specialist and doing away with bachelor's and master's degrees, which impeded classic Soviet/ Russian tradition of educating engineering and military cadres.

As was documented by numerous insiders, the four-year-long U.S. service military academies are not only in decline, they face a serious breakdown in discipline and a dramatic decline in academic standards, to such a degree that the U.S. Military Academy at West Point was considered to be relegated to a three-year military institution.[307] This is a catastrophe, one recognized by another West Point insider and graduate, Colonel Douglas Macgregor, who points out the failure not just of American military technology but also of its so-called advisers, many of who are cadre American officers and the product of U.S. military education.[308] For the Russian military, it is inconceivable to have a lieutenant graduating from any military officer college (academy) with a degree in literature or international relations. It may seem impressive to have a LSW (Leadership, Security and Warfare) degree, but one will be really hard-pressed to try to explain to a graduate of any Russian military academy what capacities a graduate degree in Leadership from a Military Academy in Sandhurst in the United Kingdom might entail. One is left guessing what Sandhurst can possibly produce by way of officer cadres in its 44 weeks program, with the Sandhurst website describing the second 14-week term as follows:

> This is the term when your focus changes. You will transition from only looking after yourself to being responsible for others. Again, there are three exercises which focus on how you operate up to company level. Once you've finished this term, you'll head off on a one-week adventurous training exercise.[309]

By simply comparing this verbiage to the way Russian military academies frame their tasks: professional academic training and service to Russia and Russian people, one can see a dramatic difference in approach to officer preparation. There is no Disneyland-like fantasy adventure terminology—it is all about readiness for war, including the ultimate sacrifice for Motherland—the recognition that the possibility of being killed comes with the territory of being a military professional, and citing the Russian pantheon of heroes who sacrificed their lives defending their country—one without equal in the world, a cold hard fact which cannot be denied by anyone with even a rudimentary knowledge of history. It is this pantheon of numerous heroes from Alexander Nevsky and the Russian volunteer army who defeated Teutonic invasion, to new heroes of SMO.

And then, of course, there is the academics. The U.S. Military Academy at West Point, while still remaining an engineering school, provides a puzzling choice of majors such as Environmental Engineering and even Philosophy, English and Economics.[310] While there is very little doubt that any officer must be well-rounded in terms of personal culture, this type of focus certainly makes one wonder how such a major can influence the study of such critical for modern war courses as Operations Research or Systems Engineering.

Four years at West Point, as is true for all U.S. service academies, are trumped by Russia's five to six years, six day a week in Specialist level officer colleges (academies).

But it is not just merely the time spent within military academics that is significant, it is the existence of a much higher level of STEM study in Russian public schools in general, that raises the academic level of public school graduates competing for entrance into Russian military officer colleges (academies) far above that in the West. Unlike U.S. service academies which accept ACT/SAT scores, Russian school graduates take standard exams in Russian, mathematics, physics/informatics and choose a specialty upfront. Take the example of the Peter the Great Academy of Strategic Missile Forces, offering such a specialty (program) as *Design, Manufacturing And Operation of Missiles and Space-Missile Complexes*; its catalogue number is 24.05.01.[311] These are extremely intensive STEM and military science programs whose equivalent in the West would be a graduate degree with military-engineering major and military science minor.

All Russian military academies, of course, provide courses in political-economy, foreign languages and, as is the case with naval academies—naval geography; all of them also provide great courses in military history. The only specialist "humanities" degree, with the exception of special linguistics, law, sociology and psychology studies at Moscow Military University, that such engineering schools provide is in military-political work—what amounts to de-communized political officers for service specifics.[312]

These are strategic differences between the West and Russia, which provide the latter with a long-term benefit in preparation of a competent officer corps and cadres for military-industrial complex. This is not just a strategic difference; it is also a profound cultural one. Here again, one must ask: how will it be possible for the U.S. to undertake such necessary changes, if it seeks to retain standing within the compass of military affairs? How long would this take?

Due to Russian state ownership of the critical strategic resources and control of military-industrial complex through massive state-owned corporations such as the giants Rostec or Rosatom, among a few others, which are only partially profit-oriented and function as vehicles for the technological and economic realization of Russia's long-term geopolitical strategy, the only possible reward for a senior officer retiring from Russia's Defense Ministry from those giants could be primarily employment in some managerial capacity. This may pay extremely well, but their role there is completely "insulated" from pursuing the kind of market rewards connected to the fictional capitalization index of the company and the price of shares, which is the main driver of American military-industrial complex, whose main driver in turn is the requirement to turn a profit. This is not to say that the private subcontractors of the Russian Defense Ministry don't care about profit, but rather that the "corporate" culture of Russia's Defense Ministry is such that those private subcontractors which cannot deliver will lose the lucrative long-term contracts whose requirements are framed largely by the General Staff's assessment of Russia's actual military needs. If one looks closer, one immediately recognizes that the type of Russia's military economy and the way it is being run, both on the "manufacturing floor" and through preparing military and civilian cadres, is remarkably reminiscent of socialist methods of management. And as the SMO demonstrated this lesson is very reminiscent of the WW II lesson of the Soviet Union, which demonstrated the immense mobilization potential of this model under the severest conditions possible, fighting the then greatest military force in history and defeating it.

Mind you, the Arsenal of Democracy was a good label for the WW II Lend-Lease program, and in effect it was just that. But it was the Soviet economy and citizenry that bore the economic and combat brunt of the WW II despite the obvious help from Lend-Lease. As Glantz and House point out, quoting in 2015 none other than Anastas Mikoyan's quip in 1945:

> If the Western Allies had not provided equipment and invaded northwest Europe, Stalin and his commanders might have taken twelve to eighteen months longer to finish off the Wehrmacht. The result would probably have been the same, except that Soviet soldiers would have waded at France's Atlantic beaches rather than meeting the Allies at the Elbe.[313]

Admitting this is a very tall order for the modern crop of American policymakers and military because it dissolves the foundation on which American military mythology rests— America's credit for defeating Nazism. Many of those people simply do not know these facts. During and in the immediate aftermath of WW II, moreover, the Soviet Union and the Red Army enjoyed unprecedented global admiration and by extension this led to the attractiveness of the Soviet economic model, which served as the foundation for the defeat of Nazism. This was a factor which neither the United States nor Great Britain could ignore.

Yet, in the year 2024 the allegedly "free market" economies of the West proved themselves impotent in a purely economic sense by making a strategic mistake of historic proportions in viewing Russia's economy through the lens of the fictitious monetarist filter, fogged by financialization.[314] This problem of the combined West cannot be resolved easily, even when applying old Cold War templates of containment and pure propaganda dehumanizing Russia and Russian people. The problem within the West itself is laid bare by its military and economic impotence in trying to defeat the Russian SMO. Russia has not only defied the West's shock-and-awe-level sanctions assault economically but is defeating it militarily and in sprouting what the combined West was always afraid of—granted in different ways and with different intensity throughout the decades of the Cold War 1.0—namely developing an idea that humanity can hold on to. A moral idea. This is the West's kryptonite, the one it cannot deal with due to a complete absence of appropriate elites and governing mechanisms which could avert the catastrophe for the West and its loss of dominant position of the last half-millennium.

CHAPTER 11.

WAR AND SOCIETY

"War is the father of all
and the king of all;
it proves some people gods, and some people men;
it makes some people slaves and some people free."

—Heraclitus, *Fragments*

WHAT HERACLITUS MEANT when talking about war related to conflict in general, is the idea which we find in what is now very much proven true Marxist dogma about the unity and struggle of opposites. It is this struggle that often results in a real war. And it is from real war that a new reality is born. Never this assertion has been more true than in the current moment in history which sees the new world emerging. The movement of some armored brigade of Russian ground forces at the line of contact with Ukrainian Forces or the launch of hypersonic Kinzhal or Zircon missiles at Western-made air defense complexes, or the lines of shiny new SU-35C fighter planes at the plant in Komsomolsk-on-Amur have orders of magnitude more bearing on the global events than all speeches and public performances by Western leaders combined or of statistical data on the EU economy.

Michael Brenner writes about the West experiencing two stunning events: a defeat in Ukraine and genocide in Palestine[315] and provides an incredibly incisive diagnosis to the abnormal mental state of people who are leading the combined West to its ultimate ruin:

> Some clues for these abnormalities are provided by their most recent responses as deteriorating conditions tighten the vise—on emotions, on prevailing policies, on domestic political worries, on ginger egos. Those

responses fall under the category of panic behavior. Deep down, they are scared, fearful and agitated. Biden et al in Washington, Macron, Scholz, Sunak, Stoltenberg, von der Leyen. They lack the courage of their stated convictions or the courage to face reality squarely. The blunt truth is that they have contrived to get themselves, and their countries, in a quandary from which there is no escape conforming to their current self-defined interests and emotional engagement. Hence, we observe an array of reactions that are feckless, grotesque and dangerous.[316]

These are the same as the reactions of Napoleon at the Borodino Battle described by Leo Tolstoy in his immortal classic:

When he ran his mind over the whole of this strange Russian campaign in which not one battle had been won, and in which not a flag, or cannon, or army corps had been captured in two months, when he looked at the concealed depression on the faces around him and heard reports of the Russians still holding their ground—a terrible feeling like a nightmare took possession of him, and all the unlucky accidents that might destroy him occurred to his mind. The Russians might fall on his left wing, might break through his center, he himself might be killed by a stray cannonball. All this was possible. In former battles he had only considered the possibilities of success, but now innumerable unlucky chances presented themselves, and he expected them all. Yes, it was like a dream in which a man fancies that a ruffian is coming to attack him, and raises his arm to strike that ruffian a terrible blow which he knows should annihilate him, but then feels that his arm drops powerless and limp like a rag, and the horror of unavoidable destruction seizes him in his helplessness.[317]

This scenario between the West and Russia has been repeated time after time for many centuries. The combined West invades Russia, a cataclysmic war happens, the West is defeated and is driven back. It recuperates and repeats its attack on Russia. This time, however, the situation is different. It is different due to the new technological realities of the war and the West being driven from the position of power it has enjoyed for the last 500 years while experiencing a highly visible process of fracturing. The new technological reality of the West vis-a-vis Russia today is such that the West has lost the arms race and gap is not closing but widening. Vladimir Putin defined this new reality in his 2020 interview, titled *20 Questions for Vladimir Putin*:

> And now we have a unique situation. I already spoke recently at the Ministry of Defense, this has not happened in the recent modern history of Russia, we have always caught up with our, let's say, competitors in strategic weapons. The atomic bomb was first made by the Americans, we caught up later, delivery vehicles in the form of strategic aviation were made by the Americans, we caught up. They made the missiles first, we were catching up. For the first time, you and I have created systems of offensive strike weapons that do not exist in the world. Now they are catching up with us. This is a completely unique situation, this has never happened before.[318]

This is a shift of an historic, tectonic scale for which the combined West wasn't ready. In fact, it was the West itself which precipitated it by failing to adequately realize or accept the above-mentioned reality. While one may debate the nature of forces which brought the West to ruin—a protracted process which we are observing currently in its devastating progress—be they nascent historic ones or objective laws of history as favored by Marxists, one cannot deny the fact that it is the world's current economic and political system that has run its course. For now, it remains the world system, imperialistic in its nature for the last 500 years.

Perhaps one has to tip the hat for the late mainstream Western scholar, Samuel Huntington, who did at least acknowledge that:

> The West won the world not by the superiority of its ideas or values or religion (to which few members of other civilizations were converted) but rather its superiority in applying organized violence. Westerners often forget this fact; non-Westerners never do.[319]

One nation stands out in the list of lands conquered by the West. It is Russia, which has successfully beaten back all the West's attempts at either conquering or altogether eliminating the Russian peoples. What is most disturbing for the West is the fact that the Russians excelled at and then surpassed the West in applying organized violence. In fact, Russia's military record is telling—it has consistently defeated the best the West could throw at it when it mattered. Russia remained of the Orthodox faith, as demonstrated by the fact that after Russian communism, which sought to expunge it, it eventually evolved into a society—especially after Trotskyism had been exorcised by Stalin—with primarily conservative values which have been very much derived from a Christian but non-Crusader historical ethos.

Not surprisingly, the Moral Code of the Builder of Communism adopted in 1961 reads very much like a secular adaptation of Jesus' Sermon on the Mount, a point made not once but by many contemporary political leaders in Russia, ranging from Russia's main communist Gennadi Zyuganov and even Vladimir Putin himself, granted that he characterized this Code as a "primitive extract from the Bible."[320] Speaking broadly, Russians have never been far removed from the faith, so much so that the late Archpriest of the Russian Orthodox Church, Dmitry Smirnov, openly challenged the notion of Soviet society being godless by pointing out that Soviet education and upbringing was much closer to Church's upbringing than what was subsequently happening in Russia in the 1990s and 2000s.[321]

This explains to a large degree the transition Russia made from the catastrophe of 1990s to a society which is presently completely self-aware and confident. In historic terms the transition was almost instant, and its main driver was initially the political rejection of the West, starting from Valdimir Putin's 2007 speech in Munich, to a complete rejection of the West on a metaphysical level, including through developing Russia's own civilizational model which is presenting an existential problem for the West. The West deluded itself as to the attractiveness of its own political and economic model, which was merely a secondary factor for the rest of the world looking inside it from the outside for the last 500 years. Rather, it was the West's real and perceived wealth and military power which have provided the main pillars sustaining the West's ability to shape the modern world, not least through robbing the rest of the world of its material riches and exploiting it.

It cannot be denied, however, that humanity still lives today in a world largely shaped by the combined West. Bear in mind: the 20th century saw the West unleashing two world wars, with the last one seeing murder and atrocity brought at the industrial level, while it was the Soviet Union that bore the brunt of it. And it was then that the phrase attributed to Marshal Georgy Zhukov, allegedly in his conversation with Marshal Konstantin Rokossovsky in Berlin in 1945, started to circulate: "We liberated them, and they will never forgive us for that."[322] This was prescient no matter if Zhukov really said it or not, because it turned out to be ultimately true—historic Russia in the form of the Soviet Union defeated the West's best military force in history and the simple fact of the West's efforts to rewrite this history by claiming that victory as theirs without acknowledgment of the USSR's greater role reveals not only an ideological agenda and shoddy scholarship, but a deep and lasting trauma. The case of stolen valor on part of the Western historiography has become so bad that calls for preservation of the truth about who bore the brunt of WW II and protesting the distortion of history are now consistently being heard from the highest political level in Russia.[323] In today's new iteration of such a trauma—the combined West cannot reconcile itself to the fact of being defeated by those whom many among Western ruling class consider subhuman, both openly or tacitly through endorsing and supporting the actions, and therefore the ideology, of the Ukrainian Nazis.[324]

The Combined West cannot allow the myth of its military power to dissipate, but it also cannot stop it from dissipating due to the battlefield reality of SMO. Once the myth of military power is removed, which is in progress, the West loses its status as a hegemon, because military power from the industrial and technological points of view provides the ultimate proof of one's claim to the status of a superpower. Military power by definition is the most important geopolitical tool, while also being the most expensive and most technologically advanced one.

And so here, the truth is really simple: the country producing an SU-57 fighter or strategic missile submarine of Borei-class will necessarily be capable of producing, as is the case now, domestically manufactured MRI machines or rolling stock if need be. But the opposite is not true—Germany produces both MRI machines and rolling stock, but it is beyond its technological and industrial capability to produce a nuclear strategic missile submarine or a fifth generation fighter, let alone produce them in quantities. War, conflict in general, always decides the issue. It would be utterly naïve to think that the combined West and its leader the United States will abdicate willingly and peacefully, but even the most pessimistic planners in Washington could not anticipate the extent of the military catastrophe into which the West has gotten itself in Ukraine. In most practical military matters, the West is no longer a real competitor to Russia, and admissions, both sotto voce and loudly, have started to come in recently, with the admission, among many others, that the West is simply not prepared to fight a modern war, one which it has failed to foresee, and which is now being fought for real. These are now wars of attrition, or in Alexander Svechin's other definition, wars of exhaustion. As Lieutenant Colonel Alex Vershinin concludes:

> Attritional wars require their own "Art of War" and are fought with a "force-centric" approach, unlike wars of maneuver which are "terrain-focused." They are rooted in massive industrial capacity to enable the

replacement of losses, geographical depth to absorb
a series of defeats, and technological conditions that
prevent rapid ground movement. In attritional wars,
military operations are shaped by a state's ability
to replace losses and generate new formations, not
tactical and operational maneuvers. The side that
accepts the attritional nature of war and focuses on
destroying enemy forces rather than gaining terrain
is most likely to win. The West is not prepared for
this kind of war. To most Western experts, attritional
strategy is counterintuitive. Historically, the West
preferred the short "winner takes all" clash of
professional armies. Recent war games such as CSIS's
war over Taiwan covered one month of fighting. The
possibility that the war would go on never entered the
discussion.[325]

Such a combined West admission is very late in coming, and
the problem with it is not that the West is incapable of sustaining
such operations as the SMO, not to speak of an all-out conventional
war on the continent, which it is not. The problem for the West is
even worse: that it will not be able to conceive of such a war in
the geographic vicinity of Russia due to the moral factor—that
no present generation of American, or for that matter British,
servicemen have fought in the defense of their own homeland,
while Russians have been forced to do it all the time, with the
present generation having a record to back it up. In war, which is
always necessarily a cultural act, Russian society mobilizes and is
ready to do whatever it takes to defeat, that is destroy, the enemy.
Modern Western societies are incapable of conducting such a war,
thus modern Western militaries are also incapable—after all, they
are an extension of the societies they serve.

Considering the fact that Russia is simply not interested
in acquiring any territories beyond what constitutes historically
Russian lands such as the Odessa and Kharkov regions, the
only war the combined West can fight against Russia is a war of
invasion and that by default means the presumable destruction of

a NATO force in Eastern Europe, if the war stays conventional, which is likely to provide enough casualties and damage to cause Western societies to either implode or initiate a radical political change including the removal of the current political class.

The combined West in general is not ready to fight such a real war, as the catastrophic failure in recruitment presently taking place in the U.S. and in Europe demonstrates.[326] Western societies, through their cultural and economic policies, have been softened to such a degree that it becomes inconceivable to see Generation Z being willing to commit to military service, let alone die for causes which absolutely do not resonate at the greater societal level. In the United States, deeply affected by the woke culture it promotes, nearly 30% of Generation Z adults identify as LGBTQ.[327] This is hardly a reliable pool for future recruits; it is also a clear path to reduction in birth rates, which are already low in the combined West. In a broader sense Western societies have been metrosexualized and prepped for dying out due to the reproduction of its population being arrested by the institutionalization of homosexuality and the dramatically increasing use of drugs—all directed at the destruction of the classic family, which is always in the foundation of the nation and its ability to defend itself from outside threats by reproducing a pool of military recruits.

In Russia, this is recognized as a reality of everyday life. But the United States has no such cultural imperative because it has no historic and cultural experience of fighting off invasions by foreign powers. The United States has been a power which only invades and therefore doesn't understand issues, especially in military sphere, related to the actual defense of a country. Hence, its utter corruption of its procurement practices and the creation of a military-industrial-congressional complex designed only for jobs programs and sustaining an electoral process favorable to same.

As the SMO demonstrated, societies like Russia continue to venerate such values as heroism, honor, service and sacrifice, especially when it comes to what is at the center of Russian psyche—the classic extended family of man, woman and their children. These are enshrined in the Russian Constitution and justly viewed as a critical instrument of national survival and longevity, as well as a social reality to be defended by the state.[328] Such legislation is simply impossible in the modern West which is sinking ever deeper into the world of cultural degeneracy and demographic withering. This is where an ultimate break between Russia and the West has occurred. The overwhelming majority of Russians don't want such a plague to spread into Russia. Russian Law also makes it clear that the advocacy of non-traditional sexual practices is strictly forbidden.[329] In other words, Russian society is not just conservative in the Western sense of the word, it values everything which is completely alien to the modern Western cultural discourse. It finds the current globalist Western discourse dehumanizing; Russian discourse is naturally humanistic and conservative.

The global majority prefers that Russian perspective and therefore sympathizes with Russia, not to mention the fact that it sees Russia alone throwing the gauntlet and successfully beating the combined West, thereby creating a genuine sense of admiration among nations of what could be termed the Global South—a fact noted by a number of reputable observers.[330] Nor have many people in the West completely lost touch with the ramifications of their present cultural reality, in addition to their economic reality, and many recognize the dystopian outcome for their respective nations if a system which is in place now will endure—native French, German or European-descent (white) American majorities may well become minorities in their own countries in the best case scenario or, in the worst case, with their cultures even a distant memory in the 21st century. Some studies posit that Generation Z will be the last white majority generation, after that white Americans will become a minority.[331]

Russians do not want such a fate, so much so that legendary commander of Akhmat brigade, Hero of Russia Apti Alaudinov, passionately called on ethnic Russians to procreate by means of having extended families of five to six children, because ethnic Russians, in his words, are founding people of Russia and the many diverse nations within the Russian Federation depend on them.[332] The difference of the attitudes toward family between Russia and the West cannot be more stark—any public figure in the U.S. calling on white Americans to procreate and justifying it by the fact that white Americans are founding people of the United States would immediately be condemned and, using modern verbiage, "cancelled" by American masters of discourse, not least because people calling for the preservation of white America will be called racist.

The Western political class, most of whom are adherents of the globalist agenda as espoused by such institutions as the World Economic Forum (WEF), cannot allow a large, powerful country such as Russia to exercise an unwanted influence on and impediment to the globalist project. But they cannot do anything about it, other than by unleashing thermonuclear war, which will assuredly end their project together with those who conceived and are trying to implement it.

This is the West's conundrum—not only is it facing a global rebellion it cannot suppress, but it cannot suppress it because, aside from the reasons addressed herein to date, it doesn't have the economic and military resources to fight a real war. As operations by Houthis against shipping slated for Israel through Red Sea demonstrated, even nuclear aircraft carriers—the most expensive and imposing of the West's military assets, which for decades served as a visual representation of primarily American power—turned out to be nearly useless against a determined opposition which has access to such strike means as drones and, however old, anti-shipping missiles. In other words, a non-state actor without a navy achieved a major naval objective of disrupting one of the most important shipping lines of communications, exposing impotence of NATO navies engaged in the operation "Prosperity Guardian"[333]—a rather silly title for an operation which exposed, as did the SMO albeit on a smaller scale, the vulnerability of the West's most advanced naval assets, which are not suited for a real war against a modern sophisticated opposition.

In terms of salvos of modern supersonic, to say nothing of of hypersonic, anti-shipping missiles, the U.S. Navy has no defense. Fixing some issues with the Aegis Combat System may improve somewhat the probability of intercepting a very limited number of old missiles by Houthis, but it cannot solve the underlying issue of the unpreparedness of Western navies to fight a modern naval war.[334] This is yet another factor to be considered by the combined West when desperately trying to preserve its weakening-by-the-minute grasp on the global "order," especially since military defeat by the SMO and the Houthis and dedollarization are two sides of the same coin—a realization which has finally come to Western elites.

"War is the father of all and the king of all." The Westphalian System of 1648, which gave birth to the nation-state, was a result of the Peace of Westphalia which concluded the Thirty Years' War—a watershed moment accepted as the world's transition to the modern era.[335] The emergence of the Bretton Woods system as well as the formation of the United Nations were a direct result of WW II. Even the collapse of the Bretton Woods in 1971 was due to war. President Nixon's decision to decouple the U.S. dollar from the gold standard was taken out of necessity to maintain the guns-and-butter economy while also financing the war in Vietnam and the Cold War, the latter expenditures being a critical factor in this decision.[336] War, conflict, is part of human life, as it is also a part of human nature and nothing can be done about this, not in the foreseeable future and certainly not by the modern West, which became the primary generator of war globally. It is most particularly manifest in the cultural, religious and political nature of the West and its leader, the United States—a deadly cocktail born out of the expansive orientation of a settler colonial state, deepened by its proselytizing spirit and complete insouciance with regard to the realities and meaning of war by America's so-called intellectual class, which has evolved to the point of expressing its world views through the degenerative woke ideology of the so-called left and moribund Cold War 1.0 ignorance on the so-called right.

But in the end, the predictions Americans give, sometimes consciously, sometimes accidentally, tell much more about Americans than about what we intended to say. One of America's foremost geopolitical authorities, John Mearsheimer, went on record in 2014, in the immediate aftermath of Russia returning Crimea back to itself, expressing the same American exceptionalist narrative as put out by Brzezinski 17 years prior. Mearsheimer went on to misidentify the most important trend of 21st century when he concluded in his 2014 program piece in *Foreign Affairs* in which he, to his greatest credit justifiably placed the responsibility for the crisis on the West, nonetheless contended that:

> Of course, some analysts might concede that NATO handled relations with Ukraine poorly and yet still maintain that Russia constitutes an enemy that will only grow more formidable over time—and that the West therefore has no choice but to continue its present policy. But this viewpoint is badly mistaken. Russia is a declining power, and it will only get weaker with time. Even if Russia were a rising power, moreover, it would still make no sense to incorporate Ukraine into NATO."[337]

The motif of "declining Russia" is foundational to the West's defeat. Be that on the political level or that of NATO's militaries, the name of the illness was iconically captured by Colonel Jacques Baud as its inability to see the world not as a still photo but as a film.[338] This is a terminal illness which afflicts the entire military-political class in the West, which is incapable of adaptation and as a result loses, and in desperation threatens the whole world with nuclear obliteration. Truly knowledgeable and cultured people are not allowed to reach the top of the political system, which ceased to function properly some time ago. Rather, the mechanism of negative selection is in place, and it cannot be removed through the "democratic process," which is now the butt of jokes all around the world. Having its most prized symbol being laughed at is a sure sign of America's losing its global standing. American "democracy," human rights, "democratic elections" and other symbols of Pax Americana no longer hold sway over the rest of the world as they used to do. In its terminal decline, the combined West is losing the remnants of its expertise and competence, the equivalent of a shot down plane spinning uncontrollably to the ground, while losing parts of its fuselage and controls in the process before the ultimate outcome—destruction.

In the ultimate iteration of a historic moment one might well rephrase famous Russian Tsar Nicholas I's quip about Turkiye being a "sick man" of Europe, with Europe itself now being the sick man of Europe. The United States itself is in a death struggle for survival as a functional society capable of upholding a modicum of orderly conduct domestically while remaining relevant economically and militarily. Rephrasing is in order, indeed. Writing in his memoirs about the fate of Russia after the collapse of the Soviet Union, George F. Kennan stressed: "Not all that went by the name of communism in Russia was bad; nor were all of those who believed in it."[339] The rephrasing is almost irresistible, if not warranted: not all that went by the name of democracy in the United States was bad; nor were all of those who believed in it. Today, Americans' trust in the Constitution and democratic process is shattered.

Dedollarization is also in a full swing with the West looking on helplessly at the growth of the BRICS and at the discussion within it about escaping dollar hegemony. Two biggest players of BRICS, China and Russia, already trade with each other primarily in their own currencies.[340] Same is true with Russia-India trade. In what would have been unthinkable even five years ago, Niger, a key African ally of the United States demanded that U.S. troops leave its territory and declared their presence in the country "illegal."[341] France is clearly losing its grip on its former colonial empire. Pro-Western regimes elsewhere will increasingly lose out to conservative nationalist forces. The conservative movement around the globe is gaining momentum. This conservatism has very little resemblance to American conservatism, which is not conservatism at all, insofar as neoliberal ideology is the cornerstone of its doctrine. That conservatism is one click away from completely abandoning the interests of its masses wherever this interferes with its profits.

But an even larger issue looms on the horizon for the United States: in 1993 Bill Postman warned about technopoly, which has become an American culture in lieu of a real one. Jeremy Rifkin warned about it too:

> Every society creates an idealized image of the future—a vision that serves as a beacon to direct imagination [*sic*] and energy of its people. . . . In the modern age, the idea of a future technological utopia has served as a guiding vision of industrial society. . . . Nowhere has the techno-utopian vision been more passionately embraced than in the United States. Technology became the new secular God, and American society soon came to refashion its own sense of self in the image of its powerful new tools.[342]

The defeat of America's weapons and tactical concepts at the battlefields of SMO thus has become a defeat of the American vision of technopoly, which is a euphemism for culture. The consequences of this are, indeed, global in scale and scope.

But even more has been accomplished by Russia in staring down a combined West. Modern Western culture has become recognized as ugly in every sense of the word, from freak shows at the demonstration of fashions, to people looking increasingly dirty from tattoos covering their bodies, to the body positive movement extolling unhealthy and aesthetically repulsive lifestyles, to the rampant use of drugs. The modern West has lost the understanding of beauty. The late Roger Scruton warned: "Beauty is vanishing from our world because we live as though it did not matter."[343] It has almost completely vanished, pushed out by the post-modernist dystopia and perversion of the Western intelligentsia. As Dostoevsky wrote in *The Idiot*, "Beauty will save the world."[344] The West has lost the meaning of and desire for beauty, thus losing the tool for its own salvation, and the world has taken note.

It still remains to be seen what kind of world we will get in the end, which beings us to the conclusion of this work, in which I will try to do what I have heretofore always avoided like the plague—try to speculate on the future of the world.

CHAPTER 12.

CONCLUSION

IT IS IMPOSSIBLE to properly finish writing on the impact of Russia's conflict with NATO's proxy, Ukraine, because the SMO operation has evolved into what Russia is now terming a war. But the outcome leaves no doubt and some preliminary conclusions and even forecasts can be made.

The most important one is the historic defeat of the combined West and its leader, the United States. How it was defeated militarily is obvious—NATO countries found themselves totally impotent in the face of an opponent with a massive and sophisticated economy and, as it stands now, the most advanced armed forces in the world. This doesn't bode well for the United States, let alone the collection of mediocre at best European military powers, which are incapable of sustaining any serious campaign on their own. U.S. military expertise, bar a few notable exceptions, turned out to be good primarily for PR and propaganda, a euphemism for non-stop confabulation of both American military history and the SMO. As former CIA analyst Larry Johnson pointed out: "Americans are by-and-large decent, genial folks. But when it comes to history, most have the memory of an Alzheimer's patient. Sam Cooke was speaking for most Americans when he crooned, 'Don't know much about history....' So, I will make this simple—America's hatred of Russia has its roots in the U.S. Government's post-WW II embrace of Nazis."[345] In the absence of a serious military history study field, with the exception of a few notable scholars, and against the background of a precipitous intellectual decline of the American ruling class, what is left is largely a hatred for any power which asserts its own right to behave as it deems necessary for the preservation of its own people and culture. Russia here checks all the boxes as the candidate for hatred, par excellence.

Once the poison of American exceptionalism was added to the mix of the neocons' fully corrupted American foreign policy and American insecurity—the clash with Russia became inevitable. Terrorism is a weapon of the weak, and as the events in Moscow's Crocus-City Music Hall massacre of innocent civilians, including children, and West's reaction to it, have demonstrated, the West is reduced to merely aiding and abetting its Nazi and terrorist tool, the Kiev regime, while trying to not get involved directly in a military conflict with Moscow. Russia's Federal Security Service (FSB), upon capturing the terrorists who massacred innocent people in Crocus-City were able to discover, almost immediately: "The criminals intended to cross the Russia-Ukraine border and had relevant contacts on the Ukrainian side."[346] This terrorist atrocity has all hallmarks of Anglo-American backing, which, when one considers America's support for genocide and crimes against humanity in Gaza by Israel, indicates the complete moral degeneration of their political conduct by the United States, and its European lapdogs, both domestically and in the international arena. The West has lost all remnants of its moral authority globally. As Larry Johnson observes the unfolding fate of NATO:

> Killing off a bureaucracy—whether civilian or military—is nigh impossible. But the impending defeat of Ukraine on the battlefield by Russia presents one of those watershed moments in history where the raison d'etre of NATO will be exposed as a fraud.... NATO's problems go beyond its inadequate military resources. The very political consensus binding NATO together is coming apart. ...NATO is a mess, yet Western leaders and NATO commanders continue to indulge the fantasy that they are ready and capable of carrying out a combined arms military conflict with Russia. They are not.[347]

NATO's geopolitical humiliation remains a secret only for the most unsophisticated strata of the Western public. *Outside of the West it is clear to pretty much everybody.* Most

societies can survive military defeats and economic hardships;
many have done so throughout history. What societies cannot
survive is moral degeneracy and the signs of that degeneracy in
the West are everywhere. In fact, the contemporary West is no
longer even the West it used to be, for all of that West's major
flaws. Today's West is an increasingly dystopian society based
on non-stop political theater. Its public narratives are fashioned
by unscrupulous corporate media, run often by sociopaths, busy
with brainwashing an increasingly ignorant and illiterate public. It
faces the disintegration of public trust and, in case of the United
States, even facing the possibility of the physical disintegration
of an already torn country which is increasingly ungovernable
into its antipathetic components. The matters of policy in the U.S.
and in Europe are increasingly matters of political demagoguery
born of the narcissism of their political class, with minuscule, if
any, practical outcomes leading toward a healthy development of
their societies. These societies cannot even produce the reaction
of a healthy organism to the penetration of a threat to itself, as the
mayhem on the U.S. southern border demonstrates.

Western societies have become increasingly unhappy. They
have also become increasingly ugly in moral and physical terms.
It seems strange for the book on military-strategic issues to talk
about beauty, but this is only so at the first glance. As late Roger
Scruton posited:

> There is an appealing idea about beauty which
> goes back to Plato and Plotinus, and which became
> incorporated by various routes into Christian
> theological thinking. According to this idea beauty
> is an ultimate value—something that we pursue for
> its own sake, and for the pursuit of which no further
> reason need be given. Beauty should therefore be
> compared to truth and goodness"[348]

These values have been rejected by the post-modernist,
post-Christian West. The less beauty—the more space is freed
to be filled with perversion, unrestrained aggression and naked

militarism. As Bronislaw Malinowski noted in 1941: "Another interesting point in the study of aggression is that, like charity, it begins at home."[349] The United States has been at war since the end of WW II practically non-stop, being involved in conflict on 18 occasions ranging from major conflicts like Korean or Vietnam wars to involvement in Afghanistan and Yemen.[350] America loves war, precisely because American society is militarily illiterate yet narcissistically bellicose. The productions of Hollywood, the main American war propaganda institution, feed the public with a sanitized image of war which has very little in common with realities, depicting the war as heroic and ego-gratifying, while failing to show its horror.[351] No doubt, there is still a place for heroism in war as the SMO demonstrated, but the American public is insulated from the real price of such heroism, which often requires an ultimate sacrifice.

For a person who is not well acquainted with American culture it would remain a complete mystery why a university football game would elicit a flyover by a group of combat aircraft of either U.S. Navy or U.S. Air Force. It is not only strange for a sports event, but also downright kitsch if not cringe-inducing, over the top, demonstration of alleged military power as sublimated throughout the game. It is one thing to sing the national anthem at a sports event, especially when it is international, totally another to tie the event to military prowess.

This is not a culturally healthy milieu, nor is that promoted by woke culture and third wave feminism—inter alia because they destroy the natural internal cohesion provided by the family and arrest national reproduction. The precipitous decline of Western culture cuts Western societies' last lifelines to reality, especially so in the United States, which is a completely torn country, whether by ethnic divisions or by political and ideological rifts that may lead to a very real and very hot civil war within the United States, ultimately finalizing its disintegration already in progress into two or even more geographic, ethnic and/or political entities. As I wrote in my previous book—there is very little in common culturally between a white farmer from Iowa, Jewish attorney from New York and Indian or Pakistani code-writers from Redmond in Washington State. Happiness is most successfully pursued in largely homogeneous societies not just with a dominant ethnic (or racial) majority but with a common shared history, with continental warfare often proving a midwife for a nation. Today the United States lacks such cohesion. Its centrifugal forces are well pronounced and getting stronger to such a degree that the upcoming elections of 2024, if they are held at all, may impact America's fortunes in a manner that will surpass that of the first American civil war.

The glue which is supposed to keep the United States together through its elites is no longer there. The American political and "intellectual" class has betrayed Americans by failing to look out for their wellbeing. The current American political system is utterly corrupt and is in pockets of foreign and domestic lobbyists, who do not care about the fate of the majority of Americans— they pursue their own best interests, and they are not tied to the happiness of the American masses, who are drowning in drugs and alcoholism. American deaths from overdose reaches 70,000 annually—this is more than the United States lost in 10 years in Vietnam War.[352]

The society's disintegration is visible on the level of individuals. Many youths and even mature people today look like they haven't showered in years—the number of tattoos on their bodies completely covers their skin. Many try to push the idea that this is beautiful. It is not, it is a return to primitive societies reflecting the loss of a connection to classic beauty and aesthetic propriety. Today, 21% of adult Americans are illiterate, 54% of adults in the U.S. have literacy levels below sixth grade.[353] These numbers are devastating and are those of a third world country— this is a national emergency and disgrace. But not so for the American globalist elites—an illiterate uneducated population is much easier to manipulate and that is the only thing the present American political class can or seeks to do. In such a case, war or the threat thereof provides an excellent whip with which to eventually corral modern Western societies into a dystopian world of mind control, inducing people to do what no normal civilized and literate person would ever do or approve of. The actions of the

American so-called "left" and the poisonous culture it generates are the best proof of that—in some places even mathematics is declared racist and tattooing and piercing one's body almost completely is called "progressive."

There is just one problem here—that there is a visible alternative to this cultural disarray. Russia has both intentionally and naturally produced a conservative idea that has begun to eclipse the American promotion of "democracy" in the eyes of the world, offering a healthy appreciation of tradition, of the need for popular wellbeing, beauty and normality.

Conservatism in the United States, on the other hand, exists primarily under the watchful eyes of American neoconservatives and promotes not just a hubristic need for supremacy, but also requires an undivided loyalty to an increasingly dangerous and frenetic Israel, due to much of its religious element being focused on "the end of times," making local and present global or even domestic wellbeing inconsequential. This is what modern American mainstream "conservatism" is.

Conservatism in many respects is an obverse side of healthy nationalism, which entails having a nation—America doesn't have one anymore, as its ideology of "Americanism" has failed to satisfy the subordinated ethnic minorities which are oppressed by its attendant white supremacy. It also doesn't have the Church, but is awash in many denominations, some of them like Catholics having difficulty grasping what is happening with America, while others, like the powerful Christians United For Israel (CUFI), have a peculiar view on Christianity with their loyalty to Israel and aggressive proselytizing. It is a salad; it is not a melting pot in any way if it ever was. It's a salad of races, ethnicities, confessions and cultures and it has stopped working in any kind of unison.

These are just a few of the societal ills, which have already begun to worry many people, given their evident destructive impact. And yet these realities seem unable to impede the blindered trajectory of the governing elites, whose attention may retain its present focus for little while longer—until the collapse of America-controlled institutions reaches a crescendo. The big one, of course, is NATO, whose impotence, i.e., American military impotence, has been exposed, possibly leading other European nations to become cannon fodder for America's incompetently planned and executed wars. Legendary CIA veteran Ray McGovern, when describing the defeat of NATO, even allows for an insane action on the Biden Administration's part such as using low yield nuclear devices to avoid, in their mind, Russia capturing a whole of Ukraine before U.S. presidential elections. McGovern, sadly, shares my view that now anything could be sold to the American public which is completely oblivious to the realities of war.[354]

Europe, increasingly deindustrialized, emasculated and "culturally enriched," is not up for a real war with the enemy that can annihilate every single member state of NATO, the United States included. The aggressive rhetoric by French President Emmanuel Macron and his promise to send 2,000 French soldiers to Ukraine amounts to nothing but PR, since those troops will not survive their encounter with a real battlefield.[355] Thus the issue of NATO's utility and existence is upon us.

Many view NATO as an obsolete alliance.[356] It is not only obsolete, it is also dangerous precisely due to a complete loss of any vision, if it ever had a real one, an insecurity born out of weakness not just in the face of Russia's military, but due to a complete failure to understand the macro forces at play. These forces are not coming for NATO only. The whole set of institutions set up by the United States in the wake of the WW II are facing complete irrelevance and, inevitably, their replacement and removal from the world stage. The list of such institutions is long and ranges from the ever self-promoting G-7 (despite being overtaken by the BRICS in GDP[357]) to the IMF, to the World Bank, to the completely politicized and corrupt International Olympic Committee, and in the end, to the United Nations. Sadly, the UN long ago turned into a tribune for the West to legitimize its own agenda, including by deflecting many initiatives, such as condemnation of Israel's genocidal behavior in Gaza, which try to address the world's injustices and even outright war crimes. United Nations must either reform itself or it will go the same way the U.S.-controlled institutions go—lapsing into irrelevance.

Removing the UN headquarters from the United States should also be considered.

The delusions, however, persist even among people who call themselves "realists" in the United States. Speaking to Lt. Colonel Davis, John Mearsheimer still thinks that under some circumstances diplomacy between Moscow and Washington is possible.[358] But Vladimir Putin has already answered this question when he stated in March 2024, while visiting the town Torzhok in Tver Region of Russia, that:

> There are many [world culture] achievements in the countries that we call unfriendly today. Although we have no unfriendly states, we have unfriendly elites in these states. ... As for the culture of these countries, we have never attempted to do anything like what the heads of those states tried to do to the Russian culture. On the contrary, we believe that the Russian culture is a part of the world culture, and we are proud to be a part of it; we view our culture in the context of the world [culture], we do not exclude anything from that context."[359]

Moscow doesn't see anyone who it can talk to in the Biden Administration. Moscow is extremely well aware of the trends in the U.S. domestic policies and of the state America is in. As Larry Johnson aptly put the destruction of the Baltimore Bridge: "As I watched the sudden and dramatic implosion of the bridge the thought crossed my mind, *Is this a metaphor for what awaits the United States?*"[360] It is.

The United States to which I and my family immigrated in the 1990s is no more. It is now an insecure nation, whose economic and political systems have ceased to function. America's only tool of enriching itself, the U.S. Dollar, had its foundation—the myth of American military supremacy—obliterated, exposing one weakness after another, ranging from malicious corrupt elites to an inability to develop a realistic strategy and procurement policy for its bloated military, which is not designed to fight a modern war against a serious enemy. That such an "enemy" might not want to attack the U.S. is beyond Washington's think-tanks comprehension.

Furthermore, why should a bankrupt nation, which has failed to adapt to the new technological paradigms in warfare and which faces physical disintegration, plan for war with China, which the United States considers its main "challenger"? The only explanation is this is either wishful thinking, a desperate attempt to grasp at the last straw of greatness past without any attempt to reconsider and maybe reverse suicidal policies which brought the United States to her knees, or simply yet another effort to direct resources towards its militarized economy.

Any real war in Asia, as usual to be false flagged by the U.S., will result in the ultimate crushing of U.S. forces and a complete destruction of the United States, which only then will recognize that it has actually fought its final war.

The problem which the new de facto multipolar world faces is to make sure that America's final war doesn't become a final war for the world which U.S. elites never knew and did not want to know.

ENDNOTES

PREFACE

1 Janna Kadri, "Putin: A Champion of the Global South?" *Al Mayadeen,* March 25, 2024. https://english.almayadeen.net/news/politics/putin--a-champion-of-the-global-south

2 Katie Crombe and John A. Nagl, "A Call to Action: Lessons from Ukraine for the Future Force," *Parameters* 53, no. 3 (USAWC Press, Autumn 2023): 25.

CHAPTER 1

3 "echo chamber," *Dictionary.com,* https://www.dictionary.com/browse/echo-chamber

4 Corelli Barnett, *The Collapse of British Power* (William Morrow & Company, Inc., 1972), 50.

5 Michael Brenner, "Lowering the Throne of America's Delusion," *Consortium News,* January 5, 2022. https://consortiumnews.com/2022/01/05/lowering-the-throne-of-americas-delusion/

6 Ibid.

7 Alexis de Tocqueville (Henry Reeve, trans.), *Democracy in America,* Chapter 16 (The University of Adelaide, 1835).

8 "Quotes: H.L. Mencken," *Good Reads.* https://www.goodreads.com/quotes/10322527-it-is-the-classic-fallacy-of-our-time-that-a

9 Мишустин посоветовал студентам получать техническое образование [Mishustin advised students to get technical education], *Vzglyad,* March 13, 2020. https://vz.ru/news/2020/3/13/1028701.html

10 Путин считает спорным отнесение политологии к науке [Putin considers it debatable to refer to political science as science], *TASS,* July 7, 2022. https://tass.ru/obschestvo/15156217

11 Andrei Martyanov, *The (Real) Revolution in Military Affairs* (Atlanta: Clarity Press, 2019), 1.

12 Raymond Williams, *Keywords: A Vocabulary of Culture and Society* (Oxford University Press, 1983 Rev. Ed.), 170.

13 James Bruno, "Russian Diplomats Are Eating America's Lunch," *Politico,* April 16, 2014. https://www.politico.com/magazine/story/2014/04/russias-diplomats-are-better-than-ours-105773/#.VKCOnP_9A1

14 Tom Nichols, "How America Lost Faith in Expertise: And Why That's a Giant Problem," *Foreign Affairs* 96, no. 2 (March/April 2017).

15 Richard Hofstadter, *Anti-intellectualism in American Life* (New York: Alfred Knopf, 1963), 34.

16 Ibid.

17 Zbigniew Brzezinski, *The Grand Chessboard: American Primacy and Its Geostrategic Imperatives* (New York: Basic Books, 1997), 23.

18 Robert H. Latiff, *Future War: Preparing for the New Global Battlefield* (New York: Alfred A. Knopf, 2017), 131.

19 Norman Polmar and Jurrien S. Noot, *Submarines of the Russian and Soviet Navies, 1718–1990* (Annapolis: Naval Institute Press, 1991), 215

20 Commander Leo Murphy, *To Catch the Quiet Ones* (U.S. Naval Institute Proceedings, July 1997), 60.

21 Anthony Cordesman and Abraham R. Wagner, *Lessons of the Gulf War: 1990–1991* (Center for Strategic and International Studies, 2013), 6.

22 Stephen Biddle, Military Power. *Explaining Victory and Defeat in Modern Battle* (Princeton University Press, 2004), 133.

23 James Slagle, "New Russian Military Doctrine: Sign of the Times," *Parameters* 24 (Spring 1994): 94.

24 Roger N. McDermott, *Russian Perspective on Network Centric Warfare: The Key Aim of Serdyukov's Reform* [report] (U.S. Military Foreign Military Studies Office, 2010), 3.

25 "The lessons Moscow learned from the 1991 Gulf War and the 2015 Syria intervention reveal much about the strategy, tactics, and weapons systems it might use (or already be using) in Ukraine." Anna Borshchevskaya, "Russia's Desert Storm: Putin's Plan to Use America's Military Playbook Against Ukraine?" [policy analysis], The Washington Institute for Near East Policy, January 23, 2022. https://www.washingtoninstitute.org/policy-analysis/russias-desert-storm-putins-plan-use-americas-military-playbook-against-ukraine

26 Angelo M. Codevilla, *America's Rise and Fall among Nations: Lessons in Statecraft from John Quincy Adams* (Encounter Books, 2022), ix.

CHAPTER 2

27 "Strategy," *Cambridge Dictionary.* https://dictionary.cambridge.org/dictionary/english/strategy

28 "Strategy," *Russian Academic Dictionary.* https://dic.academic.ru/dic.nsf/politology/4246/

29 Alexander A. Svechin, *Strategy* (Minneapolis, Minnesota: East View Information Services, 2004), 94.

30 Giulio Douhet, *The Command of the Air* (Maxwell Air Force Base, Alabama: Air University Press, 2019), 33–34.

31 Hillary St. George Saunders, *The Royal Air Force 1939–1945. Vol III, The Fight Is Won* (London: Her Majesty's Stationery Office, 1954), 167–68. http://www.ibiblio.org/hyperwar/UN/UK/UK-RAF-III/UK-RAF-III-7.html

32 Andrei Martyanov, *Losing Military Supremacy: The Myopia of American Strategic Planning* (Atlanta: Clarity Press, 2018), 131–32.

33 Ibid., 132.

34 Norman Friedman, *Network-Centric Warfare: How Navies Learned to Fight Smarter Through Three World Wars* (Annapolis, Maryland: Naval Institute Press, 2009), 240.

35 Svechin, *Strategy*, 80.

36 Captain A.T. Mahan, *The Influence of Sea Power upon History: 1660–1783* (Boston: Little, Brown, and Company, 1890), 414.

37 Ibid., 539–40.

38 Andrew K. Blackley, "Toward a New Navalism," *Proceedings* Vol. 147/12/1426 (December 2021).

39 Nicholas J. Danby, "The Roots of Roosevelt's Navalism," *Naval History Magazine* 35, no. 1 (February 2021).

40 Mahan, *The Influence of Sea Power upon History*, 541.

41 Sergey Georgievich Gorshkov, *The Sea Power of the State* (Krieger Publishing Co., 1983), 3.

42 Blackley, *Toward a New Navalism*.

43 *16"/50 (40.6 cm) Mark 7*. NavWeaps. http://www.navweaps.com/Weapons/WNUS_16-50_mk7.php#ammonote5

44 George W. Baer, *One Hundred Years of Sea Power: The US Navy, 1890–1990* (Stanford University Press, 1994), 361.

45 Ibid., 451.

46 Ibid., 286.

47 E. B. Potter (ed.) and Chester W. Nimitz (assoc. ed.), *Sea Power. A Naval History* (Englewood Cliffs, N.J.: Prentice-Hall, Inc., 1960), 881.

48 Svechin, *Strategy*, 115.

49 Alexandr Rogers, *Разница между стратегическим и проектным мышлением* [The Difference between strategic and business project thinking], lecture, YouTube video [23:49], May 5, 2023. https://youtu.be/_bNM3CpD_Ag

50 Richard Pipes, *"Why the Soviet Union Thinks It Could Fight & Win a Nuclear War,"* commentary, July 1977.

51 Lester W. Grau and Charles K. Bartles, *The Russian Way of War: Force Structure, Tactics, and Modernization of the Russian Ground Forces* (Foreign Military Studies Office, 2016), 10.

52 Mark Milley, "Strategic Inflection Point: The Most Historically Significant and Fundamental Change in the Character of War Is Happening Now—While the Future Is Clouded in Mist and Uncertainty," *Joint Force Quarterly* 110 (3rd Quarter, July 2023).

53 Carl Von Clausewitz, *On War* (Princeton, NJ: Princeton University Press, 1976), 627.

54 Anthony Cordesman and Abraham R. Wagner, *Lessons of the Gulf War: 1990–1991* (Center for Strategic and International Studies, 2013), 941.

55 Michael Peck, "Losses in Ukraine are 'out of proportion' to what NATO has been planning for, the alliance's top general says," *Business Insider,* February 5, 2023. https://www.businessinsider.com/ukraine-war-scale-out-of-proportion-with-nato-planning-cavoli-2023-2

The video of Christopher's Cavoli remarks could be seen on YouTube at *"Hard power is a reality" – Christopher G. Cavoli, Supreme Allied Commander Europe (SACEUR)* [20:05], Folk och Försvar channel, January 9, 2023. https://youtu.be/IFIhlAHnRbg

56 Natalie Brunell, *Col. Douglas Macgregor on Threat of WW3, American Dream vs. Foreign Empire, Financial System Risks*, video podcast [35:58], YouTube, November 9, 2023. https://youtu.be/P92oFl9_euQ

57 *Федеральный закон от 28.12.2010 г. № 390-ФЗ О безопасности* [Federal Law from 12/28/2010 # 390-FZ, About Security].

58 *Указ Президента Российской Федерации от 23 июля 2013 г. № 631. Положение о Генеральном штабе Вооруженных Сил Российской Федерации* [Order of the President of Russian Federation from 23 July 2013, # 631. Regulations on the General Staff of Armed Forces of Russian Federation]. http://www.kremlin.ru/acts/bank/37481

59 Mark Milley, "Strategic Inflection Point."

60 Seth Cropsey, "Mark Milley's bureaucratic proposals could lose us the next war," *The Hill,* July 24, 2023. https://thehill.com/opinion/national-security/4110122-mark-milleys-bureaucratic-proposals-could-lose-us-the-next-war/

61 Ibid.

CHAPTER 3

62 Drew Middleton, "Hitler's Russian blunder," *New York Times,* June 21, 1981. https://www.nytimes.com/1981/06/21/magazine/hitler-s-russian-blunder.html

63 Ibid.

64 "Transcript: President Obama Iraq speech," *BBC News,* December 15, 2011. http://www.bbc.com/news/world-us-canada-16191394

65 Ibid.

66 Svechin, *Strategy,* 115.

67 Robert H. Latiff, *Future War. Preparing For the New Global Battlefield* (New York: Alfred A. Knopf, 2017), 130–31.

68 David M. Glantz, *The Soviet-German War 1941–1945, Myths and Realities: A Survey Essay,* paper Presented at the 20th Anniversary Distinguished Lecture at the Strom Thurmond Institute of Government and Public Affairs (Clemson University, October 11, 2001), 5.

69 *Ukraine turning into a Graveyard w/Col Douglas Macgregor.* YouTube video [24:54], Judge Napolitano – Judging Freedom channel, August 3, 2023. https://www.youtube.com/live/9vf7Tt5KVKc

70 Douglas Macgregor, *Margin of Victory: Five Battles That Changed the Face of Modern War* (Annapolis: Naval Institute Press, 2016), 71.

71 Jan Morris, "All Trite on the Western Front," *The Guardian,* December 2, 2006. Macgregor based his unsubstantiated claims on grossly opinionated and agenda-driven, not least through pro-Polish bias, treatise by Norman Davies' book *No Simple Victory: World War II In Europe, 1939–1945.* Even the *Guardian* noted Davies' "Polish nationalism" in its devastating review of his book and its lack of fact-checking.

Alas, if this is perhaps an endearing sign of advancing years, not so forgivable is the slipshod nature of this book. The French fleet was certainly not sunk with all hands at Mers-el-Kebir. Trevor-Roper surely never wrote a book called *The Last Days of the Reich.* Geoffrey Lawrence was not the chief prosecutor at the Nuremberg trials and Lindbergh was not the first man to fly non-stop across the Atlantic. The wartime British women's military force was called the ATS, not the WRAC. Commercial journalism was decidedly not "in its infancy" during the Second World War. And how are these for a few Davies truisms, plucked from a cornucopia? "War is concerned, above all, with fighting and killing." "Courage and virtue were not the preserve of Allied fighters." "Every single one of the 10 million [POWs] was an individual person." "Soldiering is a profession whose participants have always risked death, wounds and mutilation." "All soldiers have to be trained." "All countries maintain prisons to detain criminals." You don't say, Professor! ... And if I dare end upon an anachronistic note: Davies certainly does not beat the drum for Britain, or any other nation (except perhaps his beloved Poland, and who could resent that?). https://www.theguardian.com/books/2006/dec/03/historybooks.features

72 *Sun Tzu on The Art of War* (Allandale Online Publishing, 2000), 11.

73 *Director of National Intelligence Files, Counterintelligence Reader Vol. 3*, Office of the Director of National Intelligence, National Counterintelligence and Security Center, 112–14. https://www.dni.gov/files/NCSC/documents/ci/CI_Reader_Vol3.pdf

74 Anton Kurilkin, «Других экспертов у меня для вас нет, или что не так с Юлией Иоффе» [I don't have other experts for you, or what is wrong with Julia Ioffe], *Medium,* January 14, 2018. https://rb.gy/0ht8i3

75 Rebekah Koffler, *Putin's Playbook: Russia's Secret Plan to Defeat America* (Regnery Gateway, Kindle Edition, July 27, 2021), 316.

76 *Putin's Playbook* book page, Amazon. https://www.amazon.com/Putins-Playbook-Russias-Secret-America/dp/168451374X/

77 Rebekah Koffler, *Putin's Playbook,* 7.

78 Mallory Shelbourne, "HASC Agrees to Navy's Plans to Shed Littoral Combat Ships, Moves to Abolish CAPE," *USNI News,* June 12, 2023. https://news.usni.org/2023/06/12/hasc-agrees-to-navys-plans-to-shed-littoral-combat-ships-moves-to-abolish-cape

79 Casey Michel, "Decolonize Russia," *The Atlantic,* May 27, 2022. https://www.theatlantic.com/ideas/archive/2022/05/russia-putin-colonization-ukraine-chechnya/639428/

80 *GDP (current US$) – United States, Russian Federation,* World Bank national accounts data, and OECD National Accounts data files. https://data.worldbank.org/indicator/NY.GDP.MKTP.CD?locations=US-RU

81 Fadi Lama, *Why the West Can't Win: From Bretton Woods to a Multipolar World* (Atlanta: Clarity Press, 2023), 79–80.

82 *Public debt of the United States from January 2013 to September 2023, by month.* Statista. https://www.statista.com/statistics/273294/public-debt-of-the-united-states-by-month/

83 *Russia Public Domestic Debt.* Trading Economics. https://tradingeconomics.com/russia/government-debt

84 *Объем ВВП* [The volume of GDP 2013], Rosstat. https://rosstat.gov.ru/bgd/regl/b13_01/isswww.exe/stg/d12/2-1-1-1.htm

85 Angelika Hellemann, Lydia Rosenfelder and Wolf Lux (photos) "Erstes Interview mit Neu-Verteidigungsministerin Lambrecht: 'Wir

müssen Putin ins Visier nehmen,'" *Bild,* December 19, 2021. https://www.bild.de/politik/inland/politik-inland/erstes-interview-mit-neu-verteidigungsministerin-lambrecht-wir-muessen-putin-ins-78584768.bild.html

86 Alexader Grishin, «Министр обороны Германии призвала закрыть для Путина и его окружения Париж. Чтобы они не смогли совершить шопинг на Елисейских полях,» *Komsomolskaya Pravda,* December 19, 2021. https://www.kp.ru/daily/28371.5/4521117/

87 *Total energy production/consumption, 2021,* World Energy & Climate Statistics – Yearbook. https://yearbook.enerdata.net/total-energy/world-energy-production.html

88 Ibid.

89 *December 2021 crude steel production and 2021 global crude steel production totals.* World Steel. https://worldsteel.org/media-centre/press-releases/2022/december-2021-crude-steel-production-and-2021-global-totals/

90 Melissa Pestilli, "Top 10 Aluminum-producing Countries," *Investing News,* September 5, 2023. https://investingnews.com/daily/resource-investing/industrial-metals-investing/aluminum-investing/aluminum-producing-countries/

91 "UNESCO Reveals Countries Producing the Highest No. of STEM Graduates," *Scoonews,* December 3, 2020.

92 *Pig iron 2020 and 2021.* 2022 World Steel in Figures. https://worldsteel.org/wp-content/uploads/World-Steel-in-Figures-2022-1.pdf

93 "'Russia will not lose' – EU member state. Hungary's Viktor Orban says the West should accept 'reality' and come up with a Plan B," *RT,* November 27, 2023. https://www.rt.com/news/588017-orban-russia-will-not-lose/

94 *Agreement on measures to ensure the security of The Russian Federation and member States of the North Atlantic Treaty Organiza*tion, Ministry of Foreign Affairs of Russian Federation, December 17, 2021. https://mid.ru/ru/foreign_policy/rso/nato/1790803/?lang=en&clear_cache=Y

95 Steven Pifer, "Russia's draft agreements with NATO and the United States: Intended for rejection?" *Brookings,* December 21, 2021. https://www.brookings.edu/articles/russias-draft-agreements-with-nato-and-the-united-states-intended-for-rejection/

96 Ibid.

97 "Trump charges are political persecution – Putin," *RT,* September 12, 2023. https://www.rt.com/russia/582816-putin-trump-political-persecution/

98 Andrei Martyanov, *Disintegration: Indicators of the Coming American Collapse* (Atlanta: Clarity Press, 2021), 227.

CHAPTER 4

99 Alisa Sakharova, «Как начиналась спецоперация: хронология событий 24 февраля 2022-го» [How the special operation started: Chronology of the events of 24 February 2022], *Channel 5,* February 24, 2022. https://www.5-tv.ru/news/421758/kak-nacinalas-specoperacia-hronologia-sobytij-24fevrala/?ysclid=lpluyps0eg781649916

100 «Текст обращения президента России Владимира Путина» [Text of address of the President of Russia Vladimir Putin], *Ria.ru,* February 24, 2022. https://ria.ru/20220224/obraschenie-1774658619.html

101 "Remarks by President Biden on Russia's Unprovoked and Unjustified Attack on Ukraine," White House, February 24, 2022. https://www.whitehouse.gov/briefing-room/speeches-remarks/2022/02/24/remarks-by-president-biden-on-russias-unprovoked-and-unjustified-attack-on-ukraine/

102 "OSCE Special Monitoring Mission to Ukraine (SMM) Daily Report 19/2022 issued on 22 February 2022," Organization for Security and Co-operation in Europe, February 22, 2022. https://www.osce.org/special-monitoring-mission-to-ukraine/512842

103 Chris Van Hollen, "Israel's war against Hamas is just, but it must be fought justly," *The Washington Post,* December 6, 2023. https://www.washingtonpost.com/opinions/2023/12/06/van-hollen-israel-war-gaza-hamas-conditions-aid/

104 *Біла книга 2021. Оборонна політика України* [White Book 2021: Defense Policy of Ukraine] (Kiev: Ukraine Defense Ministry, 2022), 33. https://www.mil.gov.ua/content/files/whitebook/WhiteBook_2021_Draft_Final_03.pdf

105 «Аспекты мобилизации: к вопросу о тенденциях развития Вооружённых сил Украины» [Aspects of Mobilization: The issue of trends in development of Armed Forces of Ukraine], *Lost Armor.* https://lostarmour.info/articles/vsu_mobilization_trends

106 Jakub Przetacznik with Linda Tothova, *Russia's war on Ukraine: Military balance of power*, European Parliamentary Research Service PE 729.292, March 2022. https://www.europarl.europa.eu/RegData/etudes/ATAG/2022/729292/EPRS_ATA(2022)729292_EN.pdf

107 Alexander Khramchihin, «Насколько страшна украинская ПВО» [How scary is Ukrainian Air Defense], *Независимое Военное Обозрение* [Independent Miltary Review], February 10, 2022. https://

nvo.ng.ru/realty/2022-02-10/3_1176_airdefense.html

108 Jamie McIntyre, "US and NATO credit eight years of Western training for Ukraine's combat prowess, *Washington Examiner,* April 1, 2022. https://www.washingtonexaminer.com/policy/defense-national-security/us-and-nato-credit-eight-years-of-western-training-for-ukraines-combat-prowess

109 Julian E. Barnes, Eric Schmitt, David E. Sanger and Thomas Gibbons-Neff, "U.S. and Ukraine Search for a New Strategy After Failed Counteroffensive, *The New York Times,* December 11, 2023. https://www.nytimes.com/2023/12/11/us/politics/us-ukraine-war-strategy.html

110 Ibid.

111 David M. Glantz and Jonathan M. House, *When Titans Clashed: How the Red Army Stopped Hitler* (Lawrence, Kansas: University Press Of Kansas, 2015), 256–57.

112 *Staff Organization and Operations, FM 101-5,* Headquarters, Department of the Army, Washington D.C., May 31, 1997, p. 1-1.

113 Patrick C. Sweeney, *Operational Art Primer*, United States Naval War College, Joint Military Operations Department. July 16, 2010, p. 2. https://www.moore.army.mil/mssp/PDF/nwc_sweeney_op_art_primer_16jul2010.pdf

114 Milan Vego, "On Operational Leadership," *Joint Force Quarterly* 2nd Quarter (April 2015). https://ndupress.ndu.edu/JFQ/Joint-Force-Quarterly-77/Article/581882/on-operational-leadership/

115 Alexey Leonkov, Andrei Ermolaev, Artyom Mikhailov, «Ракетное вооружение для самолетов пятого поколения» [Missile armament for the fifth generation aircraft], *Arsenal Otechestva* [Arsenal of Fatherland], August 29, 2023. https://arsenal-otechestva.ru/article/1771-raketnoe-vooruzhenie-dlya-samoletov-pyatogo-pokoleniya

116 Rick Atkinson, "Introduction," in George S. Patton, Jr., *War as I knew It* (1995), xv-xvi.

117 «ВС РФ рассматривали два варианта спецоперации: в границах ДНР и ЛНР или на всей Украине» [Armed Forces considered two variants of special operation: within borders of DNR and LNR, or at the whole of Ukraine], *TASS,* March 25, 2022. https://tass.ru/armiya-i-opk/14186363

118 Anton Troianovski, "Hopes for a peace deal center on negotiators at a palace in Istanbul," *The New York Times,* March 29, 2022. https://www.nytimes.com/2022/03/29/world/europe/russia-ukraine-peace-talks-istanbul.html

119 "Ukraine conflict could have ended in Spring 2022 – Kiev's top MP," *RT,* November 24, 2023. https://www.rt.com/russia/587945-ukraine-war-could-be-over/

120 Roman Romanyuk, «От „капитуляции" Зеленского до капитуляции Путина. Как идут переговоры с Россией» [From "capitulation" of Zelensky to capitulation of Putin. How the negotiations with Russia are progressing] *Ukrainian Pravda,* May 5, 2023. https://www.pravda.com.ua/rus/articles/2022/05/5/7344096/

121 "Johnson and Biden discussed boosting support for Ukraine-Downing Street," *Reuters,* April 12, 2022. https://www.reuters.com/world/johnson-biden-discussed-boosting-support-ukraine-downing-street-2022-04-12/

CHAPTER 5

122 Alex Vershinin, "The Return of Industrial Warfare," Royal United Service Institute (RUSI), June 17, 2022. https://www.rusi.org/explore-our-research/publications/commentary/return-industrial-warfare

123 Ibid.

124 Joshua Waddell, "Innovation and Other Things that Brief Well," *Small Wars Journal,* February 8, 2017. https://smallwarsjournal.com/blog/innovation-and-other-things-that-brief-well

125 Fadi Lama, *Why the West Can't Win,* 37.

126 *November 2023 Crude Steel Production,* Worldsteel Association, Brussels, December 21, 2023. https://worldsteel.org/media-centre/press-releases/2023/november-2023-crude-steel-production/

127 Sultan Khalid, "16 Largest Pig Iron Producing Countries," *Yahoo! Finance,* May 26, 2023. https://finance.yahoo.com/news/16-largest-pig-iron-producing-104837722.html

128 *November 2023 Crude Steel Production,* Worldsteel Association, Brussels, December 21, 2023.

https://worldsteel.org/media-centre/press-releases/2023/november-2023-crude-steel-production/

129 Melissa Pestilli, *Top 10 Aluminum-producing Countries.*

130 Eleanor Watson, "Russians are using semiconductors from kitchen appliances in military equipment, says U.S. commerce secretary," *CBS News,* May 14, 2022. https://www.cbsnews.com/news/russian-military-equipment-computer-chips-refrigerators/

131 *Gina M. Raimondo, Secretary of Commerce,* U.S. Department of Commerce. https://www.commerce.gov/about/leadership/gina-m-raimondo

132 «Доморощенный кремний. Сможет ли Россия обойтись без импортных микрочипов» [Homegrown silicon. Will Russia be able to do without import microchips], *Ria.Ru,* April 21, 2022. https://ria.ru/20220421/mikrochipy-1784536026.html

133 «В России создали комплекс для выпуска микроэлектронных наноструктур» [Russia has created complex for fabrication of microelectronic nanostructures], *Ria.Ru,* March 10, 2023. https://ria.ru/20231003/nauka-1900093372.html

134 "War in Ukraine: Is Russia's stock of weapons running low?" *BBC News,* October 13, 2022. https://www.bbc.com/news/world-63247287

135 *Louise Jones.* LinkedIn profile. https://www.linkedin.com/in/louisejones21/

136 Andrew Chuter, "British Army admits more delays in fielding enough combat forces," *Defense News,* October 12, 2020. https://www.defensenews.com/global/europe/2020/10/12/british-army-admits-more-delays-in-fielding-enough-combat-forces/

137 Martyanov, *Losing Military Supremacy,* 179.

138 Ibid.

139 John Ismay, "Russian Cruise Missiles Were Made Just Months Ago Despite Sanctions, *The New York Times,* December 5, 2022. https://www.nytimes.com/2022/12/05/us/politics/cruise-missiles-russia-ukraine-sanctions.html

140 "Dating newly produced Russian missiles used in Kyiv attacks. Ukraine Field Dispatch," Conflict Armament Research, December 2022 (updated December 2023). https://storymaps.arcgis.com/stories/81bc6b71fdc64361a05a21020c3d6d5e

141 Thomas Newdick, "Let's Talk About Russia's New Long-Range Kh-BD Cruise Missile," *The Drive,* September 19, 2023. https://www.thedrive.com/the-war-zone/lets-talk-about-russias-new-long-range-kh-bd-cruise-missile

142 "Tomahawk," *Missile Threat,* updated February 28, 2023. https://missilethreat.csis.org/missile/tomahawk/

143 "Kh-101/Kh-102," *Missile Threat,* updated July 21, 2021. https://missilethreat.csis.org/missile/kh-101-kh-102/

144 Rachel Cohen and Joe Gould, "With a mix of donated weapons, Ukraine's defenders adapt in war," *Air Force Times,* September 28, 2022. https://www.airforcetimes.com/flashpoints/2022/09/28/with-a-mix-of-donated-weapons-ukraines-defenders-adapt-in-war/

145 Joseph Trevithick, "Russian Kh-101 Cruise Missile Filmed Firing-Off Decoy Flares," *The Drive,* December 29, 2023. https://www.thedrive.com/the-war-zone/russian-kh-101-cruise-missile-filmed-firing-off-decoy-flares

146 Anton Valagin, «Дальность полета ракеты „Калибр" увеличат вдвое» [The Range of "Kalibr" missile will be increased two fold], *Rossiiskaya Gazeta,* January 8, 2019. https://

rg.ru/2019/01/08/dalnost-poleta-rakety-kalibr-uvelichat-vdvoe.
html?ysclid=lrfgdyhbdb449611986

147 «Новый „Калибр-М" меняет глобальные правила игры»
[New "Kalibr-M" changes the global rules of the game], video report
[4:15], Super.Uralov YouTube channel, October 25, 2020. https://www.
youtube.com/watch?v=6ogiXBkJLUY

148 *National Cruise Missile Defense: Issues and Alternatives,*
Congressional Budget Office, February 2021, p. 10, Fig. 1-2. https://
www.cbo.gov/system/files/2021-02/56950-CMD.pdf

149 Ibid., p. 14, Fig. 2-1.

150 Martyanov, *The (Real) Revolution in Military Affairs*, 90.

151 Peter Mitchell, "Hypersonic Hype? Russia's Kinzhal Missiles
and the Lessons for Air Defense," Modern War Institute at West Point,
May 23, 2023. https://mwi.usma.edu/hypersonic-hype-russias-kinzhal-
missiles-and-the-lessons-for-air-defense/

152 "Patriot missile system in Ukraine likely 'damaged': Report,"
Al Jazeera, May 17, 2023. https://www.aljazeera.com/news/2023/5/17/
patriot-missile-system-in-ukraine-likely-damaged-sources-says

153 David Axe, "Why Did American Patriot Missiles Fail To Stop the
Houthi's Attacks?" *The National Interest,* December 10, 2021. https://
nationalinterest.org/blog/reboot/why-did-american-patriot-missiles-fail-
stop-houthis-attacks-197764

154 Ivan Petrov, «ВКС России дважды поразили ранее неуязвимый
зенитный ракетный комплекс США» [Russia's VKS struck second
earlier considered invulnerable American air defense complex],
Rossiiyskaya Gazeta, May 31, 2023. https://rg.ru/2023/05/31/ohota-na-
patriot.html

155 Bill Gertz, "U.S. sensors unable to track Chinese, Russian
hypersonic missiles, says congressional report," *The Washington Times,*
October 11, 2022. https://www.washingtontimes.com/news/2022/oct/11/
us-sensors-unable-track-chinese-russian-hypersonic/

156 "Russia Quintupled Production of Kinzhal Hypersonic Missiles
Before Destruction of Patriot System – Reports," *Military Watch
Magazine,* May 23, 2023. https://militarywatchmagazine.com/article/
quintupled-kinzhal-production-patriotstrike

157 "Russia has launched about 8,000 missiles against Ukraine since
start of invasion, air force says," *The New Voice of Ukraine,* May 17,
2023. https://english.nv.ua/nation/russia-has-used-about-8-000-missiles-
so-far-in-its-ukraine-war-50325222.html

158 Davis Centiotti, "Kinzhal Hypersonic Aero-Ballistic Missile
Used By Su-34 In Ukraine For The First Time – Reports," *The*

Aviationist, September 4, 2023. https://theaviationist.com/2023/09/04/su-34-kinzhal/

159 Katie Krombe and John A. Nagl, "A Call to Action: Lessons from Ukraine for the Future Force," *Parameters* (Autumn 2023): 24.

CHAPTER 6

160 Laurence Peter, "How Ukraine's 'Ghost of Kyiv' legendary pilot was born," *BBC,* May 1, 2022. https://www.bbc.com/news/world-europe-61285833

161 Ibid.

162 Russian Defense Ministry Update, Official Defense Ministry TG Channel, January 19, 2024. https://t.me/mod_russia/34824

163 *Chiffres clés de la Défense – 2021* (Ministere Des Armees, 2021), 23–24.

164 Sarah Al-Arshani, "Sen. Mark Kelly flew with Russian pilots in the Navy and with NASA, and he said the Russian fighter jet running into a US drone shows 'how incompetent they are,'" *Business Insider,* March 19, 2023. https://www.yahoo.com/news/sen-mark-kelly-flew-russian-155055751.html

165 Justin Bronk, "The Mysterious Case of the Missing Russian Air Force," *RUSI,* February 28, 2022. https://rusi.org/explore-our-research/publications/commentary/mysterious-case-missing-russian-air-force

166 *Weltkrieg in Nahost: US-Colonel Macgregor über die grössten Gefahren der Gegenwart* [World War in the Middle East: US Colonel Macgregor on the greatest dangers of the present], *Die Weltwoche* interview [1:31:10], YouTube, January 14, 2024. https://www.youtube.com/watch?v=DtCS7vxuhyQ

167 Anthony Cordesman and Abraham R. Wagner, *Lessons of the Gulf War: 1990–1991* (Center for Strategic and International Studies, 2013), vii.

168 Ibid., 372.

169 Alexandr Khramchikhin, «Насколько страшна украинская ПВО» [How Scary is Ukrainian Air Defense], *Независимое Военное Обозрение* [Independent Miltary Review], February 10, 2022. https://nvo.ng.ru/realty/2022-02-10/3_1176_airdefense.html?ysclid=lrokrirppj770940815

170 Dmitry Gorenburg, "Russia's Syria Operation Reveals Significant Improvement in Military Capability," *The National Interest,* November 16, 2015. https://nationalinterest.org/blog/the-buzz/russias-syria-operation-reveals-significant-improvement-14356

171 *The Depot-Level Maintenance of DoD's Combat Aircraft: Insights for the F-35*, Congressional Budget Office report (February 2018), 7. https://www.cbo.gov/system/files/115th-congress-2017-2018/reports/53543-depotmaintenancef35.pdf

172 «Истребители переходного периода» [Fighters of a transitional period], *Kommersant*, August 21, 2007. https://www.kommersant.ru/doc/795697?ysclid=lrpxql9ane76996857

173 «Глава Ростеха сравнил стоимость летного часа Checkmate и F-35» [The head of Rostec compared the cost of flight hour of Checkmate and F-35], *Sibnet.Ru*, April 11, 2021. https://info.sibnet.ru/article/602039/

174 "Boeing to extend USAF F-15 fleet service life," *Air Force Technology*, November 25, 2011. https://www.airforce-technology.com/news/newsboeing-to-extend-usaf-f-15-fleet-service-life/

175 Hercules Reyes, "F-35 Not as 'Survivable' as Thought: House Armed Services Committee Chief," *The Defense Post*, September 1, 2021. https://www.thedefensepost.com/2021/09/01/f-35-not-survivable/

176 Sergei Andreev, «Удар по элите ВВС: Почему Киев потерял всех опытных лётчиков-истребителей» [The strike at Air Force elite: Why Kiev lost all experienced fighter pilots], *Life.Ru*, August 16, 2022. https://life.ru/p/1516754

177 Ibid.

178 Maxim Tucker, "Ukraine air chief: my best pilots are dying while we wait for F-16s, *The Times*, March 19, 2023. https://www.thetimes.co.uk/article/ukraine-air-chief-our-pilots-can-master-f-16-jets-in-under-six-months-dz7bfvqn5

179 "The US military 'gets its ass handed to it' in World War 3 simulation – researchers," *RT*, March 11, 2019. https://www.rt.com/usa/453550-us-loses-world-war-three/

180 Ibid.

181 Ashish Dangwal, "First Kill? Russian Su-57 Stealth Fighter Downs Ukrainian Su-27 Jet With New Long-Range Missile – Media Claims," *The Eurasian Times*, October 19, 2022. https://www.eurasiantimes.com/first-kill-russian-su-57-stealth-fighter-downs-ukrainian-su-27-jet/

182 Dmitry Kornev, «'Длинная рука': ракета Р-37М расширила возможности ВКС РФ по уничтожению воздушных целей» ["Long hand": R-37 expanded capabilities of Russia's VKS in killing aerial targets], *Rossiiskaya Gazeta*, December 11, 2023. https://rg.ru/2023/12/11/dlinnaia-ruka-raketa-r-37m-rasshirila-vozmozhnosti-vks-rf-po-unichtozheniiu-vozdushnyh-celej.html?ysclid=lryetzqpga574707196

183 «Источник: новая российская ракета показала уникальную точность в рамках СВО» [Source: new Russian missile has shown a unique accuracy during SMO], *Ria.ru,* March 11, 2023. https://ria.ru/20230311/raketa-1857168173.html

184 *Kh-31PD High-speed anti-radar missile,* Rosoboronexport presentation, YouTube. April 14, 2023. https://youtu.be/oj22QMqm1Kw

185 "AMRAAM: Advanced Medium-Range Air-to-Air Missile," *NAVAIR,* Naval Air Systems Command. https://www.navair.navy.mil/product/AMRAAM

186 Anton Valagin, «Российская система ПВО установила мировой рекорд» [Russian Air Defense system set the world record], *Rossiiskaya Gazeta,* October 16, 2022. https://rg.ru/2022/10/16/rossijskaia-sistema-pvo-ustanovila-mirovoj-rekord.html?ysclid=ls0yf2cwwr166925904

187 Viktor Bodrov, «Заглянуть за горизонт: как ВС РФ уничтожают украинские самолеты на сверхдальних дистанциях» [To look beyond the horizon: How Russian VKS shoot down Ukrainian aircraft at the extreme range], *TASS,* November 21, 2023. https://tass.ru/armiya-i-opk/19337985

188 *Combat Aircraft Journal* 24, no.6 (June 2023): front page.

189 Martyanov, *The (Real) Revolution in Military Affairs,* 121–22.

190 Jon Lake, "From Seven to Four," Combat Aircraft Journal 24, no. 6 (June 2023): 29.

191 Ibid., 30.

192 *Scott Ritter: Russia and the Middle East,* YouTube video [1:07:02], Judge Napolitano – Judging Freedom channel, January 30, 2024. https://www.youtube.com/live/w3IAwqSIxXM

193 Vijainder K Thakur, "Russia 'Doubles' Su-57 Production; Ukraine's F-16 Fighters Likely To Face The Wrath Of RuAF Stealth Jets," *Eurasian Times,* December 28, 2023. https://www.eurasiantimes.com/russia-doubles-su-57-production-ukraines-f-16-fighters/

194 Greg Hadley, "Air Force Now 'Very Weak', New Report Says, But Space Force Is Gaining Strength," *Air and Space Forces Magazine,* January 24, 2024. https://www.airandspaceforces.com/heritage-report-air-force-readiness-down/

195 "Kiev knew Ukrainian POWs were on plane it downed – Putin," *RT,* January 26, 2024. https://www.rt.com/russia/591341-kiev-knew-pows/

CHAPTER 7

196 Christopher Klein, "Fooling Hitler: The Elaborate Ruse Behind D-Day," *History,* June 27, 2023. https://www.history.com/news/fooling-hitler-the-elaborate-ruse-behind-d-day

197 Graham Jenkins, "The Mask of the Bear: Soviet Deception in Operation Bagration," *Automatic Ballpoint* [blog], May 4, 2010. https://automaticballpoint.com/2010/05/04/the-mask-of-the-bear-soviet-deception-in-operation-bagration/

198 Christopher M. Rein, "Weaving the Tangled Web: Military Deception in Large-scale Combat Operations," *Military Review* (September-October 2018). https://www.armyupress.army.mil/Journals/Military-Review/English-Edition-Archives/September-October-2018/Tangled-Web/

199 Alex Horton, John Hudson, Isabelle Khurshudyan and Samuel Oakford, "U.S. doubts Ukraine counteroffensive will yield big gains, leaked document says," *The Washington Post,* April 10, 2023. https://www.washingtonpost.com/national-security/2023/04/10/leaked-documents-ukraine-counteroffensive/

200 Ibid.

201 Jacques Baud, "Russian Armed Forces Personnel," in *The Russian Art of War: How the West led Ukraine to defeat* (Max Milo Editions, January 17, 2024).

202 "Miscalculations, divisions marked offensive planning by U.S., Ukraine," *Washington Post,* December 4, 2023. https://www.washingtonpost.com/world/2023/12/04/ukraine-counteroffensive-us-planning-russia-war/

203 «У ВСУ нет шансов в контрнаступлении – Путин» [VSU have no chance in counteroffensive], *Ria.Ru,* June 16, 2023. https://crimea.ria.ru/20230616/u-vsu-net-shansov-v-kontrnastuplenii--putin-1129442059.html

204 Losses table by periods, «Потери Украины за время специальной военной операции (СВО)» [Ukraine's losses during special military operation], *Mskvremya.ru,* 2023. https://mskvremya.ru/article/2023/1520-poteri-ukrainy-za-vremya-spetsoperatsii

205 «МО раскрыло потери российских войск в ходе операции на Украине» [Ministry of Defense disclosed losses of Russian troops in SMO], *Izvestiya,* March 3, 2022. https://iz.ru/1299805/2022-03-03/mo-raskrylo-poteri-rossiiskikh-voisk-v-khode-operatcii-na-ukraine

206 *Vladimir Trukhan and I: Answering Questions on SMO and warfare,* YouTube video [2:00], February 1, 2024. https://youtu.be/L0bEsh201Os

207 Arpan Rai, "Ukraine says whole of Russia will 'panic' when counteroffensive begins: 'They will suffer the consequences,'" *Independent,* US edition, May 8, 2023. https://www.independent.co.uk/news/world/europe/ukraine-counteroffensive-russian-losses-putin-b2334687.html

208 *Пленный военнослужащий ВСУ Дыбиц Федор,* Situational Reporting, Russian Defense Ministry video [05:14], *VK Video,* February 5, 2024. https://vk.com/video-133441491_456274027

209 «Мы пока не столкнулись с основным ударом ВСУ. Военный эксперт Леонков – о главном направлении украинского наступления» [We haven't encountered the main blow of AFU yet. Military expert Leonkov about main axis of Ukrainian offensive], *Rossiyskaya Gazeta,* June 10, 2023. https://rg.ru/2023/06/10/voennyj-ekspert-leonkov-o-glavnom-napravlenii-ukrainskogo-nastupleniia.html

210 Sergei Nakhimov, «Количество сил ВСУ и танков в наступлении на Запорожском и Южно-Донецком направлении. Мнение» [Number of AFU forces and tanks on Zaporozhie and South-Donetsk axes. Opinion], *Amalnews,* June 18, 2023. https://amalantra.ru/kolichesto-sil-vsu-i-tankov-v-nastuplenii/

211 «Главный вопрос спецоперации: Что такое „линия Суровикина"» [The main question of Special Military Operation: "What is Surovikin Line"], *Tsargrad,* June 13, 2023. https://dzen.ru/a/ZIiVOx36y0SBBPjN

212 Anatoly Matveichuk, «Через три-четыре недели у ВСУ иссякнет боевой запал» [In three-four weeks AFU battle fuse will fizzle out], *Rossiyskaya Gazeta,* June 7, 2023. https://rg.ru/2023/06/07/voennyj-ekspert-anatolij-matvijchuk-ukrainskaia-armiia-vedet-boevye-dejstviia-strogo-po-standartam-armii-amerikanskoj.html

213 Martyanov, *Losing Military Supremacy,* 70.

214 «Полоса Обеспечения (Зона Прикрытия)», War and Peace Terms and Definitions, *Academic.Ru.* https://war_peace_terms.academic.ru/588/

215 «Полоса обеспечения», *Military Encyclopedic Glossary* (Moscow: Military Publishing House of Ministry of Defense of the USSR, 1986), 571.

216 *Field Manual no. 3-0,* Operations, Headquarters Department of the Army Washington, D.C. (October 1, 2022): 6-36–6-37. https://armypubs.army.mil/epubs/DR_pubs/DR_a/ARN36290-FM_3-0-000-WEB-2.pdf

217 Mikhail Rodionov, «Хроника 24 июня. Как начался и к чему привел вооруженный мятеж Евгения Пригожина» [Chronicles of June 24th: How the armed mutiny of Evgeniy Prigozhin has started and what it led to], *Gazeta.ru,* June 25, 2023. https://www.gazeta.ru/army/2023/06/24/17189018.shtml

218 "Miscalculations, divisions marked offensive planning by U.S., Ukraine," *Washington Post,* December 4, 2023. https://www.washingtonpost.com/world/2023/12/04/ukraine-counteroffensive-us-planning-russia-war/

219 Ilia Davlyatchin, «Бурная молодость «кремлевского ресторатора» [A stormy youth of "Kremlin restarauter"], *Rosbalt,* September 21, 2018. https://www.rosbalt.ru/piter/2018/09/21/1733712.html

220 «*Известия* раскрыли подробности заработка Евгением Пригожиным миллиардов рублей» [*Izvestiya* revealed the details of Evgeniy Prigozin earning billions of rubles], *Izvesiya,* July 10, 2023. https://iz.ru/1542052/2023-07-10/izvestiia-raskryli-podrobnosti-zarabotka-evgeniem-prigozhinym-milliardov-rublei

221 Shane Harris and Isabelle Khurshudyan, "Wagner chief offered to give Russian troop locations to Ukraine, leak says," *The Washington Post,* May 14, 2023. https://www.washingtonpost.com/national-security/2023/05/14/prigozhin-wagner-ukraine-leaked-documents/

222 «Кремль отреагировал на публикацию о якобы желании Пригожина сдать позиции ВС РФ» [Kremlin reacted to publication of alleged Prigozhin's desire to give up positions of Russian Armed Forces], *Lenta.ru,* May 15,2023.

223 "Miscalculations, divisions marked offensive planning by U.S., Ukraine," *Washington Post,* December 4, 2023. https://www.washingtonpost.com/world/2023/12/04/ukraine-counteroffensive-us-planning-russia-war/

224 «ВСУ потеряли 159 тысяч военных с начала контрнаступления, заявил Шойгу» [AFU lost 159 thousands of personnel since the start of the counteroffensive], *Ria.ru,* December 19, 2023. https://ria.ru/20231219/poteri-1916703085.html

225 «Военный эксперт: ВСУ в первоначальном виде были уничтожены к маю 2022 года» [Military expert: AFU in their original form have been annihilated by May 2022], *Ria.ru,* January 16, 2024. https://ria.ru/20240116/ukraina-1921606684.html

226 *Lt Col Tony Shaffer: Does Putin intend to make a move on #NATO?* YouTube video [02:10], Judge Napolitano – Judging Freedom channel, February 8, 2024. https://youtu.be/LgZOS37-2hg

227 Katie Crombe and John A. Nagl, "A Call to Action: Lessons from Ukraine for the Future Force," *Parameters* 53, no. 3 (Autumn 2023): 25.

228 V.O. Korepanov, «Моделирование Военных, Боевых и Специальных Действий» [Modelling of Military, Combat and Special actions], *V.V. Shumov Voennaya Mysl,* no. 1 (2023): 31.

229 Leo Tolstoy, *War and Peace* (1867).

CHAPTER 8

230 Richard Pipes, "Why the Soviet Union Thinks It Could Fight & Win a Nuclear War," *Commentary,* July 1977. https://www.commentary. org/articles/richard-pipes-2/why-the-soviet-union-thinks-it-could-fight-win-a-nuclear-war/

231 Ibid.

232 Reynolds School of Journalism staff, "Nine Inspiring Media Quotes: Journalism, Public Relations and Visual Communication," *Nevada Today,* March 23, 2017. https://www.unr.edu/nevada-today/ news/2017/nine-media-quotes-journalism

233 *President Nixon Warns Against The "Media Elitist Complex"* (recorded in 1983), Richard Nixon Foundation YouTube video [4:19], January 16, 2024. https://youtu.be/TEX6ONLvJg0

234 Thomas Newdick, "Russian Submarine Shows Massive Damage After Ukrainian Strike," *Yahoo News: The War Zone,* September 18, 2023. https://www.yahoo.com/news/russian-submarine-shows-massive-damage-165654878.html

235 «Источник назвал незначительными повреждения подлодки „Ростов-на-Дону"» [The source called the damage to submarine Rostov-on-Don insignificant], *TASS,* September 24, 2023. https://tass.ru/ armiya-i-opk/18830811

236 David Ignatius, "The West feels gloomy about Ukraine. Here's why it shouldn't," *The Washington Post,* July 18, 2023. https://www. washingtonpost.com/opinions/2023/07/18/ukraine-war-west-gloom/

237 *David Ignatius,* Linked-In. https://www.linkedin.com/in/david-ignatius-50a6847/

238 "Sociopathy," *Psychology Today.* https://www.psychologytoday. com/us/basics/sociopathy

239 *Zanny Minton Beddoes - The Economist | The Daily Show,* The Daily Show YouTube video [12:53], February 12, 2024. https://youtu. be/7cmWbSv-GOE

240 Hunter S. Thompson, *Fear and Loathing in Las Vegas: A Savage Journey to the Heart of the American Dream* (Vintage, 2nd edition, July 23, 2010). Transcript online at MIT. http://web.mit.edu/tibbetts/Public/ fear_and_loathing.txt

241 Svechin, *Strategy*, 132.

242 *Russian Army Ad Makes Woke US Army Ad Look Like a Joke for Kids,* YouTube video [4:33], *The Rubin Report,* May 24, 2021. https://youtu.be/P5ar7vYg0pY

243 Patrick Buchanan, "Nobody's Quaking in Their Boots, Anymore," *The American Conservative.* https://www.theamericanconservative.com/nobodys-quaking-in-their-boots-anymore/

244 "Zelensky ally's revelations betray motive to stage Bucha – Moscow," *RT,* November 29, 2023. https://www.rt.com/russia/588220-revelations-zelensky-ally-bucha-staged/

245 Foreign Minister Sergey Lavrov's opening remarks at a meeting with Martin Griffiths, UN Under-Secretary-General for Humanitarian Affairs, Moscow, April 4, 2022. Foreign Ministry of Russian Federation. April 4, 2022. https://mid.ru/en/foreign_policy/news/1807721/

246 Martin Armstrong, "Bucha – the False Flag to Cross the Rubicon," *Armstong Economics,* April 5, 2022. https://www.armstrongeconomics.com/world-news/war/bucha-the-false-flag-to-cross-the-rubicon/

247 *SY HERSH Meets the Press – Live from the National Press Club, Washington DC,* YouTube video [1:25:10], *Consortium News,* March 14, 2023. https://www.youtube.com/live/LbYRcVF8frc

248 John Vandiver, "Airborne arrivals: 101st brigade, 82nd unit headed to Eastern Europe on rotation," *Stripes,* September 21, 2023. https://www.stripes.com/branches/army/2023-09-21/101st-airborne-82nd-airborne-europe-11434410.html

249 John Jackson, "NATO Allies Would Run Out of Ammo Within Days of War With Russia: Report," Newsweek, February 13, 2023. https://www.newsweek.com/nato-allies-would-run-out-ammunition-within-days-war-russia-report-says-1780851

250 Patrick Smith, "Russian troops 'forced to fight with shovels' as ammo shortage undermines Bakhmut advance," *NBC News,* March 6, 2023. https://www.nbcnews.com/news/world/russian-troops-fight-shovels-ammo-shortage-bakhmut-prigozhin-wagner-rcna73501

251 Valeria Gorodetskaya, «Украинский военный рассказал об участии ОБСЕ в постановочных съемках про «'успехи' ВСУ» [Ukrainian military told about participation of OSCE in staged reporting about "successes" of AFU], *Vz.ru,* February 16, 2024. https://vz.ru/news/2024/2/16/1253849.html

252 Veronika Prokhorenko, «'Сдача' Авдеевки – НЕ категорическое поражение: Мусиенко дал хороший прогноз» ["Abandoning" Avdeevka is NO a categorical defeat: Musienko gave a good forecast], *Unian,* February 19, 2024. https://www.unian.net/war/avdeevka-eto-na-samom-dele-pobeda-musienko-dal-horoshiy-prognoz-12547788.html

253 Holly Evans, "Canadian parliament accidentally honours Nazi – with Zelensky and Trudeau applauding," *Independent,* September 26, 2023. https://www.independent.co.uk/news/world/europe/canada-nazi-parliament-trudeau-yaroslav-hunka-b2418536.html

254 «Интервью Путина набрало около миллиарда просмотров, заявила Симоньян» [Putin's interview has been viewed around one billion times, Simonyan], *Ria.ru,* February 11, 2024. https://ria.ru/20240211/intervyu-1926732274.html

CHAPTER 9

255 What the Pentagon has learned from two years of war in Ukraine. Alex Horton. The Washington Post. February 22, 2024.

https://www.washingtonpost.com/national-security/2024/02/22/ukraine-war-pentagon-lessons-learned/

256 Ibid.

257 Leadership in Adversity. Colonel Harry Summers. *Military Review* LXXI, no. 5. May 1991, p.3.

https://apps.dtic.mil/sti/tr/pdf/ADA252791.pdf

258 2022 National Defense Strategy. US Department of Defense. October 27, 2022, p.1.

https://media.defense.gov/2022/Oct/27/2003103845/-1/-1/1/2022-NATIONAL-DEFENSE-STRATEGY-NPR-MDR.PDF

259 Ibid., 7.

260 National Security Strategy. The White House. October 12, 2022, p.7.

https://www.whitehouse.gov/wp-content/uploads/2022/11/8-November-Combined-PDF-for-Upload.pdf

261 Matt Purple, "We Must Fight Them Over There So We Don't Have to Fight Them Over Here," *The American Conservative,* January 15, 2021. https://www.theamericanconservative.com/we-must-fight-them-over-there-so-we-dont-to-fight-them-over-here/

262 *2022 National Defense Strategy,* US Department of Defense (October 27, 2022): 5. https://media.defense.gov/2022/Oct/27/2003103845/-1/-1/1/2022-NATIONAL-DEFENSE-STRATEGY-NPR-MDR.PDF

263 «Военная доктрина Российской Федерации (в редакции от 25 декабря 2014 г.)» [Military doctrine of Russian Federation (in December 25, 2014 edition)], Ministry of Foreign Affairs of Russian Federation, December 25, 2014. https://www.mid.ru/ru/foreign_policy/official_documents/1584621/

264 *Russian Tactics: ATP 7-100.1,* Headquarters Department of the Army, Washington, D.C. (February 29, 2024): 2–7. https://armypubs. army.mil/epubs/DR_pubs/DR_a/ARN40121-ATP_7-100.1-000-WEB-2.pdf

265 Lester W. Grau and Charles K. Bartles, *The Russian Way of War. Force Structure, Tactics, and Modernization of the Russian Ground Forces* (Foreign Military Studies Office. 2016), 56. https://www. armyupress.army.mil/portals/7/hot%20spots/documents/russia/2017-07-the-russian-way-of-war-grau-bartles.pdf

266 Nick Paton Walsh, Florence Davey-Attlee, Kostyantin Gak, and Brice Lâiné, "'Nowhere to hide': The question troubling Ukrainian troops amid a grinding counteroffensive," *CNN,* August 1, 2023. https:// edition.cnn.com/2023/08/01/europe/ukraine-neskuchne-question-counteroffensive-intl/index.html

267 «В ВС России набрали 486 тысяч добровольцев» [486 thousand personnel have volunteered for service in in Russian Armed Forces], *Ria.ru,* December 14, 2023. https://ria.ru/20231214/dobrovoltsy-1915737767.html

268 *Russian Tactics: ATP 7-100.1,* Headquarters Department of the Army, Washington, D.C. (February 29, 2024), D-2. https://armypubs. army.mil/epubs/DR_pubs/DR_a/ARN40121-ATP_7-100.1-000-WEB-2.pdf

269 "Russia says it shot down long-range US missiles given to Ukraine," *Reuters,* October 25, 2023. https://www.reuters.com/world/europe/russia-says-it-shot-down-long-range-us-missiles-given-ukraine-2023-10-25/

270 *Russian Tactics: ATP 7-100.1,* Headquarters Department of the Army, Washington, D.C. (February 29, 2024), 1–2. https://armypubs. army.mil/epubs/DR_pubs/DR_a/ARN40121-ATP_7-100.1-000-WEB-2.pdf

271 Richard Pipes, "Why the Soviet Union thinks it Could Fight and Win a Nuclear War," *Commentary,* July 1977. https://www.commentary. org/articles/richard-pipes-2/why-the-soviet-union-thinks-it-could-fight-win-a-nuclear-war/

272 *Incompetence is Killing the US | Col. Larry Wilkerson,* Dialogue Works YouTube video [42:33], March 1, 2024. https://youtu.be/m1i1w0Hp5EI

273 Gar Alperovitz and Martin J. Sherwin, "Opinion: U.S. leaders knew we didn't have to drop atomic bombs on Japan to win the war. We did it anyway," *The Los Angeles Times,* August 5, 2020. https://www. latimes.com/opinion/story/2020-08-05/hiroshima-anniversary-japan-atomic-bombs

274 Glantz and House, *When Titans Clashed*, 359.

275 "Putin delivers key address to Russian lawmakers: As it happened," *RT*, February 29, 2024. https://www.rt.com/russia/593352-putin-federal-assembly-address/

276 "Admiral Lisa Franchetti, Chief of Naval Operations," *America's Navy*. https://www.navy.mil/Leadership/Flag-Officer-Biographies/BioDisplay/Article/3148210/admiral-lisa-franchetti/

277 Евменов Николай Анатольевич, Деловой Петербург [[Evmenov Nikolai Anatolievich, Business Petersburg], *DP.ru*. https://whoiswho.dp.ru/cart/person/1937805

278 *Joseph Schumpeter, Capitalism, Socialism, and Democracy* (Taylor & Francis e-Library, 2003), 153. https://periferiaactiva.files.wordpress.com/2015/08/joseph-schumpeter-capitalism-socialism-and-democracy-2006.pdf

279 Chris Sullentrop, "Douglas Feith: What has the Pentagon's third man done wrong? Everything," *Slate*, May 20, 2004. https://slate.com/news-and-politics/2004/05/douglas-feith-undersecretary-of-defense-for-fiascos.html

280 *Jacques Baud And Me Interview*, SmoothieX12 YouTube interview [59:52], February 29, 2024. https://youtu.be/QirQ0LLM4IQ

281 Ibid.

CHAPTER 10

282 Jack Mendelsohn, "NATO's Nuclear Weapons: The Rationale for 'No First Use,'" *Arms Control Today*, Arms Control Association, July 1999. https://www.armscontrol.org/act/1999-07/features/natos-nuclear-weapons-rationale-first-use

283 Robert H. Gile, *Global War Game, Second Series 1984–1988*, Naval War College, Center for Naval Warfare Studies, Newport Paper no. 20 (2004): 45. https://digital-commons.usnwc.edu/cgi/viewcontent.cgi?article=1020&context=usnwc-newport-papers

284 O.V. Antipenko, «Основные факторы, влиявшие на тактику танковых соединений и частей в обороне в 1980-е — начале 1990-х годов» [Main factors influencing the tactics of tank formations and units in defense in 1980s—early 1990s], *Voyennaya Mysl* no. 2 (2024): 52.

285 Paul F. Gorman, *U.S. Intelligence and Soviet Armor*, June 1, 1980 (approved for Release March 2004): 1. https://www.cia.gov/readingroom/document/0000624298

286 O.V. Antipenko, «Основные факторы, влиявшие на тактику танковых соединений и частей в обороне в 1980-е», 49.

287 Ibid., 50.

288 "Russian TOR-M2 air defense missile system shows high efficiency against Ukrainian drones," *Army Recognition*, July 8, 2022. https://armyrecognition.com/ukraine_-_russia_conflict_war_2022/ russian_tor-m2_air_defense_missile_system_shows_high_efficiency_ against_ukrainian_drones.html

289 Sergei Ptichkin, «Чем уникальны антидроновые ракеты, которые скоро поступят в зону СВО» [What is the actuality of antidrone missiles, which soon will arrive to SMO zone], *Rossiiskaya Gazeta*, January 23, 2024. https://rg.ru/2024/01/23/drony-pancir-ne-probiut.html

290 «Российские военные рассказали, как уничтожили первый "Абрамс"» [Russian military told how they destroyed first Abrams], Ria. ru, March 1, 2024. https://ria.ru/20240301/abrams-1930582111.html

291 Ibid.

292 Chris Osborne, "M1 Abrams: The Best Tank in the World For A Reason," *The National Interest*, October 24, 2020. https://nationalinterest. org/blog/buzz/m1-abrams-best-tank-world-reason-171331

293 «Спецоперация, 6 марта: ВС России подбили третий американский танк Abrams» [SMO, March 6: Russian military destroyed third American Abrams tank], *Ria.ru*, March 6, 2024. https:// ria.ru/20240306/spetsoperatsiya-1931556187.html

294 Michael P. Locasso, "An Unerring Sense of Locality: Ukraine and the Future of Armored Warfare," *Modern War Institute*, May 2, 2023. https://mwi.westpoint.edu/an-unerring-sense-of-locality-ukraine-and-the-future-of-armored-warfare/

295 Denis Telmanov, «Javelin должен был сжечь всю нашу технику, но этого не произошло» [Javelin was supposed to burn all our equipment, but it didn't happen], *Gazeta.ru*, April 19, 2022. https:// www.gazeta.ru/army/2022/04/19/14752790.shtml

296 «Танки Т-14 "Армата" планируют доработать по результатам применения в СВО» [T-14 Armata tanks are planned to be finalized based on the results of deployment in SMO], *TASS*, August 22, 2024. https://tass.ru/armiya-i-opk/18555527

297 Jacques Baud, "Operational Control," in *The Russian Art of War: How the West Led Ukraine to Defeat* (Max Milo Editions, January 17, 2024).

298 David Axe, "A Russian Drone Spotted a Ukrainian Patriot Air-Defense Crew Convoying Near The Front Line. Soon, A Russian Hypersonic Missile Streaked Down," *Forbes*, March 9, 2024. https:// www.forbes.com/sites/davidaxe/2024/03/09/a-russian-drone-spotted-a-ukrainian-patriot-air-defense-crew-convoying-near-the-front-line-soon-a-russian-hypersonic-missile-streaked-down/

299 «Российский "Спутникс" планирует запуск более 100 космических аппаратов в 2024 г» [Russian "Sputnix" plans the launch of more than 100 satellites in 2024], *Interfax,* December 26, 2023. https://www.interfax.ru/russia/937998

300 «Ожидания от космонавтики-2024: пуск „Ангары", спутники и новые рекорды» [Expectations from cosmonautics-2024: The launch of "Angara," satellites and new records], *Ria.ru,* January 11, 2024. https://ria.ru/20240111/kosmos-1920726628.html

301 Roman Kretsul and Alexey Ramm, «Морской рой: как российские военные корабли будут защищаться от дронов» [A Sea Swarm: How Russian navy ships will defend themselves from drones], *Izvestiya,* July 13, 2023. https://iz.ru/1543336/roman-kretcul-aleksei-ramm/morskoi-roi-kak-rossiiskie-voennye-korabli-budut-zashchishchatsia-ot-dronov

302 «Минобороны работает над увеличением скорости гиперзвуковых комплексов» [Defense Ministry works on increasing the speed of hypersonic complexes], *TASS,* December 28, 2019. https://tass.ru/armiya-i-opk/7441479

303 Martyanov, *The (Real) Revolution in Military Affairs,* 92–93.

304 A.N. Kostenko and V.A. Vakhrushev, «Геополитика Российской Федерации в современном мире» [Geopolitics of Russian Federation in the modern world], *Voyennaya Mysl* no. 2 (2024): 18.

305 J. William Fulbright, *The Arrogance of Power* (New York: Random House, 1966), 222.

306 «Россия выходит из Болонской системы: кого и как это коснётся» [Russia exits Bologna system: Who and how will be affected], *RBC.ru,* May 28, 2022. https://www.rbc.ru/spb_sz/28/05/2022/628e297 49a794747a1ee085d

307 Tim Bakken, *The Cost of Loyalty: Dishonesty, Hubris, and Failure in the U.S. Military,* Kindle edition (Bloomsbury Publishing, 2020), 282.

308 *Interview: A Washington vanity project | George Galloway, MP,* YouTube video, December 15, 2023. https://youtu.be/OEI1LyoNv6g

309 "What happens at Sandhurst | Intermediate Term (14 weeks)," *Training to Be An Officer,* Royal Military Academy Sandhurst. https://jobs.army.mod.uk/how-to-join/training/officer-training/

310 USMA Academic Program | Majors and Minors, USMA at West Point, 2024. https://courses.westpoint.edu/static/index.htm#t=Part_4_-_Majors_and_Minors.htm

311 «Проектирование, производство и эксплуатация ракет и ракетно-космических комплексов в ВАРВСН» [Design, Manufacturing and Operation of Missiles and Space-Missile Complexes], *VUZOpedia,* VARVSN, 2023. https://vuzopedia.ru/vuz/922/napr/220

312 «Военно-Политическая Работа» [Military-Political Work], *VUZOpedia,* VARVSN, 2023. https://vuzopedia.ru/vuz/922/napr/488

313 Glantz and House, *When Titans Clashed,* 359.

314 "Russia's economy once again defies the doomsayers," *The Economist,* March 10, 2024. https://www.economist.com/finance-and-economics/2024/03/10/russias-economy-once-again-defies-the-doomsayers

CHAPTER 11

315 Michael Brenner, "Michael Brenner: The West's Reckoning?," *Sheerpost,* March 8, 2024. https://scheerpost.com/2024/03/08/michael-brenner-the-wests-reckoning/

316 Ibid.

317 Leo Tolstoy, *War and Peace* (1867), Book Ten: 1812, Chapter XXXIV, translated by Louise and Aylmer Maude (Project Guttenberg, 2001; last updated June 14, 2022). https://www.gutenberg.org/files/2600/2600-h/2600-h.htm

318 «20 Вопросов Владимиру Путину» [20 Questions for Vladimir Putin], Part 6, *TASS,* March 2, 2020. https://putin.tass.ru/ru/ob-armii/#translation

319 Samuel Huntington, *The Clash of Civilizations and the Remaking of World Order* (New York: Simon & Schuster, 2003 paperback edition; originally published 1996), 51.

320 «Путин сравнил коммунистическую идеологию с христианством» [Putin compared communist ideology to Christianity], *TASS,* January 14, 2018. https://tass.ru/obschestvo/4872596

321 *Советское общество не было безбожным* [Soviet Society Wasn't Godless], Прот. Дмитрий Смирнов [Archpriest Dmitry Smirnov] YouTube video [03:43], March 4, 2016. https://youtu.be/vD9akymBC3M

322 «Ничему Не Учатся» [They Are Learning Nothing], *Литературная Россия* [Literary Russia], May 1, 2022. https://litrussia.su/2022/05/01/nichemu-ne-uchatsya/

323 «Путин: Россия не позволит искажать историю Великой Отечественной войны» [Putin: Russia will not allow to distort the history of the Great Patriotic War], *Ria.ru,* February 23, 2020. https://ria.ru/20200223/1565121055.html

324 Foreign Minister Sergey Lavrov's interview with RIA Novosti and Rossiya 24 TV on current foreign policy issues, Moscow, The Ministry of Foreign Affairs of Russian Federation, December 28, 2023).

Excerpt: There is a selection of quotes about what Ukrainian officials think about Russians. After the state coup, then Prime Minister of Ukraine Arseny Yatsenyuk said that Russians are "subhuman." Later, Petr Poroshenko said that their children would attend schools and kindergartens while children in Donbass would be sitting in basements. Zelensky was asked before the special military operation what he thought about the people living in Donbass and their demand for the implementation of the Minsk agreements. He said that there were people and then there were "creatures" and that those who lived in Ukraine and were Ukrainian citizens but felt association with the Russian language and culture should "beat it to Russia." He said this in August 2021. Therefore, those who call on the world to support the demand for returning Ukraine to the 1991 borders are supporting the call for genocide. https://mid.ru/en/foreign_policy/news/1923676/

325 Alex Vershinin, "The Attritional Art of War: Lessons from the Russian War on Ukraine," *RUSI*, March 18, 2024. https://www.rusi.org/explore-our-research/publications/commentary/attritional-art-war-lessons-russian-war-ukraine

326 Richard Sisk, "The Military Recruiting Outlook Is Grim Indeed. Loss of Public Confidence, Political Attacks and the Economy Are All Taking a Toll," *Military.com,* January 22, 2024. https://www.military.com/daily-news/2024/01/22/uphill-battle-boost-recruiting-military-faces-falling-public-confidence-political-attacks-economic.html

327 Matt Lavietes, "Nearly 30% of Gen Z adults identify as LGBTQ, national survey finds," *NBC News,* January 24, 2024. https://www.nbcnews.com/nbc-out/out-news/nearly-30-gen-z-adults-identify-lgbtq-national-survey-finds-rcna135510

328 *The Constitution of Russian Federation,* Article 72, Kremlin (updated July 1, 2020), p. G.

«ж1) защита семьи, материнства, отцовства и детства; защита института брака как союза мужчины и женщины»; [g) defense of family, motherhood, fatherhood and childhood; defense of the institute of marriage as the union between a man and a woman].

http://www.kremlin.ru/acts/constitution/item#chapter3

329 «КоАП РФ Статья 6.21. Пропаганда нетрадиционных сексуальных отношений и (или) предпочтений, смены пола» [KoAP RF Article 6.21. Propaganda of non-traditional sexual relations and (or) preferences, change of gender], *Konsultant. ru.* https://www.consultant.ru/document/cons_doc_LAW_34661/d4344568bd586d541d39273855ba64ba9d18e84a/

330 *Putin's Landslide Victory as NATO is Losing | Dmitry Orlov,* Dialogue Works YouTube video [40:51], March 21, 2024. https://youtu. be/h-Eqk8BCFzg

331 Daniel De Vise, "America's White Majority is Aging Out," *The Hill,* August 7, 2023. https://thehill.com/homenews/race-politics/4138228-americas-white-majority-is-aging-out/

332 «Командир „Ахмата": русские, вы государствообразующие, рожайте! Иначе вымрете!» [The Commander of "Akhmat": Russians, you are state founding people, procreate! Otherwise, you will die out!], *Pravda.ru,* May 13, 2023. https://www.pravda.ru/news/politics/1834091-alaudinov/

333 Agnes Chang, Pablo Robles, and Keith Bradsher, "How Houthi Attacks Have Upended Global Shipping," *The New York Times,* January 21, 2024. https://www.nytimes.com/interactive/2024/01/20/world/middleeast/houthi-red-sea-shipping.html

334 Megan Eckstein, "US Navy making Aegis updates, training changes based on Houthi attacks," *Defense News,* March 21, 2024. https://www.defensenews.com/naval/2024/03/21/us-navy-making-aegis-updates-training-changes-based-on-houthi-attacks/

335 Joshua J. Mark, "Thirty Years' War," *World History Encyclopedia,* August 11, 2022. https://www.worldhistory.org/Thirty_Years%27_War/

336 Michael Hudson, *Super Imperialism: The Origin and Fundamentals of U.S. World Dominance* (London-Sterling, Virginia: Pluto Press, 2003), 17.

337 John J. Mearsheimer, "Why the Ukraine Crisis Is the West's Fault," *Foreign Affairs,* August 18, 2014. https://www.foreignaffairs.com/articles/russia-fsu/2014-08-18/why-ukraine-crisis-west-s-fault

338 *Jacques Baud And Me Interview,* SmoothieX12 YouTube interview [59:52], February 29, 2024. https://youtu.be/QirQ0LLM4IQ

339 George F. Kennan, *At a Century's Ending: Reflections 1982–1995* (W.W. Norton & Company, 1996), 52.

340 Jennifer Sor, "China and Russia have almost completely abandoned the US dollar in bilateral trade as the push to de-dollarize intensifies," *Business Insider,* December 21, 2023. https://markets.businessinsider.com/news/currencies/dedollarization-dollar-dominance-brics-currrency-china-russia-trade-yuan-ruble-2023-12

341 Ruth Maclean and Eric Schmitt, "Niger Orders American Troops to Leave Its Territory," *The New York Times,* March 17, 2024. https://www.nytimes.com/2024/03/17/world/africa/niger-orders-american-troops-out.html

342 Jeremy Rifkin, *The End of Work: The Decline of the Global Labor Force and the Dawn of the Post-Market Era* (New York: G.P. Putnam Sons, 1995), 42–44.

343 "Roger Scruton quotes," *Good Reads.* https://www.goodreads.com/quotes/7378672-beauty-is-vanishing-from-our-world-because-we-live-as

344 Vladimir Solovyov, "The Meaning of Dostoevsky's 'Beauty Will Save the World,'" St. Peter Orthodox Church. https://stpeterorthodoxchurch.com/the-meaning-of-dostoevskys-beauty-will-save-the-world/

CHAPTER 12

345 Larry Johnson, "Western Hatred of Russia Rooted in Support for Nazis and Bureaucratic Sclerosis," *A Son of the New American Revolution,* March 21, 2024. https://sonar21.com/western-hatred-of-russia-rooted-in-support-for-nazis-and-bureaucratic-sclerosis/

346 "Suspects behind Moscow terrorist attack: What we know so far," *RT,* March 23, 2024. https://www.rt.com/russia/594815-suspects-moscow-terrorist-attack-known/

347 Larry Johnson, "Can NATO Survive a Loss in Ukraine?" *A Son of the New American Revolution,* March 17, 2024. https://sonar21.com/can-nato-survive-a-loss-in-ukraine/

348 Roger Scruton, *Beauty: A Very Short Introduction* (Very Short Introductions) Illustrated Edition (OUP Oxford: Kindle edition, March 24, 2011), 1.

349 Bronislaw Malinowski, *An Anthropological Analysis of War: War Studies from psychology, sociology, anthropology* (New York: Basic Books, 1964), 251.

350 Martin Kelly, "American Involvement in Wars From Colonial Times to the Present," *ThoughtCo,* November 4, 2020. https://www.thoughtco.com/american-involvement-wars-colonial-times-present-4059761

351 Robert H. Latiff, *Future War: Preparing for the New Global Battlefield* (New York: Alfred A. Knopf, 2017), 131.

352 Drug Abuse Statistics: Drug-Related Deaths. National Center for Drug Abuse Statistics. https://drugabusestatistics.org/

353 Alvin Parker, "US Literacy Rates 2024: Statistics and Trends," *Prosperity,* March 8, 2024. https://www.prosperityforamerica.org/literacy-statistics/

354 *NATO Lost it Hands Down as Russia Crushed Ukraine's Army –* *Terrorist Attack in Moscow* | *Ray McGovern,* Dialogue Works YouTube video [32:58], March 29, 2024. https://youtu.be/BGSBxotojHk

355 Ibid.

356 Wayne Allensworth, "An Obsolete Alliance Turns 75," *Chronicles,* March 2024, 15.

357 "BRICS and G7 countries' share of the world's total gross domestic product (GDP) in purchasing power parity (PPP) from 2000 to 2023" [graph], *Statista,* 2024. https://www.statista.com/statistics/1412425/gdp-ppp-share-world-gdp-g7-brics/

358 *John Mearsheimer Special Encore: What's said Behind Closed Doors – Ukraine, Russia, China & NATO,* Daniel Davis / Deep Dive YouTube video [20:21], March 29, 2024. https://www.youtube.com/live/8M02pL2xev4

359 "Russia has no unfriendly states, only unfriendly elites—Putin," *TASS,* March 27, 2024. https://tass.com/society/1766847

360 Larry Johnson, "USG Can't Get Its Story Straight on Terrorist Warning to Moscow, While Baltimore Bridge Collapse Seems Apt Metaphor for America," *The Son of the New American Revolution,* March 27, 2024. https://sonar21.com/usg-cant-get-its-story-straight-on-terrorist-warning-to-moscow-while-baltimore-bridge-collapse-seems-apt-metaphor-for-america/

INDEX